'*Transfaith* offers compassionate Christians an intelligent discussion about transgender people and their concerns which has been desperately needed for decades. Starting with a review of past attempts to frame policy responses, this comprehensive and accessible new book addresses both Biblical and pastoral considerations and makes practical suggestions.'

Christine Burns MBE
Author and Transgender Activist

'*Transfaith* is a much needed resource and inspiration for the journeys individuals, families, congregations and other groups are now taking as we explore God's gifts of gender and love among us today. Blending deep pastoral care and insight with renewed commitment to scripture, and crucially placing trans people themselves at the centre, it offers us hugely valuable Christian pathways both to understand and affirm transgender people and to open up fresh vistas of biblical vision and awareness. May it be taken up and used both by transgender people in our own spiritual lives and by our churches which have the power to liberate and empower.'

The Revd Dr Jo Inkpin
Lecturer in Theology & Senior Tutor, St Francis College Brisbane.

'As a relative newcomer to the discussion of transgender people and the Church, I have been favourably impressed by this weighty, comprehensive book entitled *Transfaith*. The authors provide data, analyse contexts and connections, raise questions, encourage reflection and produce eye-opening insights. Undoubtedly *Transfaith* will be a major resource and reference work for many years to come.'

Dr Renato Lings
Copenhagen-based translator, theologian, lecturer, and writer.
Author of *Love Lost in Translation: Homosexuality and the Bible*

'The Church of England has, at last, begun to engage with the fact that trans people are members of its parishes, congregations, and clergy. The 2017 General Synod debate of the Blackburn Motion on welcoming and affirming trans people showed that progress is being made, but we are not there yet! Much work still needs to be done to inform church members of the situatio[...] brothers, and there has been a shortage what it means to be a trans person, created in God's image, in Church and world today. *Transfaith* is a timely book, which is accessible to all readers, and which provides us with a theology to underpin our pastoral encounters with trans people, and to hear their precious voice which helps us all better to understand how they and we are all fearfully, and wonderfully made".'

The Revd Chris Newlands
Vicar of Lancaster Priory, Proposer of the Blackburn
Motion

'Chris Dowd and Tina Beardsley have created a rich resource which will be of great assistance to both individuals and groups wanting to engage seriously with the gifts and needs of trans persons. Based on wide scholarship, including original research into the faith lives of trans folk, and drawing on their extensive personal experience and pastoral encounters, there is much wisdom here for us all, and many practical resources, including Bible studies, liturgies and pastoral guidelines. Every pastor and theologian should have this book on their shelves; though it won't sit on the shelf for long.'

Professor Nicola Slee
Director of Research at the Queen's Foundation,
Birmingham
Professor of Feminist Practical Theology at the Vrije
Universiteit Amsterdam

'If it is true that for those who are disciples of Christ there is no male and female (Galatians 3.28), then the Churches must have some interesting things to say about gender in general and transgender people in particular. This book proves that is so, perhaps not so much in the synods and official documents but most certainly in the lived theology of transgender people themselves whose voices have often been excluded from official pronouncements on their lives. Those of us who are not transgender need to listen to the voices of those that are, for Christ speaks to us through them and we are all part of his one body. *Transfaith* will help us do so. It is written with a clarity, sensitivity and depth not always evident in official documents on 'the issue'. It demonstrates that engaging openly and positively with transgender people can pull all of us deeper into the radical heart of the Gospel.'

Professor Elizabeth Stuart
Deputy Vice-Chancellor, University of Winchester

'We live in a more open and accepting society as our knowledge and understanding of human identity has developed. This has found expression in safeguarding, in law, of equality and inclusivity. With more work to be done this book offers us a framework within which to understand the nature of transition, identity and gender.

'The particular quality of this text is reflected through Chris and Tina's experience, learning, and pastoral sensitivity. The reader is asked to pay close attention to language and to explore what it is that might enforce silence, oppression and inadequate pastoral care. This approach to understanding trans people is based upon a thorough understanding of the cultural and theological background into which too many of our discussions have distorted and silenced individuals. There is a theological wisdom and depth to this reflective and practical book that illuminates challenges and informs. It attends closely to the stories that we have so often silenced and deserves the widest possible readership. It will strengthen your commitment to an imaginative and compassionate pastoral theology.'

The Revd Canon Professor James Woodward,
Principal Sarum College

'This book will be an invaluable resource for Christians who would like to be better informed about the "transgender debate." Unlike other writing on the subject, it does not present trans people as a problem or simply talk about them: it is the fruit of much reflection following in-depth interviews with trans people. It contains, in addition, a very helpful overview of current medical thinking on the issue and an account of how Christians have written about it in the past, as well as some fascinating Bible studies and potentially helpful liturgies for those ministering to trans people.

'The authors make clear at the outset that their book takes a positive stance about trans people. It will not, as such, make easy reading for some Christians. It is, however, something that I feel all involved in ministry should read since it provides, in the authors' words, 'an opportunity for all of us 'to explore what we think we know about God, gender, and to challenge the lazily comfortable assumptions we have come to believe as fact.' I commend highly.'

Dr John Inge, Bishop of Worcester

Transfaith

a transgender pastoral resource
includes Bible studies and liturgies

**Chris Dowd and Christina Beardsley
with Justin Tanis**

DARTON·LONGMAN+TODD

First published in 2018 by
Darton, Longman and Todd Ltd
1 Spencer Court
140 – 142 Wandsworth High Street
London SW18 4JJ

Royalties from sales of this book with be donated to The Sibyls.

ISBN: 978-0-232-53311-8

A catalogue record for this book is available from the British Library

Printed and bound in Great Britain by Bell & Bain, Glasgow

Contents

To Will,

without whose support, love and encouragement this book
could not have been written.

The Authors

Chris Dowd was originally a minister in the LGBT-identified Metropolitan Community Churches for over a decade, planting a queer friendly fresh expression called Journey in the West Midlands. At the same time, he served as a special category minister for the United Reformed Church as a University Chaplain at Aston University. He retrained as a minister of Word and Sacrament within the United Reformed Church and currently serves as a Chaplain at Hull University and as minister for several churches.

Christina (Tina) Beardsley, a Church of England priest, worked in parishes for twenty-two years, and as a healthcare chaplain for sixteen years, the last eight as Head of Multi-faith Chaplaincy at Chelsea & Westminster Hospital, London. Tina is an honorary assistant priest at St John's Church in Fulham. Educated at Sussex, Cambridge and Leeds universities, she lectures and writes on chaplaincy, spirituality, gender and Victorian religion. An advocate for trans inclusion in the Church, Tina is a member of the Sibyls, Christian spirituality for transgender people, and co-editor with Michelle O'Brien of 'the Sibyls' book', *This is My Body: hearing the theology of transgender Christians* (2016) also published by DLT.

Justin Tanis is Managing Director of the Center for LGBTQ & Gender Studies in Religion at the Pacific School of Religion, Berkeley, CA. A Master of Divinity, Harvard Divinity School, Justin's Doctor of Ministry dissertation from San Francisco Theological Seminary, published in 2003 as *Transgendered: Ministry, Theology and Communities of Faith*, was a finalist in the Lambda Literary Award that year. He is a contributor to *The Queer Bible Commentary* and *Take Back the Word: A Queer Reading of the Bible*. Justin has served congregations in Boston, Honolulu and San Francisco and was a denominational executive for nine years, coordinating leadership and educational programmes in twenty-two countries. With a long history of grassroots activism, including ACT-UP and Queer Nation in the 1980s, Justin's work includes advocacy for LGBT rights with several US national non-profit organisations. An artist and photographer, Justin has a lifelong passion for the arts, and his scholarly interests include the theology expressed by LGBT artists.

Introduction

There is really no way of knowing how many trans people there are in our churches. For people secure in their gender identity, such an intense desire to completely change such a fundamental aspect of personhood is so confronting and troubling we don't consider it until we are confronted with it. The issues trans people raise for the Church are troubling and require thought and reflection. We believe this is not because trans people themselves are deeply troubling people, but because they force cisgender people (folk who are not transgender) to confront assumptions and prejudices they barely recognise exist within themselves.

Chris likes to think this book began in the 1980's when he found himself sharing a flat with several friends. Suddenly one of these friends moved out and abruptly severed contact with the other members of the flat share. We all wondered what we had done to offend them so badly. It was only years later in a chance encounter in a supermarket that he discovered this friend had transitioned.

Later, as a pastor Chris supported several people in their transition to live out their gender identity. He was often completely unclear if he had helped them at all. Certainly, at times he felt he had little to offer. While he had several trans friends and colleagues, he never felt it was appropriate to ask them all the questions his experiences had raised for him. Nor could he find any book that answered them.

We have tried to produce an easy to read piece of helpful pastoral theology. For Chris this is the book he has been looking for but was unable to find. By the time you have reached the end of this book we hope you will agree that we have at least managed to achieve part of that ambition.

This book is based on Chris's doctoral thesis. What you are reading are the fruits of several years of academic research using sociological research and theological reflection. The results of the research are not always comfortable reading, but they are academically valid.

We can't pretend this book doesn't take a positive stance about trans people. This is no academic or theological hatchet job. Chris is avowedly an ally, and its subject matter is a personal one for Tina who is a published author in this area. The aim of this book is not to present trans people as a problem for the Church, but as an opportunity for the rest of us to explore what we think we know about God, gender, and to challenge the lazily comfortable assumptions we have come to believe as fact.

This book is designed for those who find themselves in the situation of supporting someone and those close to them through their gender journey. It is not a 'how to' book in the normal sense because each situation will be different and the medical, social and religious situation of trans people is changing all the time.

Instead, it is designed as a resource to dip in and out of and to read and use parts as they become relevant. We have written this book because we honestly believe it is needed and we hope that you find it helpful.

We are extremely fortunate that trans theologian Justin Tanis has written a chapter for the book addressing the US context.

We are particularly grateful to those who read and commented on some or all of the manuscript: Arnold Browne, Christine Burns MBE, Bishop John Inge, Jo Inkpin, Renato Lings, Chris Newlands, Michelle O'Brien, Stephen Passmore, Sally Rush, Liz Stuart, Jay Walmsley, Alex Clare-Young and James Woodward. Some of them have also kindly written commendations which we greatly appreciate.

Finally, we wish to express our thanks to Nicola Slee for her careful supervision of the doctoral research which elicited the evidence base for the pastoral insights outlined in these pages.

Chris and Tina

General definitions used in this book.

Androgyny – A term derived from the Greek words for man and woman, so meaning one who combines the qualities of the two.

Berdache – A term invented by European observers to describe gender nonconforming/cross-gender living Native American Indian people who had an acknowledged place, and sometimes a sacred role in their society. The term can be offensive, especially due to European attempts to erase this aspect of indigenous culture.

Cisgender person – Denoting or relating to a person whose gender identity conforms to their biological sex as assigned at birth.

Coming out – Refers to the process by which an individual accepts that they are trans and begins to disclose this identity to others.

Gender confirmation surgery (GCS) – Denotes a surgical procedure undertaken with the intention of changing one's primary and/or secondary sex characteristics in the interests of gender transition.

Gender Dysphoria – Refers to the diagnosis or experience of discomfort or distress (dysphoria in contrast to euphoria) at discrepancy between a person's gender identity and their assigned/presumed gender, and the expectation that they will conform to their society's gender norms. The term 'gender dysphoria' has replaced 'gender identity disorder' and 'transsexualism' in the clinical literature, but trans people themselves are increasingly unhappy about being reduced to a diagnosis and tend to opt for non-medical labels.

Gender expression – Denotes how a person outwardly expresses their gender in terms of masculinity/femininity/androgyny/other.

Gender identity – Refers to 'a person's innate sense of their own gender, whether as male, female or something else, which may or may not correspond to the sex assigned at birth' (Stonewall 2017: 38).

Gender journey – Refers to the process whereby a trans person moves from an experience of incongruence to one of congruence between their gender identity and their gender expression and role.

Gender non-conformity – Denotes people whose behaviours or appearance disrupt cultural norms relating to gender role and expression. Not all trans people are gender nonconforming. Not all gender nonconforming people identify as trans.

Genderqueer – A term that can encompass gender nonconforming expression/someone who identifies as both man and woman/as neither man nor woman/as a combination of the two/as an unnamed gender.

Gender Reassignment – A term used in legislation to describe the gender transition, and which need not imply medical, including surgical intervention has taken place.

Gender Reassignment Surgery (GRS) – Refers to the surgical procedure(s) people may undertake as part of transition. We prefer 'Gender Confirmation Surgery' (GCS) – see entry above.

Gender variance – Although used in the technical literature this term lacks the stigmatising resonance of other more clinical terms, and conveys that being trans is simply a human variation.

GIRES – The UK based organisation, Gender Identity Research & Education Society.

Heteronormativity – The social privileging of the belief that male and female are distinct, complementary, with specific roles, and that heterosexual orientation is the norm.

Natal Gender - Refers to the gender assigned at birth. In this book it is used of someone's assigned or perceived gender, especially prior to transition.

Non-binary gender identity – A term that encompasses the combination of masculine and feminine/an identity between male and female (intergender)/neutral gender (e.g. agender)/multiple gender identities (bigender or pangender)/gender identity that varies over time (gender fluid)/a partial connection to gender identity (demi-gender).

Passing – This term originated in the era of racial segregation in the US to described biracial Americans' efforts to be perceived as white in order to access education and employment, or to avoid social stigma. Trans people use it to mean that their gender expression is such that no one would guess that their natal gender had differed from their gender identity. The other term used is 'stealth'.

Sex – Refers to the biological body as indicated by the genitals, i.e. the sex assigned at birth (which is not always the same as the person's chromosomal sex). The historic options have been either male or female but recently some jurisdictions have introduced a gender neutral option.

Sex Reassignment Surgery (SRS) - Refers to the surgical procedure(s) people may undertake as part of transition. We prefer 'Gender Confirmation Surgery' (GCS) – see entry above.

Social gender – Refers to the gender role allocated to an individual by society, or assumed by an individual.

Transition – Denotes the process (which need not be medical) whereby trans people assume the gender role (man/woman/other) and expression that confirm their gender identity. Many trans people experience transition as a time of emotional and spiritual growth.

Transgender/trans person – These are umbrella terms for a range of gender identities and are discussed in detail in Chapter 1.

Transsexual person – An older clinical term for trans people, it especially denotes someone who intends to, is undergoing, or has undergone gender reassignment.

Trans people – This is the term that is used most often in this book. It is used as a collective noun for transgender people.

Trans man – Refers to Female-to-Male (FTM) trans people, i.e. those whose birth sex was assigned as or perceived to be female, but whose gender identity and expression is male.

Trans woman – Refers to Male-to-Female (MTF) trans people, i.e. those whose birth sex was assigned as or perceived to be male, but whose gender identity and expression is female.

(N.B. The terms male-to-female (MTF) and female-to-male (FTM) fail to convey that prior to transition trans women (MTF) identified as female, and trans men (FTM) identified as male, but they are commonly used, including by trans people themselves.

WPATH – The World Professional Association for Transgender Health, formerly the Harry Benjamin International Gender Dysphoria Association (HBGDA), is the multi-professional, evidence based authority in the field.

Chapter 1

On our own terms: trans people and their terminology

As a hospital chaplain Tina learned that an important touchstone of respect is the readiness to use the terms with which the other person identifies.

When meeting a trans person for the first time, some people worry they might say the 'wrong' thing. This will only make you more nervous! The most important consideration is that you are meeting another human being and a fellow child of God. Relating to other people as made in the image of God is fundamental to Christian personal encounter. Some trans people may wish you to be aware of their trans identity and to acknowledge it, but others may not. Allow them to lead you to the name and pronouns they would like you to use.

> Practical tips:
> Always remember the trans person's humanity and that, first and foremost, they are a child of God.
>   Let the trans person guide you regarding their preferred name and pronouns.
>   Pronouns may be the familiar 'she' or 'he' but could be gender neutral, e.g. 'they', 'ze'/'zie', 'hir'/'zir'/'per'.

There is an array of terms for and about trans people. Many originated fairly recently, with a rapid evolution in the last few years, when a rich variety of descriptors and terms has arisen. This chapter reviews historical and contemporary Western terminology to describe trans people, and some non-Western examples are also mentioned. It recounts the rise of the medicalisation of trans people, and describes current treatment options. It also examines changing perceptions of 'sex' and 'gender', and ends by noting some connections between gender variance and the sacred.

General

Some Christian authors (O'Donovan 2007:3 [1982]; Roberts 2016:13) describe trans people as a recent cultural phenomenon. It's true that the medical treatment of trans people has been available only for roughly a century. The medical profession, though, observed and classified gender variant people prior to that, and the language of early sexologists in the late nineteenth and early twentieth century – based on what their gender variant patients told them – largely shaped the terminology about trans people.

These clinical terms unintentionally pathologised sexual minorities and gender variant people. The French theorist Michel Foucault (1998: 101) noted that, at a later stage, this terminology would become a badge of pride to the people concerned, a process he called 'reverse discourse'. A third stage occurs when people begin to question the adequacy of these clinically derived terms compared to their own self-understandings.

These three phases – the development of technical terminology; its adoption as reverse discourse; disenchantment with it – are apparent in the continuing evolution of language about trans people. Currently, trans people have begun to emerge from 'the clinical gaze' (Foucault 2003: 146) and self-define their reality. The coining of newer terms like 'gender queer', 'non-binary', 'a-gender' (for further information see 'General definitions used in this book' on p.3ff, suggests that the process is far from over.

The (re-)claiming of language can also apply to formerly derogatory terms. The rehabilitation of the word 'queer' – once a term of abuse – as a positive identity, for example 'gender queer', is a striking example. For some older lesbian, gay, bisexual and transgender (LGBT) people, the negative associations of 'queer' remain, leaving them unable to embrace the new meaning. As language evolves, members of the same community may interpret the same word differently.

Intergenerational differences are apparent among trans people – Chris's research identified at least three paradigms (see Chapters 3 and 6; Insight 4 on p. 138). Interpretation can also cut across generations. The GIRES' – Gender Identity Research & Education Society – paper *Terminology* (2015) notes that 'transsexual' and 'transsexualism' are now considered old-fashioned terms. Neither is a heading in the Glossary section of Stonewall's *A Vision for Change: Acceptance Without Exception for Trans People 2017-2022* (2017). Yet some trans people still wish to use these terms.

> Be cautious about using terms unless you are sure of their
> meanings and how they might be received.

Specifics

As the GIRES document notes, the concept of 'typical gender identity' as a man or a woman, which renders trans people atypical, is itself unsatisfactory. It remains, nevertheless, how many people think and recent linguistic creativity by trans people is presumably a reaction against it. Despite the numerous terms, clarity is still possible.

'Trans' is the Latin word for 'across', or 'beyond'; as in the biblical expression 'Transjordan', meaning the other side of the Jordan. It conveys a person's internal sense that their gender identity is at odds with their sex as assigned at birth. It is less suited to the process of transition. Like the dated and unhelpful notion of 'sex change' (a term to be avoided), the implication that one is 'crossing' from one gender to another is misleading. Many trans people experience an unchanging sense of gender identity, which transition merely enables them to express. Note here the limitations of language, even in the case of 'trans', a term widely favoured by trans people themselves.

Those who do not share the trans person's experience of discordance with their birth assigned gender are often referred to today as being cisgender. 'Cis' too is a Latin word, as in 'Cisjordan', meaning on 'this side of the Jordan'. For cisgender people their gender identity is 'on side' with their gender as assigned at birth.

In the UK 'transgender' and, more recently 'trans' have become 'umbrella' terms, and include a wide range of gender variant people: 'those whose gender is not the same as, or does not sit comfortably with, the sex they were assigned at birth' (Stonewall 2017: 38). 'Gender variance' or 'gender nonconforming' are the terms often used in the literature; 'trans' in everyday speech.

Gender dysphoria is a diagnosis of discomfort or distress (dysphoria in contrast to euphoria) at discrepancy between a person's gender identity and their assigned/presumed gender, together with distress at the expectation that they will conform to their society's gender norms. The term 'gender dysphoria' has replaced 'transsexualism' in the clinical literature, but trans people, increasingly unhappy about being reduced to a diagnosis, are opting for non-medical labels.

The terms transsexual person (someone whose gender identity does not match their assigned gender, and who may have undergone, is undergoing, or intends to undergo, gender transition) and transvestite person (someone who cross-dresses, but is cisgender), though still found in legal and clinical settings, are becoming less common.

Some definitions:

Gender identity: 'a person's innate sense of their own gender, whether as male, female or something else, which may or may not correspond to the sex assigned at birth' (Stonewall 2017: 38).

Cisgender person: someone whose gender identity aligns with their biological sex as assigned at birth.

Trans person: someone who experiences disjunction between their gender identity and the biological sex they were assigned at birth.

Gender expression: how a person outwardly expresses their gender in terms of masculinity/femininity/androgyny/other. Clothing, hair styles, makeup, facial hair or its absence, speech patterns and body language can all be forms of gender expression. Many trans people seek to match their gender expression with their gender identity.

Gender non-conformity can indicate variation from cultural norms relating to gender roles and expression. Not all trans people are gender nonconforming. Not all gender nonconforming people identify as trans. Cisgender people can be gender nonconforming. Gender nonconformity is often mistakenly confused with sexual orientation.

Transition: the process whereby trans people assume the gender role (man/woman/other) and expression that confirm their gender identity.

Gender identity v cross-dressing

Trans can also be the preferred term for those who 'cross-dress intermittently for a variety of reasons including erotic factors (also referred to as transvestism)' (GIRES 2015: 2); not least because the term 'transvestite' has carried considerable stigma. The historical account below describes how clinicians gradually differentiated between those who cross-dress and are cisgender, and those whose gender nonconformity is indicative of discrepancy between their gender identity and their assigned gender, and who are likely to explore transition.

One of the UK's most high-profile cross-dressers, Grayson Perry (2016: 5), has asked, 'how can I, brought up as a man, know anything about the experience of being a woman?' He means 'brought up as a boy', of course, and that having absorbed the messages aimed at boys he grew up to be a man, albeit a cross-dressing man. A biological boy with a female gender identity, on the other hand, thinks of themselves as a girl, and reinforces their gender identity by absorbing messages aimed at girls, and behaving, as far as possible, as girls are expected to behave. Even when this dynamic is not obvious to others because the child is concealing it, the boy concerned could be said to be bringing up themselves to be a woman, and vice versa for a biological female with male gender identity. There are other children who will grow up unable to identify with either gender.

That the single term 'trans' can apply to people whose gender identity conflicts with their sex appearance, and also to gender nonconforming people who are cisgender, can be confusing, but acknowledges genuine complexity. For example, someone who has for several years cross-dressed only intermittently, may subsequently permanently transition their gender role; presumably, in response to increasing awareness of their true gender identity.

The trans umbrella also enables people who are intermittently gender non-conforming to access the legal protections available to those who transition, as they are often perceived to be the same and, unhappily, can be the targets of similar hate crime and discrimination.

Drag (possibly an acronym for 'dressed as a girl') performance – cross-dressing for theatrical purposes – is very obviously different from trans people's experience, but has sometimes enabled trans people to experiment and offered a means of employment. For example, the young April Ashley worked as a female impersonator prior to her transition, and more is said below about that historical era. The media sometimes conflates drag performance and transgender people but they are quite distinct.

Gender identity v sexual identities
Gender identity and sexual orientation
Trans people's self-understanding relates primarily to their gender identity, not their sexual orientation. Trans people can be attracted to

people of the same sex, the opposite sex, both sexes, or they may be asexual. The self-understanding of cisgender lesbian, gay and bisexual (LGB) people relates principally to their sexual orientation, not to their gender identity. Sexual orientation and gender identity interface and overlap, but are significantly different.

In the popular mind though there can be confusion between trans people and LGB people. How has this come about? Here are some likely reasons.

Gender identity and gender expression

Most LGB people describe themselves as cisgender, but some experience a sense of alienation from prevailing models of masculinity and femininity. A few might even self-identify in terms of their gender nonconformity, in which case they would be more accurately said to be trans, especially if they no longer identify as cisgender.

The interface between cisgender LGB identities and transgender identities is most apparent in relation to gender expression. Gender expression refers to the ways in which gender is performed, and can conform to or conflict with societal norms. Some cisgender LGB men and women may display gendered behaviours that others consider atypical for their assigned gender. These behaviours alone are not indicative of a transgender identity. The person may simply prefer not to conform to how society expects men and women to behave. This may also be true for some people who identify as cisgender and heterosexual.

Children whose gender expression is considered atypical are sometimes referred to clinicians. Not all of these children articulate that they belong to a gender different to their assigned gender (though some do), but they may be engaging in cross-gender play, behaviours and dress. Studies suggest that, on becoming adults, a small percentage of these children will identify as transgender. Many though will identify as lesbian, gay, bi or heterosexual. Variant gender expression is not linked to sexual orientation.

The LGBTI+ alliance

In recent decades, a justice alliance has emerged among LGB&T people to promote equality. Sometimes the list is longer, and includes queer, questioning and intersex people along with other identities.

> Intersex people's reproductive, genetic, genital, or hormonal configurations vary from typical male or female biology. Being intersex is quite different from being trans, though some trans people may be intersex, and some intersex people transition.

The differing interests of the various constituencies are usually acknowledged by these alliances, but powerful groups can dominate. For example, when literature or publicity claiming to be LGB&T focuses on sexual orientation, and omits gender identity. A similar dynamic occurs when gender variant people in history are interpreted as cisgender LGB pioneers.

From the 1950s onwards, following medical advances, the press reported the high-profile transitions of Christine Jorgensen, Michael Dillon, Roberta Cowell, Sir Ewan Forbes and April Ashley. The media then spoke crudely of sex-change. Colloquially the language for sexuality and gender remained blurred and some trans people socialised in venues that were safe spaces for gay and lesbian people. Even as late as the 1970s, the term 'gay' could still include those who would now be described as trans people in the category of '"drag" culture' (Brooker 2017: 147), i.e. cross dressing for entertainment purposes. The word 'gay' was itself an umbrella term that embraced multiple identities, including people who would now identify as trans.

The Sexologists

Another conflating of trans people with cisgender LGB people arose from the theoretical assumptions of sexologists in the second half of the nineteenth century. Early sexologists like Richard von Krafft-Ebing (1840-1902) analysed atypical sexual orientation and gender expression in contrast to an emerging norm of heterosexuality. The idea that gender variance might be distinct from homosexuality took time to emerge.

The term heterosexual first appears in the 1892 and subsequent editions of the US translation of Krafft-Ebing's classic work *Psychopathia Sexualis (Sexual Psychopathy: A Clinical-Forensic Study)*, published in German 1886. This influential text defines all sexual desire unrelated to procreation as perversion, though it also argues that homosexuality has a biological basis.

Points to note:
The assumption that heterosexuality and cisgender identity are the 'gold standard', mean that variant sexual orientation and gender variance are conceived as 'other' or even as 'deviant'.

But the essence of heterosexuality and cisgender identity are often assumed rather than examined.

The privileging of heterosexuality and cisgender identity is often referred to as heteronormativity.

The association of atypical sexual orientation and atypical gender identity with sexual deviance added social stigma that had not previously existed. Cross-dressing, for instance, was frequently tolerated as harmless eccentricity (Gilbert 1926) until it was pathologised as transvestism. On the other hand, the medicalisation of homosexuality often replaced the harsh punishments inflicted in jurisdictions where it was criminalised (Whittle 2002: 35).

The theories of two of the leading early sexologists, Karl Heinrich Ulrichs (1825-95) and Magnus Hirschfeld (1868-1935), both of whom were gay, and passionate homosexual law reformers, also compounded the conflation of sexual orientation and gender identity. In fact, Hirschfeld's study, *Transvestites: The Erotic Drive to Cross-Dress* (1991 [1910]) first published in 1910, clearly distinguished cross-dressing and cross-gender identification from auto-eroticism, homosexuality, fetishism and masochism.[1] Based on seventeen case studies, Hirschfeld's text is, for its date, an astonishing example of evidence-based medicine. His findings indicated that most cross-dressers (a category that, for Hirschfeld, included those who would now be said to have a transgender identity) were heterosexually orientated. This means that a contemporary conservative Christian scholar like Robert Gagnon (2007), who regards transsexualism as

---

1   Pfäfflin (2015: 13) claims that Hirschfeld created the category of transvestites in response to a gay scandal at the German court in 1905 and that it included 'all effeminate homosexuals'. Even if this were the origin, in his book Hirschfeld (1991 [1910]: 147f) is at pains to differentiate gender variance from homosexuality, and categorises (1991:222) transvestites as intermediary in their 'emotional characteristics' as distinct from their sexual orientation.

'an extension of the issue of homosexuality', is ignoring research that is over a century old.

Hirschfeld developed a 'theory of intermediaries'. Based on four categories – the sexual organs, other physical characteristics, sexual orientation and emotional characteristics – he speculated that the total number of possible variations of masculine and feminine was over forty-three million (Hirschfeld 1991 [1910]: 227). Ulrichs, contrastingly, had adopted a simplistic model that conceptualised gay and lesbian people as gender variant. He believed that gay men were unusually feminine, and lesbian women pronouncedly masculine, overlooking that these individuals were simply the most visible examples. Indeed, it was Ulrichs, writing in 1862, who described a male who loved another male in the gendered terminology now used of trans women: *anima muliebris virili corpore inclusa* – 'a female soul confined in a male body' – and vice versa for a gay woman.

'Trapped in the wrong body' – a case study

Two famous English popularisers of Ulrichs' ideas were the gay theorists John Addington Symonds (1840-93) and Edward Carpenter (1844-1929). In *A Problem in Modern Ethics: Being an Inquiry into the Phenomenon of Sexual Inversion* (1896: 92), Symonds outlines Ulrichs' theories in detail and then summarises: 'Ulrichs maintains that the body of an Urning [gay man] is masculine, his soul feminine, so far as sex [i.e. gender] is concerned.' Carpenter's *The intermediate Sex: A Study of Some Transitional Types of Men and Women* published in 1912 was based on his 1896 essay. As the title suggests, Carpenter (1948 [1896]: 132) simply repeats Ulrichs' idea that some gays and lesbians are gender variant, 'born … as it were on the dividing line between the sexes': 'that while belonging distinctly to one sex as far as their bodies are concerned they may be said to belong mentally and emotionally to the other'. Carpenter (1948: 141) concedes that these are 'extreme' types and goes on to describe what he considers the 'more normal and perfect' type – those who conform to stereotypically masculine or feminine body types and gender expression – but still, in his view, retain a cross-gendered core.

It's intriguing to find what has become a standard trope of trans people's narratives in historical texts about homosexuality. When this theory was advanced gender variant people were not readily distinguishable from gay and lesbian people. The men and women Carpenter describes as 'extreme types' might well have identified as trans today. Once the model proved wanting in relation to sexual orientation, it was apparently re-applied to gender variant people, though again without total success.

The notion of being 'trapped in the wrong body' may sound like convenient shorthand, but many trans people increasingly disown it as descriptive of their experience. Kate Bornstein (1994: 6) calls it an 'unfortunate metaphor', and the notion that there is a 'right' body could suggest economic and racial privilege. The image of 'reaching gendered homes' is therefore being replaced by that of 'borderlands', where people make sense of their experiences (Alsop *et al.* 2002: 209ff). Nevertheless, the experience of some trans people is precisely that of the self being trapped in the 'wrong' body, with transition as the journey that undoes the incongruence by making the body a 'right match' for their gender identity.

The Bible study on John 11 (see Chapter 8 below) attempts to rehabilitate the metaphor of being 'trapped within' by pairing it with that of 'coming out'.

Medicalisation: towards transsexualism

People who would now be considered trans were identified by clinicians in 1838 and 1853 (Pfäfflin 2015: 12) but not studied comprehensively until the late nineteenth century. Krafft-Ebing's term 'metamorphosis sexualis paranoia' which dates from 1877, suggests gender transformation, but was specifically linked to mania and so avoided by Hirschfeld (1991 [1910] 234). Likewise, the term 'eonism' – named after the cross-dressing French aristocrat and diplomat, Le Chevalier d'Éon de Beaumont (1728-1810) – favoured in the early twentieth century by British sexologist Havelock Ellis was not widely adopted.

Hirschfeld sought to liberate patients from personal turmoil or social ostracism, but his clinical approach, suited to the professional, academic culture of the emerging social sciences, began to objectify and problematize trans people. His choice of the term 'transvestite', Latin for cross-dresser, is probably based on earlier usage, including the theatrical term 'travesti' for cross-gender performance. The 'first specific name for a transsexual person' (Pfäfflin 2015: 13) it made sense then, just prior to the emergence of surgical options, when clothes were still the key marker of gender variance, though Hirschfeld (1991 [1910]: 233) acknowledged its limitations: 'One disadvantage of the term is that it describes only the external side, while the internal is limitless.'

It is interesting that the term 'transvestite' survived (or maybe the author misunderstood) for someone seeking hormonal and surgical treatment in the 1960s novel *I Want What I Want* (Brown 1966: 203) when the protagonist, Wendy, keen to complete her transition by hormones and surgery, refers to herself by this term. As noted above, 'transvestite' now applies exclusively to those (usually males, though Hirschfeld's study included a female example) who alter their gender expression, but are cisgender. Over time, though, the link between crossdressing and sexual arousal, noted by Hirschfeld, has been stressed, rendering this cohort vulnerable to stigmatization as sexual deviants; and hence the increased preference for the less clinically-sounding term, 'cross-dresser', and the neutrality of 'transgender'.

Hirschfeld eventually distinguished gender variance from transvestism. He oversaw the bilateral mastectomy of a female to male (FTM) patient as early as 1912 (Whittle 2002: 36), and supervised the transition of Dora-R [Dorchen Richter] in 1921, including her gender confirmation surgery, and is associated with that of Lily Elbe in 1930. Hirschfeld even referred to the 'psychic transsexual', but his work was interrupted by the Nazi terror which destroyed his research institute. Harry Benjamin (1885-1986) has credited David O. Cauldwell with popularising the term 'transsexual' in 1949 (Bullough & Bullough 1998: 17). These were immensely significant developments. Trans people's experience was being recognised as a real phenomenon and not as a delusion, facilitating their rescue from clinicians who used suppressant drugs or electro-convulsive therapy to 'cure' them. Older trans people may still be recovering from the trauma associated with these interventions.

Benjamin was alerted to what he would call transsexual people by a referral from the sexologist Alfred Kinsey. An endocrinologist, he became a major advocate of hormone treatment and surgery for this population. When he published *The Transsexual Phenomenon* in 1966 he had seen over three hundred patients and would treat another thousand (Ettner 1999: 12ff). His most famous case was Christine Jorgensen, 'the GI who became a blond beauty' in 1953 (Meyerowitz 2002: 51ff).

Sex-reassignment surgery (SRS) was also available in the UK at this time, though mainly among the upper classes (King 1996: 88). People from other social backgrounds travelled abroad to places like Casablanca, April Ashley being the most well-known. 'Reassignment', in this context, is intended to convey the relabelling of a person's social gender, their gender identity remaining unchanged, but might be taken to imply, incorrectly, that a person's gender has been changed. Gender confirmation surgery (GCS) is a more accurate and, for many, the preferred description.

Scientific developments enabled clinicians to administer cross-gender hormone therapy to masculinise FTM clients and feminise male to female (MTF) clients. The working hypothesis emerged that gender identity arose from prenatal hormone exposure, making it unlikely that the mind could be adjusted to the body. The body, therefore, must be adjusted to the mind (Bullough & Bullough 1998: 18f). Initially, surgeries had to be negotiated with the medical establishment. Benjamin's regimen of hormone therapy and gender confirmation surgery is standard treatment in most countries today. The World Professional Association for Transgender Health (WPATH) and its Standards of Care (SOC) were originally named after him.

Points to note:
Cross-gender hormone therapy has been used to assist gender transition for about eighty years.

Gender transition involving surgery has been taking place for over a century.

A number of surgical procedures are available.

It is more appropriate to speak of gender confirmation surgery (rather than reassignment surgery).

The terms male-to-female (MTF) and female-to-male (FTM) fail to convey that, prior to transition, trans women (MTF) identified as female, and trans men (FTM) identified as male, but they are commonly used, including by trans people themselves.

Treatment options

In the UK trans people may access a psychosocial assessment for gender dysphoria from a suitably qualified health professional. Gender identity clinics and specialists are available both in the NHS and the private sector. While many trans people access hormones and surgery to address their gender dysphoria, some take up only one of these options. Others require neither and integrate their transgender identity into the gender role associated with their assigned gender, without feminizing or masculinizing their bodies. Changing gender expression may be sufficient for others. It has become increasingly obvious to those working with trans people that there is no 'one size fits all' treatment for gender dysphoria. Consequently, pathways have become much more individualized.

Hormone therapy

One of the first UK people to receive hormone therapy treatment to assist transition was Michael Dillon/Lobzang Jivaka, who was prescribed testosterone in the late 1930s by a sympathetic doctor. Dillon subsequently trained as a physician, and made his own contribution to sexology. The editors of Dillon/Jivaka's recently published autobiography, *Out of the Ordinary* (2017) claim that his 1946 book *Self: A Study in Ethics and Endocrinology* is actually the first published work on the ethics of gender transition. It predates Benjamin's *The Transsexual Phenomenon* by two decades and is written by someone transitioning rather than merely observing it.

Dillon and his contemporaries were the first generation of trans people to benefit from the synthesizing of testosterone, which had been pioneered in Holland in 1935. The effects of testosterone on the secondary sex characteristics of trans men greatly assist transition. Oestrogen is used to similar effect on trans women. Cross-gender hormone therapy remains a standard treatment today, though some people transition without it.

The current criteria for hormone therapy include persistent, well-documented gender dysphoria, capacity for consent, and the age of majority - 18 years old in the UK. (Note, though, the Gillick Competence, a medical law protocol, can determine whether a child under 16 years of age may consent to their medical treatment without parental permission or knowledge.) Some people self-prescribe using the internet or other non-regulated suppliers, but this is inadvisable due to the potential health risks. The administration of such powerful drugs should be properly supervised and their effects monitored by competent medical staff.

Older clinical protocols required the trans person to transition for a year or more before hormones could be prescribed. This could invite abuse and discrimination. Transitioning without hormone therapy rendered some trans people vulnerable by their visibility. For example, trans women with male facial markers, or trans men with unbroken voices. Those who could afford it often approached private clinicians to avoid this. Today's clinicians are usually more flexible and willing to prescribe earlier.

Surgeries

Often portrayed by the media as essential to gender transition, many trans people do not undergo gender confirmation surgery. Even those for whom it is an important milestone see it as only one aspect of the transition journey. Its importance is as a new beginning for further self-affirmation rather than as the end point of the gender journey.

The uptake of genital surgery has always been less among trans men compared with trans women. This is due partly to the complexity of the surgeries and the higher risk of unsatisfactory outcomes, though techniques have become more sophisticated and successful. Michael Dillon was the UK's first recorded trans man to undergo genital reconstruction during a series of multiple operations that began in 1945. The surgeon Sir Harold Gillies, famous for advancing plastic surgery techniques through his treatment of wartime casualties, diagnosed Dillon as 'acute hypospadic' (a genital variation in males) to conceal these innovative and, at that time, controversial, procedures. For trans men transitioning today, disguising breast tissue by binding is a common first step. A double mastectomy may follow in due course. 'Top surgery', as it is colloquially known, is usually more significant for trans men than genital surgery, as it was for Dillon.

Similarly, facial feminization surgery can assist trans women who have undergone puberty, by removing testosterone induced 'male markers' such as 'brow bossing' (bony projection on the forehead), bony eye sockets, heavy and square jaw-line. Those who can afford this surgery – it is unavailable on the NHS – might prioritise it even before genital surgery, as it can assist social interaction early in transition. However, these procedures are best delayed until female hormones have had maximum impact on the face. In 2000 Tina co-founded the Clare Project in Brighton and Hove, for people dealing with issues of gender. Several members had facial feminization surgery and for most this was their initial 'gender confirmation' procedure.

For trans men a series of procedures are available in addition to mastectomy: hysterectomy (removal of the womb), oophorectomy (removal of the ovaries) – although testosterone can cause atrophy of the ovaries, so the latter may not be necessary – and phalloplasty (surgical construction of the penis) which involves several stages. The genital reconstruction of trans women, known as vaginaplasty, is less complex, though it can be a two-stage procedure. It includes, or may be preceded by, orchiectomy (removal of the testes). These are all major surgeries and recovery normally requires several weeks, or even months, absence from work depending on the procedure. Gender reassignment is a protected characteristic under the UK Equality Act 2010, and employers and Human Resources departments are obliged to accommodate leave for appropriate procedures.

Other procedures

Chondrolaryngoplasty, commonly called a tracheal shave, is a procedure that some trans women undergo to reduce the 'Adam's Apple' or thyroid cartilage. It is sometimes combined with feminsation laryngoplasty, designed to raise the pitch of the vocal cords. Testosterone usually causes trans men's voices to break but is not always successful so speech therapy may be necessary to deepen the pitch, but oestrogen cannot reverse testosterone's effects on a trans woman's voice if it has already broken. Trans women who wish to feminize their voice without surgery often access speech therapy to alter intonation and pitch.

Testosterone is usually more obvious in its effects on trans men than oestrogen is on trans women, as it stimulates the growth of facial hair and, in some cases, male pattern baldness, besides redistributing body fat and altering body shape. Although oestrogen can stimulate a trans woman's breast tissue, soften her skin, and reduce body hair, it has minimal impact on facial hair, which requires electroepilation (electrolysis), laser, or a combination of the two, to remove it. Facial hair removal can be a long and costly process, but is available today in some NHS settings.

Passing

The term 'passing' originated in the era of racial segregation in the US. It described biracial Americans' efforts to be perceived as white in order to access education and employment, or to avoid social stigma. Being 'read' or 'clocked' meant someone had guessed one's racial history, and failure to 'pass' their scrutiny. Trans people have adopted this terminology. For many trans people 'passing' is paramount. It means that no one would guess one had transitioned. It is not about deceiving others. Rather, one's gender identity and expression are now aligned, leaving no trace of the gender assigned at birth that may have caused internal distress.

Hormone therapy, surgeries and other procedures assist trans people to 'pass', but not everyone accessing these treatments 'passes' convincingly in society according to their gender identity. Their gender history is apparent. Perhaps they have only just begun taking hormones. It could be their pitch of voice, or that their height, hand or foot size lies outside the average for their gender identity and expression. Maybe socialization in their birth assigned gender has affected their speech patterns, mannerisms or behaviour, especially if they have tried to hide or deny their gender identity. Most trans people can live with these discrepancies, if such they are. Transition was the goal. Passing is a bonus.

Psychotherapist and photographer Alex Drummond is a trans woman who has transitioned without hormones and surgery – and has a beard. Alex explains her unconventional appearance by arguing that, as someone transitioning in middle age, it would be difficult for her to pass as a woman. She sees her distinctive gender nonconformity as broadening 'the bandwidth of gender', thereby creating a space for transgender people who are unlikely to pass, but would like to come out, and could benefit and contribute much by living as their authentic selves.

'Passing privilege', as it is sometimes called, may be due to youthfulness, i.e. transitioning before natal hormones have taken full effect; physical advantages prior to transition, such as wide hips in a trans woman, height or upper body mass in a trans man. It could be thanks to social advantages, like the income to access expensive procedures. Passing is sometimes critiqued by trans people, feminists, and others for reinforcing gender stereotypes. For many trans people passing is simply an attempt to be themselves and to live safely without being abused, attacked or victimized. Chris and Tina both believe society will be healthier when everyone can be open about their past. Otherwise passing becomes yet another closet, isolating the trans person from their community and inhibiting them from working for greater gender equality for all.

Trans health

The specific health needs of trans people who have accessed medical treatment are increasingly recognized. Annual blood checks for side-effects are essential for those on hormone therapy, which is usually administered for life. Trans women in the appropriate age bracket are called for breast screening like other women, but trans men may need to access cervical screening, and trans women the prostate-specific antigen (PSA) test. NHS clinics should be sensitive to trans people who approach them for these apparently cross-gender procedures. The social care needs of older trans people are also being highlighted.

Disentangling Sex and Gender

It seems surprising that the term gender has come to denote the differences between men and women only during the past sixty years. Prior to that, men and women were usually distinguished by referring to differences of sex. This earlier usage can still be heard; for example, when women are referred to as 'the fair sex'. Previously, 'gender' tended to be limited to textbooks on grammar where, intriguingly, neuter was an option – an alternative only rarely contemplated when sex denoted male or female persons.

During the same six decades, the term 'sex' has come to connote sexuality and sexual union, rather than the differences between male and female, though it retains that meaning. The term 'transsexual' illustrates this change. As employed by Benjamin and his contemporaries, 'sexual' meant pertaining to male and female, not to sexual intercourse: gender not sexuality. Some trans people object to the term transsexual for implying that being trans is about sexual orientation, but that was not intended by those who first used the term. This 'new' association arose because the term sex became equated with sexuality, rather than the anatomical and other differences between male and female. Presumably 'gender' was adopted to describe sex difference partly because 'sex' increasingly meant sexuality.

The rise of gender

Gender has emerged in general parlance as the preferred term for sexual difference. The connection between gender and biology (male and female bodies) was loosened by Freudian, feminist and Jungian theory. Two individuals influenced the preference for the term gender in relation to trans people: one a clinician, the other a trans person and campaigner.

Robert J. Stoller (1924-91), a US professor of psychiatry, was the author of *Sex and Gender: On the Development of Masculinity and Femininity* published in 1968 and based on his extensive research with trans people. In it he noted that many behaviours, feelings, thoughts and fantasies related to the sexes lack biological connotations. He also distinguished between gender identity and gender role.

The significance of Virginia Prince (1912-2009), an advocate for heterosexual male cross-dressers, is increasingly recognized, notably in *Virginia Prince: Pioneer of Transgendering* (2006) edited by Richard Ekins and Dave King. Prince's bi-monthly magazine, *Transvestia*, first published in 1960, lasted two decades and documented the trans community's self-understanding, rather than the views of interested specialists. Prince's preference for the term gender, rather than sex, relates to her transition as female without surgical intervention. Tina recalls watching a television interview in the late 1960s, or very early 1970s, in which Prince insisted that she had undergone a change, not of sex, but of gender.

Although 'gender change' held this specific meaning for Prince, her usage assisted the emergence of 'transgender' as a popular generic term for many types of trans people.

The gender binary

As the language of 'sex', 'gender' and 'sexuality' gradually evolved, this model developed. It is often referred to as the gender binary:

Male	*biological sex*	Female
Man	*gender identity*	Woman
Masculine	*gender expression*	Feminine
[To women	*sexual orientation*	To men]

According to the gender binary, biological sex means one is either male or female, but this ignores the existence of intersex people whose chromosomes and/or sexual anatomy (primary or secondary sex characteristics) are atypical. Since the development of the internet, which enabled intersex people to network, their voices are being heard, in contrast to clinicians' opinions about them. Many claim their lives were blighted by non-consensual childhood surgeries designed to conform their bodies to male and female physical ideals dictated by the gender binary.

The gender binary conceptualises gender identity as the experience of being a man with a male body or a woman with a female body, but this overlooks transgender people whose gender identity does not align with their bodies, and non-binary people and others unable to relate to the dichotomy of man or woman.

Within the gender binary, gender expression is conceived in terms of stereotypical masculine and feminine behaviours, but these restrict everyone and transgender and non-binary people in particular.

In terms of sexual orientation, the gender binary assumes that sex, gender identity and gender expression will align to produce a cisgender, heterosexual outcome.

Even when not acknowledged explicitly, the gender binary has dominated Western culture since the Enlightenment. Theorist Thomas Laqueur argues that this 'two sex' conceptualization, which polarizes men and women as complementary opposites, emerged in the eighteenth century. From that date, the 'two sex' model gradually replaced the long-standing 'one sex' model of the human person, which had stressed the similarities between men and women's bodies, including the potential, at least, of gender fluidity (and for men in particular, sexual attraction to both men and women).

The very notion of 'sex change', or even 'gender change', rests on the presumption of a binary: one is either male or female, and hence, when someone begins to express their cross-gender identity, they must be 'changing' from female to male, or vice versa. The gradual differentiation of biological sex – chromosomes, gonads, hormones and phenotype (external sex characteristics of the body) – and gender identity (one's internal self-understanding), combined with mounting evidence that they can be at variance, has clarified that someone who transitions is living into, or confirming, rather than changing, their gender.

Although it regarded women as an inferior version of the male, thus provoking anxieties about male feminization, the pre-Enlightenment 'one sex' model had conceptualized gender as a spectrum, along which, theoretically, people could move. Twentieth-century research into the development of the human embryo demonstrated an initial lack of sex differentiation in the womb, promoting interest in, if not a return to, the one sex model. That men and women emerged from 'a common ground-stuff' was also obvious to nineteenth-century theorists like Symonds (1896: 91). In traditional cultures, where gender transition is culturally legitimized, a one-sex model may operate, or several gender identities may be recognized, as in classical Judaism which has six different terms.

The cisgender, heterosexual expectations of the two sex model have been problematic for trans people. For example, in the 1950s and early 1960s, clinicians often assumed that 'genuine' transsexuals would be heterosexual after transition, and thus that their sexuality on presenting would appear to be 'homosexual'. This conflation of gender identity and sexual orientation may even have caused some cisgender homosexual people to present for transition to avoid the stigma then attached to their sexuality, with inevitable surgical regrets.

Johns Hopkins University Hospital, a pioneering US academic treatment centre for trans people from 1965, cited such 'mistakes' among its reasons to discontinue gender confirmation surgery in 1979. This decision is often quoted by those opposed to gender transition, but it was based on the belief that trans people were mentally ill, and that their minds could be altered. Those who quote it are unlikely to acknowledge that this withdrawal of treatment was the catalyst for improving the care of trans people and led to the first version of the international Standards of Care on transgender health, published in 1979. The current WPATH Standards of Care, Version 7, state that it is unethical to attempt to alter someone's gender identity, as well as citing evidence of its ineffectiveness. In 2016 Johns Hopkins announced that gender-affirming surgery would be restored to its care programme.

Leaving the psychiatrist's couch

During the 1970s, as gender and sex were disentangled, and gender identity was increasingly perceived as innate and immutable, gender dysphoria (Fisk 1973) – indicating unease at the disjunction between one's sex and one's gender identity – began to replace the term 'transsexualism' (Ekins & King 1996: 94-6, 110). Initially, this shift from 'species' to 'disease', from the 'actor' to the condition, increased the authority of clinicians, as the 1979 Standards of Care enhanced the consultant psychiatrist's role in surgical referral (Bullough & Bullough 1998: 28) specifically to exclude those with mental health problems.

The term 'transsexualism' first appeared in the 7th edition of the US *Diagnostic and Statistical Manual of Mental Disorders* (DSM II) in 1974 (the year that the designation of homosexuality was altered though it was not removed until 1987). Re-designated as gender dysphoria in 1990 (Whittle 1996: 197), it was listed as 'gender identity disorder' in DSM III (1980), but recent consultation revealed widespread dissatisfaction with the notion that trans people are (mentally) disordered. DSM V (2013) has adopted the less clinical classification 'gender dysphoria'.

A clinical terminology timeline:	
1960s	Transsexualism
1980s	Gender Identity Disorder
2000s	Gender Dysphoria

Even in the 1970s, transsexualism tended to be located, as it had been in the late nineteenth century, on a continuum with effeminate homosexuality and transvestism, distinguished by its non-erotic motivation, anti-homosexual feelings, and strong desire for surgical intervention (Billings & Urban 1996: 105). A diagnostic distinction was made between the transsexual's sense of cross-gender identity, and the cross-dresser's temporary assumption of female attire, sometimes for purposes of arousal, though Ettner (1999: 70) thinks it was 'overly simplistic and therapeutically unproductive'. DSM III (1980) replaced the term 'sexual deviance' with 'paraphilia' to indicate that a deviation (para) relates to an object to which the person is attracted (philia). The change was hardly an improvement. DSM V speaks of 'paraphilic disorder' and includes what it describes as 'transvestic disorder'.

Ray Blanchard, who chaired the DSM V Paraphilia Working Group, classifies transsexual women into two basic types: those attracted to males, and those attracted to females. He attributes autogynephilia (love of oneself as a woman) to the latter. The notion is hardly original. A century earlier Hirschfeld (1991 [1910]: 140) had observed that some of his case studies were 'attracted … by the women within themselves', only to reject it as an explanation (1991 [1910]: 156). Blanchard has less to say about his third type, the female-to-male transsexual man who is sexually orientated to women. Absurdly over-simplistic, Blanchard's theory has been widely criticized for restoring the long discredited link between sexual orientation and gender identity; though some trans women happily identify as autogynephilic.

As these examples illustrate, despite greater awareness of trans people's self-understanding, and the development of humane treatment pathways, some clinical literature has maintained the pathologising medical culture of earlier decades. Many trans people believe its time is over, and the associations with mental illness and sexual perversion have been increasingly questioned (O'Keefe & Fox 1996: 1; Israel & Tarver 1997: 27; West 2004: 4, 18) and are emphatically denied in the evidenced-based WPATH Standards of Care. In Holland, for example, trans people's transitions are overseen by endocrinologists, while in the UK, where it has been the prerogative of consultant psychiatrists, a multi-disciplinary team approach is becoming more common, and a specialist's background might be general practice rather than psychiatry.

Gender – essentialism v social constructionism
Assaults on the medical model

Transitioning with the help of hormone therapy and surgeries is a lifeline to many people and to question these pathways can appear personally undermining. Janice Raymond's *The Transsexual Empire*, (1979) is a well-known radical feminist critique of the medical-psychiatric hegemony for perpetuating restrictive female gender roles and, in her opinion, encouraging trans women to 'colonise' women's space and bodies (Ekins & King 1996: 171ff). When Raymond wrote, of course, trans women were expected to conform to their (predominantly male) clinicians' ideas of femininity to access treatment.

One legacy of Raymond's book is the continuing rhetoric that trans women are not 'real' women. Yet it was as much an assault on patriarchy as an attack on trans people. It also contributed to a questioning of the gender binary and gender stereotypes whereby a broader range of transgender experience has found a voice. Raymond, though, perpetuated the prevailing gender hierarchy by targeting those she assumed were male (trans women), and largely ignoring trans men.

Raymond is especially alert to professionals' commercial exploitation of trans people and the encouragement of consumerist solutions to personal problems that would be better addressed by self-understanding and politics. Here gender confirming surgeries are understood as reaffirming traditional gender roles (Billings & Urban, 1996, p 111ff), but not everyone has genital surgery, especially FTMs (Ekins & King 1996: 31, 212; Bullough & Bullough 1998: 31).

Although still voiced, the concern that gender transition might undermine feminist gains appears dated, not least by its binary assumption that the personal expression of one's gender identity precludes political action to overthrow patriarchy, when one could do both.

Nature v nurture

This perennial debate applies to many aspects of human life and rarely results in a conclusive outcome. Superficially, since most people experience congruence between their birth sex and their gender identity, gender expression appears to be a given. This is the 'common sense' basis for gender essentialism. Yet even a cursory knowledge of other societies suggests that many supposedly masculine or feminine traits are interpreted differently elsewhere around the globe. This cross-cultural awareness informs the view that gender expression is largely socially constructed, and feminism has long questioned demarcation of gender roles.

Many trans people and their significant others value scientific evidence 'that pre-natal sex hormones ... and/or direct genetic effects ... have an indelible impact on brain development' and the claim that brain studies substantiate the hypothesis that gender variant people 'are intersexed at brain level' (Reed 2016: 98-99). This essentialist perspective on variant gender identity is one theoretical basis for transition. As are assessments that acknowledge the interplay of nature and nurture, such as Reid et al. (1996: 6.7), who state that 'the weight of current scientific evidence suggests a biologically-based, multi-factorial aetiology for transsexualism.'

For some trans people these debates are inconsequential: their experience simply 'is'. For others, recognising the social construction of gender has created the opportunity to discover their gender identity beyond the constraints of societal norms.

Gender as performance

First published in 1990, the intent of Judith Butler's influential text, *Gender Trouble* is evident from its subtitle: *Feminism and the Subversion of Identity*. Unlike second wave feminists like Raymond, with their essentialist notion of 'real' (biologically/anatomically) natal women, Butler's post-modernism appears to destabilize the very idea of 'gender identity'. Her belief that 'Gender is a kind of persistent impersonation that passes as real' (quoted in Alsop et al. 2002: 101), threatens both feminist and transgender essentialism. For Butler, gender is largely performative, rather than a given: an elaborate construct formed of multitudinous repeated gestures and habits.

Many feminists disapprove of drag, especially female impersonation, as demeaning of women, due to its stereotyping of femininity. Butler appreciates drag for demonstrating the artificial unity of sex, gender and performance, and thus, subverting the heterosexist gender binary. Her response to de Beauvoir's famous phrase 'one is not born a woman, but becomes one', is that '"woman" need not be the cultural construction of the female body, and "man" need not interpret male bodies' (Butler 2006 [1990]: 152). It has proved popular with some trans people, for obvious reasons. Hardly an easy read, Butler's text offers theoretical underpinning for those who are gender fluid or genderqueer. A manifesto for the playful exploration of gender roles and expression, it resembles pre-modern approaches to gender like the cross-gender performances in Shakespeare's plays and Baroque opera.

Butler's ideas have indeed proved 'troubling' to those for whom gender identity is biologically based. That being transgender might have a biological basis has been an important development, so as Kate Bornstein notes, if gender is predominantly fluid then 'It's hard to cross a boundary that keeps moving' (Whittle 1996: 211). Bornstein's response is that, whatever the latest theorist opines about gender, 'we simply feel ours is either right or complete or it isn't' (Bornstein, 1998, p. 161). Butler's work, though, has established common ground between feminists and gender variant people, and her belief that gender is performative has been significant.

In 1997 Tina participated in the five-day workshop, 'Gender in Performance' led by drag king the late Diane Torr, at Chisenhale Dance Space, London. Although not referenced, Butler's text presumably inspired it. Torr's 'Man for A Day' workshops have enabled women to experience masculine presentation and expression, particularly how men inhabit space. During 'Gender in Performance', Tina – then pre-transition – finally learnt how she ought to have been standing, sitting and moving as someone presumed to be male! She also learnt more about feminine movement. This workshop confirmed that she did not wish to oscillate between female and male, as drag performers and some trans people, do. Exploring gender through performance revealed that she would probably transition permanently.

Cabaret and pubs

The other participants in Diane's workshop were actors and there for work purposes, rather than to explore their identity. In the UK, though, trans people are associated with theatre in popular imagination, due mainly to the publicity surrounding April Ashley in the 1960s and 1970s. A performer at Le Carrousel de Paris, famous for its male and female impersonators, Ashley became a model, as did Caroline 'Tula' Cossey, a high profile UK trans woman of the next generation. Both were 'outed' by the media: Ashley in 1961, Cossey two decades later, having appeared as an extra in the latest James Bond film.

Theatre, cabaret, and pubs were safe spaces, not just for trans people to visit, but as workplaces, in an era when social ostracism limited their employment opportunities. Yet trans people are as varied as any other social group. Only a few will want to pursue a theatrical career. Legal changes from the late 1990s advanced equality for UK trans people, enabling those who transition to pursue a wide range of occupations. This is when the presumed link between trans people and male and female impersonation began to fracture. The media have yet to catch up.

The UK legal framework

Outed in the early 1960s, April Ashley dominated the headlines again at the end of the decade during her divorce case, Corbett v Corbett, in which her transition became the point at issue. The court acknowledged that Ashley had 'changed' gender. However, it ruled that, since marriage is the union of a man and a woman, as defined by sex (chromosomes, gonads, genitals), rather than gender (a psychological factor like transsexualism), Ashley's marriage to the Hon. Arthur Corbett was *void ab initio* (invalid from the outset).

This landmark ruling ended the unofficial amending of birth certificates for trans and intersex people that had prevailed for at least two decades (e.g. Michael Dillon in the 1940s). Henceforth, trans people could legally change name, updating their passport and other documents, but their birth certificate, when required, revealed their gender history. Transition left them unable to marry someone of the opposite sex. Mark Rees, a trans man who transitioned prior to women's ordination to the priesthood, was disqualified from the discernment process for ordained ministry in the Church of England because his birth certificate still stated that he was female. Rees and others challenged these injustices in the European Court of Human Rights, assisted by the inspirational human rights lawyer, David Burgess, who would subsequently transition as Sonia. The UK government proved slow to respond, and in 1992 the organization Press for Change was formed to campaign for full legal recognition for British trans people, including the right to marry.

Following a European Court of Justice ruling, the UK government introduced the Sex Discrimination (Gender Reassignment) Regulations 1999, making it unlawful to discriminate in employment or vocational training when someone intends to, is undergoing, or has undergone gender reassignment. Although trans people still face discrimination at work, this legislation effected significant protection, as previously many trans people were simply dismissed from their jobs when they transitioned.

The next major milestone of UK trans equality was the Gender Recognition Act (GRA) 2004 in which Press for Change played a significant role. The legislation, which followed a ruling of the European Court of Human Rights, gives full legal recognition, in what it calls their 'acquired' gender, to trans people who can demonstrate a diagnosis of gender dysphoria, and have transitioned for a two year minimum. Full legal recognition facilitates the issue of a new birth certificate in the acquired gender. Sex confirmation surgery is not a requirement for full gender recognition; as surgery is not always part of transition, especially for trans men. A forthcoming consultation on the UK's Gender Recognition legislation proposes removing the requirements of a gender dysphoria diagnosis and medical documentation.

The GRA 2004 enables those with full gender recognition to marry someone of the opposite sex in their Church of England parish church, if there are no legal impediments, though clergy who have conscientious objections to the trans person's gender history (if known) are not obliged to perform the ceremony themselves. Prior to the UK's Marriage (Same Sex Couples) Act 2013, married trans people could only obtain full gender recognition by divorcing their cisgender spouse. If they wished to remain together they could then contract a civil partnership with the former spouse. Full gender recognition is now possible without dissolving an existing marriage, but the 2013 legislation introduced the requirement of 'spousal consent'. To quote the Stonewall (2017: 30) document:

> In England and Wales, those who are married and want to have their gender legally recognised, need the written permission of their spouse in order to do so if they want their marriage to continue. If their spouse does not give this permission, the trans partner cannot have their gender legally recognised and remain married. This means that a spouse can effectively block their partner's decision to have their gender legally recognised.

Prior to 2013, trans people in civil partnerships (introduced under separate legislation in 2004) who transitioned, had to dissolve the partnership to obtain full gender recognition, and could then marry the former partner. Under the 2013 legislation a trans person in a civil partnership who transitions and wishes to obtain full gender recognition, must either convert their partnership to a marriage or dissolve it, as heterosexual civil partnerships remain illegal.

These legislative anomalies affecting trans people's relationships have had considerable emotional impact on their lives. The UK's equal marriage legislation (which does not yet apply in Northern Ireland) is a huge improvement but transition can be a testing time for couples.

Some will remain together, while others will part. Chapter 9 contains liturgies to mark these and other aspects of the journey.

These legal changes have also had far-reaching linguistic and conceptual consequences in that 'The meaning of Sex has been expanded to include Gender and Gender Identity' (Jillian T Weiss 2014: 3). Thus, while the GRA (2004) 'poses no challenge to the idea that there are legally only two sexes', 'the act does undermine the binary of two morphologically distinct sexes' and 'what it means to be legally recognised as a man or a woman has now been redefined as it is not based on the body or biology' (Whittle & Turner 2007).

'Gender reassignment' is a protected characteristic under the UK Equality Act 2010. Complaints that this surgical terminology is unduly narrow, restricting protections to a single category of trans people, have been countered by successive governments. They argue that the legislation covers anyone who is perceived to be trans, and thus a broad range of gender variant people. This concern will be further addressed by the forthcoming consultation on the UK's gender recognition legislation, which includes the possibility of recording one's sex as 'X'.

Some newer terms:

Genderqueer: can imply gender nonconforming expression/the person identifies as both man and woman/ as neither man nor woman/ as a combination of the two/ as an unnamed gender.

Non-binary gender identity: can mean the combination of masculine and feminine (androgynous)/an identity between male and female (intergender)/neutral gender (e.g. agender)/multiple gender identities (bigender or pangender)/ gender identity that varies over time (gender fluid)/a partial connection to gender identity (demi-gender).

Summing up

Western gender variant people are emerging from a period dominated by a medical model and clinical terminology that rendered them transgressive. Being trans is now understood as a human variation, not a medical diagnosis. The recent rapid proliferation of terms for gender variance, mostly generated by trans people themselves, demonstrates increased confidence and creativity. This linguistic pluralism suggests that the West is recovering a fluid, playful approach to gender that existed in the pre-modern era. Further back still in time – as in some traditional cultures today – gender variant people were honoured as sacred figures, their blurring or crossing of boundaries suggestive of transcendence rather than transgression.

Gender and the sacred
Shamanism

Richard Green's essay on historical and cross-cultural instances of gender variance, first published in 1966 (Green 1998: 3-14), like the examples cited by Hirschfeld (1991 [1910]: 245ff) over half a century earlier, counters the belief that transgender people are a recent phenomenon. Many of these examples trace a connection between cross-gender living and the mediation of the sacred, often referred to as shamanism.

Historically, shamanism has frequently been androgynous, but modernity is said to have unravelled 'the ancient inextricable connexion between the gods, spirituality, shamanism and transsexuality' (Ettner 1999: 9). The Hijra of India and Pakistan, often referenced in this context (O'Keefe & Fox 1996: 118; Califia 1997: 145; Hubbard 1998: 48; Ettner, 1999: 8; Mollenkott, 2001: 145) are one exception. Even when their lifestyle repels (circumstances force some hijra to become sex workers) they retain traditional religious functions, blessing rites of passage like birth or marriage.

Hirschfeld (1991 [1910]: 248ff) included historic accounts of Western perceptions of Native American men who lived as women, and women who lived as men in his classic study. More recently these third and fourth gender people were interpreted through gay (sexual) paradigms that are now giving way to transgender interpretation (Califia 1997: 120ff). The association of two spirit people with death and its rituals in Native American society (Roscoe 1998: 206f) also resonates with contemporary experience of transition as 'dying' to a former gender role, and bereavement (Bornstein 1998: 79, 185) at its loss, by loved ones or the self, as well as rebirth.

Despite the attempted erasure of gender variant people among the Americas' indigenous populations, respectfulness survives and Native Americans are unsurprised when people apparently 'choose' their gender: 'To us a man is what nature, or his dreams make him. We accept him for what he wants to be' (O'Keefe & Fox 1996: 150). Prominent in the Bible and other religious texts, in that society dreams are attended to, rather than dismissed, as in cultures dominated by science, technology and the industrial-military complex. Freud and Jung, however, have encouraged Western people to notice their dreams, and Jung envisaged the union of masculine and feminine as the goal of spiritual growth.

To honour the trans person's journey as a sacred calling, conferred by the Spirit, rather than a neurosis discovered by white medicine (Feinberg 1998: 63), one need not colonise another culture. The historic western tradition of shamanism also involved sexual transformation. The wisdom of the blind seer Tiresias, for example, in Ovid's great poem of gender and other transformations, *Metamorphoses*, is associated with his having lived as both man and woman. In her scintillating review of the amazon and the anodrogyne in Western art and literature, Camille Paglia (1991: 45) wonders provocatively:

> The shaman is an archaic prototype of the artist, who also crosses sexes and commands time and space. How many modern transsexuals are unacknowledged shamans? Perhaps it is to the poets they should go for counsel, rather than surgeons.

Paglia's either/or option is unexpectedly binary. Why not visit both? Modern culture has made it easier for trans people to access clinicians, but has neglected this archaic paradigm of the shaman, or mediator. Trans people may not necessarily be insightful into both genders, but their wisdom differs from those who have not shared their particular experience.

The Bible

The Bible too has its shamans, such as the roving bands of ecstatic prophets discussed by Theodore Jennings (2005: 81ff), who also notes the 'transgendering' (*sic*) of Israel by the prophets Amos and Hosea, Jeremiah and Ezekiel. The nation, composed of men and women, has a patriarchal name, but these prophets imagine it as a female in relation to God. Re-examining the Joseph narrative in Genesis, Jennings posits Joseph's robe as a female garment. Joseph's cross-dressing, and his facility to interpret dreams, renders him a classic shaman. He is also a eunuch, in one sense of the word, that is, a court official. In Scripture eunuchs often play a mediating role; in the Book of Esther for example. As well as Joseph and the eunuchs the Bible also contains several gender nonconforming people: among them, the only female Israelite Judge, the prophetess, Deborah (Judges 4 & 5), and, as Kessler (2005) discusses, Moses's Midianite wife, Zipporah

(Exodus 2:21; 4:20-26; 18;2-3,6), who circumcises (a male duty) her son, and Mordechai, who in rabbinic literature nurses (a female role) his adopted daughter, Esther. The Bible studies in Chapter 8 below explore the Joseph narrative and other biblical passages in more detail.

Spirituality and religion

The focus of this book is the significance of Christian spirituality and religion for gender variant people. Those from other faith traditions also testify to the importance of spirituality. In affirming his gendered self, Michael Dillon/Lobzang Jivaka made a spiritual pilgrimage from Church of England Christianity, via Gurdjieffianism, to Buddhism and ordination as a Buddhist novice-monk (*getsul*) in a Tibetan monastery in Ladakh, India (Dillon/Jivaka 2017 & 1962). Persia West (2015), who follows an eastern meditation practice, regards spirituality as fundamental to her emerging gender expression:

> I am ... in essence a creature of the spirit, which means that intangible – the mind, the heart, the spirit, feelings, emotions. I recreated myself from my own feelings, my longings, the ache to restore myself to the fullness of my own being, to become authentic to who I was and am. My body was not the foundation of my true identity; I was not defined by flesh. Finally, my flesh was defined by my inner being; the flesh followed the spirit.

The late Angela Heather Hammerton, a member of the UK network the Sibyls, Christian spirituality for trans people, made this observation: 'My transition has been about spirituality from start to finish.' In 2015 at a Sibyls weekend, Tina surveyed thirteen Sibyls' members about the role of spirituality and religion in their experience as gender variant people. Six responded. All were female and described themselves as spiritual. Their definitions of spiritual included the word 'God'. Four described themselves as religious; two did not. Their spiritual practice was mainly traditional Christian, though one used the phrase 'Live life to the full', suggestive of contemporary (non-realist) spirituality (Cupitt 1999: 58). The two people who did not consider themselves to be religious defined religious practice as 'Rulebook faith; institutional faith; cultural faith'; 'Following ritual and practices'.

All six respondents said spirituality had been an important part of their journey as a trans person. It had contributed positively for five of them, of whom two said it been both positive and negative. One respondent found it particularly affirmative: 'Spirituality has been revealed, deepened as a result of my greater self-knowledge.

It is absolutely bound together in a dual journey.' The impact of religion was more mixed, a consequence perhaps of the tone of Church statements and theorising about gender variant people, discussed in the next chapter. In terms of how religion and/or spirituality might contribute to trans people's well-being there was striking recurrence of the word 'acceptance':

> *'A sense of right and wrong; an acceptance; a loving.'*
> *'Acceptance without prejudice.'*
> *'Self-acceptance of identity was such a hurdle for me. Knowing God accepted me was a massive help and bonus.'*
> *'Being accepted for what we are is such a boon.'*
> *'Religion tolerates trans people rather than accepts them.'*

In line with the account of trans people's growing and critical ownership of the terminology, as outlined in this chapter, one person envisaged a future in which religion or spirituality might contribute to transgender people's wellbeing by 'Self-affirmation and transition to true gender without sole reliance on medical or psychiatric advice, and legal acceptance.'

Chapter 2

Setting the Scene

Source materials for Church writings on trans people.

To properly understand the arguments within the Church about trans people, it is important to consider what has been written about them. This chapter looks at the main source materials that have been used by the Church when writing policy and then explores how these source materials have been used in the reports themselves.

Two very different types of writing have emerged from these materials. The first type is a response to the perceived threat created by the existence of trans people. This describes the life experience of trans people as one of mental illness that has created unhappy, sinful and unstable people. It seeks to reinforce a conservative theological viewpoint on matters of gender and human sexuality.

The second type of writing invites the reader to learn, explore and see old paradigms with new eyes. It also seeks to provide information to help churches welcome trans people and work with them pastorally. While some of it may seem less than a ringing endorsement now, they must be recognised as a genuine attempt to engage openly with a complex issue.

It is also important to remember that there has been little written on the subject that has been used by the Church and much of it is quite old. Much of the newer writing includes a response to what the Church has said as well as being an indication of growing confidence of the trans community and a broader interest in it.

Oliver O'Donovan – *Transsexualism and Christian Marriage*

O'Donovan's aim is to explore whether gender reassignment surgery produces a genuine change of gender. His concern is about transsexual people marrying and if this is actually same sex marriage in another guise. He concludes that transsexuals cannot change their God-given chromosomal gender and so they remain in their birth gender and therefore cannot marry.

The key scripture used is Genesis 1:27. O' Donovan sees this as the basis for a God ordained binary gender. He believes that transsexuality disrupts this divine plan and should be resisted (O'Donovan 1982: 6).

Other Scripture is not explored but quoted as a set of self-evident assertions. For example, he uses Mark 10.6 on marriage (O'Donovan 1982: 6) and 1 Corinthians 6.18, claiming that there is an analogy between Paul's condemnation of fornication and transsexualism (O'Donovan 1982: 16). He uses the tale of Ananias and Sapphira, who did not give all they possessed to the Church (Acts 5-11), as an analogy for transsexual marriage. He believes it leaves transsexuals as exposed in judgement for forsaking their birth gender (O'Donovan 1982: 19) as these two early converts. He argues that conducting what he regards as para marriages (O'Donovan 1982: 21) devalues both the vocations of singleness and heterosexual marriage.

Instead of Scripture, his main source of authority when considering transsexual marriage appears to be the legal ruling Corbett v Corbett which defined the status of transsexual people until the 2004 Gender Recognition Act. While it is recognised that this legal ruling did set the precedent for the legal status of trans people at the time he was writing, O'Donovan seems unaware this could be changed by a later ruling or legislation and thus removing the authority for his argument.

O'Donovan is also selective in how he uses the available published materials available at the time. An example is the testimony of Nicholas Mason (Mason 1980) about the struggles he faced in transitioning gender. O'Donovan completely ignores this biographical account and merely uses it to show that some doctors refer to the birth rather than the declared gender of trans people.

When considering GCS, O'Donovan mainly refers to the work of John Money and the Johns Hopkins medical centre. He disagrees with the expert position that being trans is a form of intersexuality and that sex can be reassigned, but does not cite dissenting opinions or authors to prove his assertion (O'Donovan 1982: 17). By doing this he discards the only medical evidence he presents.

Instead, he believes gender dysphoria is a psychological illness (O'Donovan 1982: 17) that can be cured by the acceptance of the God-given gendered body, and that medical procedures produce only a facsimile rather than a genuine change of gender (O'Donovan 1982:16). While he does advocate surgery as a treatment of last resort to relieve the profound distress experienced by some transsexual people (O'Donovan 1982: 17), he is critical about healthy bodies being altered to conform to what he considers a mental illness. The weakness of O'Donovan's beliefs about the causes of transsexuality is that they are completely uncorroborated by medical evidence. It is the opinion of someone with no expertise in transsexualism.

Central to O'Donovan's writing is his investigation of the 'transsexual claim' which he believes is based on three assertions:

> *my body is an accident that has befallen the real me, the real me has a true sex, male or female; and I know immediately what that sex is without needing anyone to tell me (O' Donovan 1982: 10).*

His arguments to counter this claim are unconvincing. He provides no evidence that the 'gender accident' is psychological rather than physical in nature. His attempt to refute trans people's assertion of their real gender does not recognise the value of lived experience and the importance of self-identity. His third point overlooks that our gender system teaches us clear gender roles for men and women. People have more than enough information to make an informed decision about which gender they are.

He also introduces a puzzling charge of Gnosticism against transsexuals (O'Donovan 1982: 11). He argues that the body is not something that is divorced from the spirit, but that both body and spirit should inform each other. He seems unaware that this argument could be used exactly the opposite way to affirm transsexuality. This argument also ignores the Christian tradition of asceticism that seeks to allow the spirit to triumph over the body.

It is important to remember that this was written almost forty years ago, when social attitudes were very different. The problem is that it is still being used as an authoritative text by churches on the issue of transsexuality. It is the basis of both the Anglican and Evangelical Alliance's published papers on the issue which are explored later in this chapter.

David Horton – *Changing Channels? A Christian response to the Transvestite and Transsexual.*

Horton's aim is to provide a pastoral response to people who cross-dress or who are transsexuals. He disagrees with O'Donovan about the given-ness of binary gender and considers that people may be both physically and psychologically intersex (Horton 1994: 45). He believes there is a large, undiscovered community and is aware of organisations such as the Beaumont Society (which is a social group for transsexuals and cross-dressers). He also mentions analogous people in other cultures such as the lady-boys of Thailand, and the Berdache of the First Nation Peoples of the Americas.

Horton writes with knowledge about his subject. He makes the distinction between transgenderists (those who do not seek GCS), and transsexual people (those who do). He believes that potential partners need to be told early on about gender dysphoria, and that wives need time and help to adjust to any disclosure. He believes that faith can be an enormous support for both transgender people, their families and friends. He believes the Church has a role to play in seeking justice for trans people in society, and laments that support and help for them are found in the gay community rather than the Church (Horton 1994: 48).

Horton explores the scriptures and concludes there is no biblical impediment to transsexualism. Like O'Donovan, he is concerned about the decoupling of soul and body, but considers that surgery is better than the lasting distress and risk of suicide he has observed in his pastoral work with those who are unable to get treatment to resolve their gender dysphoria. Of interest is his challenge to the reader when he asks:

> Do we represent Christian values to those who are different, or do we merely seek their conformity to our patterns of behaviour to save ourselves embarrassment? (Horton 1994: 56)

But while Horton argues for inclusion within the Church, he also considers that 'odd' people may drive away children and families. He considers that it may be more acceptable for trans people to appear as their birth gender at church or be given chaplaincy services in their home. While this may not be a ringing endorsement it is a genuine attempt to sympathetically explore and engage with the pastoral issues regarding trans people from thirty years ago.

Rodney Holder – *Crucible articles on transsexuality.*

Holder produced a two-part article that appeared in the Anglican Journal *Crucible* over two successive issues in 1998. His concern is both pre-operative and post-operative transsexual people. The first article examines transsexualism as a medical condition and concludes that transsexuality is 'to be determined very early in life and not a matter of individual choice' (Holder 1998a: 94). Like Horton, he concludes that there are no biblical impediments to transsexuality, and cites God's acceptance of eunuchs in Isaiah 56, Matthew 19 and Acts 8 as evidence. While he condemns cross dressing as outlined in Deuteronomy (because he considers there is an erotic element to it), he considers preoperative transsexual people presenting as their acquired gender as 'aiming for a sense of wholeness' (Holder 1998a: 96).

In the second article Holder refutes O'Donovan's concerns about surgery on healthy bodies. He argues that many types of surgical and medical interventions are used to promote wholeness, and makes the helpful distinction between the intention behind the surgical procedure and the surgical procedure itself. He concludes that gender confirmation surgery is an attempt towards wholeness and there should be no objection to it provided there are appropriate safeguards to prevent inappropriate surgical decisions.

He also disputes O'Donovan's position that gender is chromosomal, arguing that gender is more than genetics and that social identity and external genitalia must be considered. He also disagrees with O'Donovan regarding the marriage of post-operative transsexuals, provided it is within a heterosexual union. He believes those who have married when they were preoperative should remain celibate, and that the marriage contracted in their birth gender is still valid and unable to be dissolved.

Victoria Kolakowski – 'An ethical response to transsexual persons' and other writings

Victoria Kolakowski is the only transsexual writer to be quoted directly in Church reports about trans people. In 'An Ethical Response to Transsexual Persons' (1997b) she argues that transsexuality is a modern phenomenon that is not really addressed within Hebrew Scriptures such as Deuteronomy 22:5.

Her main contribution to the debate is the linking of transsexual people with biblical eunuchs. Her argument is that if eunuchs are approved in scripture, then transgender people are also approved. This is also explored further in 'The Concubine and the Eunuch: Queering Up the Breeder's Bible' (Kolakowski 1997a). It will be discussed later in this chapter.

Fraser Watts – 'Transsexualism and the Church'

This article is an attempt to sum up the writings on transgender people up to its publication date in 2002. Watts concludes that hard facts about the causes of transsexualism are in short supply (Watts 2002: 64). He does not believe gender dysphoria is a mental illness. Instead he argues that the psychological illness often associated with gender dysphoria is just as likely to be caused by the stress of living in an unsympathetic society.

Like Horton, he is aware of several societies with gender liminal roles such as the Berdache and recognises they have an element of the sacred within them. He also points to Christian traditions of religious celibacy and speaks of the Church Father Origen who practiced a self-orchiectomy to become a eunuch for the Kingdom.

Watts appraises the work of O'Donovan and the Evangelical Alliance. While he believes O'Donovan's concerns about surgery have some merit, he also argues that the wholeness of a person is more than the integrity of the body. In evaluating the Evangelical Alliance report Watts is suspicious of the insistence on a psychological cause of transsexuality arguing, that it is likely that there is at least some biological basis for transsexuality (2002: 77). He is uneasy about how the Evangelical Alliance report pits the 'truth of someone's sex' against their 'false gender beliefs' (2002: 78). He points out that dualism has a respectable place in the Christian tradition and that the use of the term Gnosticism in relation to transsexual people is 'a very loose use'. He is also concerned over the reliance on Genesis 1:27 as an exclusive statement when there are demonstrably intersex folk who do not fit in a gender binary. Given this biological reality, he contends it may be logical to assume that trans people are another category (2002: 79).

Watts also considers the impact on transsexual clergy. He suggests they should take time out of ministry while they adjust to their gender transition and then the Church should attempt to find a place for a committed transsexual minister who wishes to continue ministry.

In summary

These early writings are concerned with transsexuality, rather than with trans or gender queer folk, but they form the basis by which all trans people are viewed in the reports in the next section. Except for O'Donovan, these early writings are cautiously sympathetic. The writers assess scripture and find little impediment to the acceptance of trans people. Some see eunuchs in the Old and New Testaments and Church Fathers like Origen as likely precedents. They express concerns but also point to pastoral opportunities, and (in the case of Kolakowski) new insights into scripture.

All writers concede that gender confirmation surgery may be the best option for transsexual people, even if they see it as an action of last resort. It is therefore surprising that these writings are the primary source materials for the reports from the Evangelical Alliance and the Church of England whose response has been overwhelmingly negative.

What the Church has said

The Christian Church in Britain has spent very little time considering trans people. There are no statements from many of the smaller mainstream denominations such as Methodism, the Society of Friends or The United Reformed Church (URC). Much of their conversation and energy has focused on the issues that gay and lesbian people present, especially in recent times around same sex marriage. The Methodist Church is a good example. Their paper *Common Human Sexuality* (1990) mentions trans people only once in passing, though their recently produced *Equality and Diversity Inclusion Toolkit, Module 5, Gender*, rectifies this omission.[1]

The denominational responses to trans people from the UK Church are the Evangelical Alliance's *Transsexuality* (2000) and the Church of England Reports *Issues in Human Sexuality* (1991), *Some issues in human sexuality: A guide to the debate* (2003) and The Pilling Report (2013). These will now be explored.

The Evangelical Alliance – *Transsexuality*

The Evangelical Alliance published their report called *Transsexuality* in 2000. Their aim was to explore transsexuality from a conservative Christian viewpoint and to provide a policy statement for their member churches to follow. A later version was produced that included observations on equality legislation in 2005 which has since been withdrawn from circulation.

Understanding of transsexuality in the report

The report explains there are non-operative trans people as well as transsexuals and makes a distinction between transvestitism (which they deem has an erotic element) and being trans. While it admits that most transsexual people are happy with gender confirmation surgery (2000: 24), it argues that the duty of Christians is obedience to God and that birth gender should be a clear intention of God's will. It contends that the onus of proof should be on transsexual people and the medical establishment to claim the reality of transsexualism rather than the onus of proof being on Christians to justify their position on the issue (2000: 52). The report recognises that the Church is seen by society as 'strong on condemnation and weak on compassion' (2000: 53) and a denier of human rights (2000: 52). It justifies this stance as

1   http://www.methodist.org.uk/ministers-and-office-holders/equality-diversity-and-inclusion/edi-toolkit

being countercultural against the 'me-first culture' and the 'deification of sex' (2000: 54).

Halfway through the report the central concern against transsexuality is explored. This concern is that if transsexuality is real, it renders the gendered distinctions between male and female 'infinitely plastic' (2000: 57). This plasticity would threaten the conservative understanding of gender promoted by the Evangelical Alliance (2000: 48). This concern is further explored in the ethical implications section where it affirms that a given biological sex is fundamental. Any revision of a conservative theology of gender is a form of unacceptable Gnosticism which makes gender subjective and contingent. This argument is borrowed directly from O'Donovan.

Transsexuality further argues that sex and gender are a biological reality (sic) and a matter of public fact, and that these facts are more important than self-perception. While it acknowledges that some people may see not this reality (sic) it argues they should be dissuaded from their false gender beliefs and be led to the truth of their biological sex (2000: 65). It considers GCS is only appropriate in matters of pastoral emergency (2000: 67) as a way of managing symptoms rather than curing the problem.

Use of Sources

The report offers a review of scientific literature. This section begins by asserting that science does not have greater authority in this area than Scripture. It also dismisses much of the science it discusses as 'one off' results and a deliberate skewing of results to appease unspecified 'single issue lobby groups' (2000: 15).

Transsexuality begins by referencing work by evangelical Christians Whitehead and Whitehead (1999) whose work is neither published in an academic publication nor peer reviewed. When the report engages with peer reviewed literature it only quotes selectively from it. An example of this is how it establishes the incidence of transsexuality (Gallarda et al. 1996). While the report correctly quotes the statistics from the article, it ignores the article's finding that medical intervention is the only way to improve the clinical condition of transsexual people. This omission is presumably because it would undermine the EA's contention that surgery is a last resort after all other options have failed.

Another example occurs when discussing Bosinski et al. (1997). This study showed that 83.3 per cent of untreated female to male transsexuals had above normal values for at least one measured androgen (male hormone) as opposed to 33.3 per cent of a female control group. While the authors consider this significant, *Transsexuality* does not report this finding. Instead it attempts to explain that the masculine body shape of the FTM participants observed in the study meant that they were treated differently than other women (sic). The report contends that this treatment was the cause of their transsexuality rather than the greater presence of androgen. This can only be a misinterpretation of the article which clearly argues a biological link to transsexuality.

Transsexuality also criticises the work of Gooren (Zhou et al. 1995). It attempts to throw doubt on his study, arguing that brain structures change in response to behaviour. As evidence it cites an article in the popular science magazine *Scientific American* (Kandel & Hawkins 1992) rather than peer reviewed clinical studies.

The report then argues that since a biological cause has not been established, the obvious answer is that the cause must be psychological. In evidence the report misquotes Holder as endorsing psychological causation (2000: 22). What he is discussing at this point is his concern that a proved biological basis for transsexualism could be tested in utero and may prompt parents to abort transgender foetuses (1998a: 92). Later on he is further misquoted as having cited a high incidence of regret after GCS (2000: 25). Whereas what he was recommending was that the Harry Benjamin Gender Dysphoria Guidelines (now the WPATH Standards of Care) should be used because they increase the probability of a successful gender transition (Holder 1998a: 94). This misquotation implies that there is a great deal of dissatisfaction with GCS. Peer reviewed studies such as Lawrence (2003) report the exact opposite.

Transsexuality also cites Cohen-Ketternis and Arrindell (1990) who show trans people remembered their parents were more emotionally distant than a cisgender control group. What is not quoted is the discussion about the impact of subsequent events on the interpretation of memory (1990: 619), and the possibility that a trans person who had subsequently experienced difficulties with parents may find a change in their interpretation of their personal histories.

The overwhelming impression is that this material has been included to give a veneer of scientific respectability to the report. A mixture of popular science, Christian pseudoscience, misquotation and the selective quoting of peer reviewed sources does not help the reader to come to an understanding of the origins of gender dysphoria or transsexuality. What the reader is left with is a vague impression that transsexuality is psychological in basis and that both trans people and their parents are to blame. This is neither a useful nor an accurate summary of the cited material.

Use of Scripture

Given the Evangelical Alliance's assertion of the primacy of Scripture, very little space is given to the exploration of it. Of the eighty-seven pages only three and a half pages are specifically devoted to the exploration of Scripture. These discuss the possibility of a progression from the prohibition of Deuteronomy 23:1 to the recognition of Matthew 19 and to the acceptance of the Ethiopian Eunuch in Acts 8:26-39. An attempt is made to wrestle honestly with the complexities discussing whether Deuteronomy can apply to transsexuality and the applicability of Matthew 19 (2000: 46). Instead of continuing this biblical work, the report then veers off into a doctrinal discussion of Creation and marriage (2000:48), The Fall, Redemption and Final Restoration (2000: 51).

Impact on Church practice

The authors believe that with prayer, guidance and support, reversion to birth gender is possible for some transsexual people, but they also acknowledge this may not be possible for all. They accept their member churches have a pastoral responsibility towards trans people but consider it should take the form of 'heavy shepherding' towards gender conformity (2000: 83).

The report concludes with advice to churches on issues such as dealing with marriage (where it concludes that divorce or separation may be the best option); whether the repentant transsexual person should receive baptism and communion (this is left to individual churches but with a warning that privileging (sic) a transsexual person may lead to resentment amongst congregants) and a discussion concerning whether transsexual people could be in church leadership (not recommended because they are said to be poor role models).

On matters of pastoral care, it recommends a healing (sic) of disunity between body and spirit (2000: 81). It discusses compassionately the need to allow openly trans members to be part of a church to save them from self-harm and suicide, but counsels a gentle heavy shepherding where possible (2000: 82). The report clearly states that the only appropriate Christian response for a transsexual person who refuses to return to their birth gender is celibacy (2000: 78).

While it is less than enthusiastic about trans people, the report recognises the pastoral reality that most trans people are happy post-transition. While coming from the conservative social and theological position of its membership, it does accept member churches have a pastoral responsibility to trans people and attempts a compassionate response within its own understandings.

Trans Reactions to the report

Justin Tanis (2003: 98) is particularly concerned about the recommendations of shepherding back to gender conformity and the 'last resort' option of GCS. He asks how much misery a person should be put through at the cost of their inclusion in the Christian community. He is also very suspicious of the charge of Gnosticism, arguing that trans people fully inhabit their bodies and that is what makes the pain of gender dysphoria so intense (2003: 100). He is also deeply concerned that the onus of action to promote acceptance is entirely put on the transsexual person, and that the Evangelical Alliance does not suggest any form of education or enabling of congregations to accept transsexual members (2003: 101).

Tina's critique of the Evangelical Alliance report is that it is disingenuous because it supports medical intervention to 'correct' intersex conditions but does not advocate surgery for trans people because they are born with normal (sic) bodies. She dismisses the claim that GCS is experimental, noting that there is nearly eighty years of experience (Beardsley 2007: 14), considering the report 'simplistic and rigid' (Beardsley, O'Brien and Woolley 2012: 261) and overly dogmatic in its insistence on a psychological cause for transsexuality. She is also critical that it has not engaged with trans people to gain their perspectives (Beardsley 2007: 14).

In conclusion

It would be hard to see *Transsexuality* as particularly helpful. It is truly the child of O'Donovan and recycles many of his original arguments. It also continues his tradition of ignoring expert opinion and lived experience in favour of championing an ideological position that cannot be arrived at in any academically credible way. But what is the most distressing about *Transsexuality* is the lack of humility or humanity in this report. Even with its obvious flaws it is unshaken in its own self-confidence. It also places a theological viewpoint before any compassion, kindness or pastoral sensitivity. It is my fondest hope that the Evangelical Alliance will reconsider their position and withdraw from circulation a document that is neither helpful nor hopeful in any sense.

The Church of England: *Issues in Human Sexuality, Some issues in human sexuality: A guide to the debate* and *Report of the House of Bishops Working Group on human sexuality* (the Pilling Report)

The Church of England has produced three reports that mention trans people: *Issues in Human Sexuality: A statement by the House of Bishops* (1991), *Some issues in human sexuality: A guide to the debate* (2003) and *Report of the House of Bishops Working Group on human sexuality* (the Pilling Report) (2013).

Issues in Human Sexuality and the Pilling Report only mention trans people tangentially. They do not discuss any of the source material or explore Scripture regarding transsexuality. They provide neither guidance nor insights. *Issues in Human Sexuality* merely notes in section 3.19 that 'human sexuality is a fragile system, easily distorted and broken' (1991: 26). It lists those distorted sexualities as those unwilling to have intercourse with their spouse and trans people.

While the methodology section of the Pilling Report tells us that trans people were interviewed as part of the consultation process the working group undertook, trans people are referred to only three times in the report. The first mention is in paragraph 30 where it concludes that the issues trans people encounter are about feelings of shame and exclusion and not primarily about sexuality (2013: 7). The second reference admits that 'transgender and intersex conditions raise important theological issues' (2013: 9) but this is explored no further. The third is Paragraph 198 which states that 'Unlike people with intersex conditions, their [meaning trans people] bodies are unambiguously either male or female' (2013: 61). With this observation, it directs readers to *Some issues in human sexuality* to explore these matters further.

The Pilling Report does not give any guidance on transsexuality because its focus is same sex marriage and it does not consider the complexities of marriage for intersex and transgender people. The list of interviewees in Appendix 2 lists two specifically transgender groups, Sibyls and the Trans Awareness Group, and also respected academics such as Dr Susannah Cornwall. To have not considered marriage for trans and intersex folk seems a missed opportunity.

Some issues in human sexuality: A guide to the debate

Bishop Richard Harries explains in the foreword 'The title of this study exactly defines its purpose' (House of Bishops 2003: ix). The aim of the report was to expand on the earlier *Issues in Human Sexuality* and add material to act as a guide rather than change Church of England teaching.

Understanding of transsexuality

The report gives two definitions of transsexuality. The first is from the Home Office's Report of the Interdepartmental Working Group on Transsexual People (2000). This report is the product of senior civil servants who consulted with many organisations with experience of trans people including the Beaumont Society, the British Medical Association, the Gender Identity Research & Education Society (GIRES,) Liberty, Northern Concord, Press for Change, FTM Network, The Gender Trust, and experts such as Dr Zoe-Jane Playdon and Professor Louis Gooren and Dr Stephen Whittle. What is quoted in *Some issues in human sexuality* is a less than complete reproduction of the definition given by the Working group's report. It leaves out the following underlined sections:

> *1.1 <u>People with gender dysphoria or gender identity disorder live</u> with a conviction that their physical anatomy is incompatible with their true gender role. They have an overwhelming desire to live and function in the opposite <u>biological</u> sex. <u>Some people become aware of their transsexualism as children while others discover their feelings later in life. Once experienced these feelings are unlikely to disappear.</u>*

> *1.2 <u>The cause of the condition remains obscure. Many transsexual people benefit from counselling and others live happier lives following hormone treatment and gender reassignment surgery</u> (2000: 3).*

In stark contrast the second definition is from *Transsexuality* describing transsexuality as a psychological illness 'in which the mind can no longer accept the body' (2003: 223). *Transsexuality* cannot claim such a vast representation or expertise as the Home Office Report. Prof Zoe-Jane Playdon specifically addresses the issue of psychological illness inherent in the Evangelical Alliance definition:

> ....in 1984 the American Psychiatric Association gave diagnostic criteria. At that point, the circumstance [transsexuality] might be described as a physiological condition which was subject to

verification by psychiatric analysis - the analysis verified, or proved, that the individual was not mentally ill (Home Office 2000:40).

In *Some issues in human sexuality* the possible causes of transsexuality are listed as physiological (either with a genetic or hormonal component), psychological (because of poor parenting) and social (as a reaction against a too rigid gender system) (2003: 226). While it acknowledges that people do not choose transsexuality it goes on to make the confusing claim that people can choose not to be transsexual by accepting their natural (sic) gender.

This is an important point and is the crux of the logic followed in *Some issues in human sexuality*. If transsexuality is a psychological illness it can be cured. If it is a choice, and trans people continue to choose transsexuality, they can be blamed for doing so. While the report is willing to consider these possibilities, it is not willing to explore a third option: that transsexuality is naturally occurring and is a complex interplay between many factors over which the individual has very little control.

It is this refusal to consider this possibility that is the reason that *Some issues in human sexuality* champions the understanding of transsexuality as a psychological illness. If this is not the case, the interpretation of Genesis 1:27 as a divinely ordered rigid dichotomy of male and female begins to break down. Gender may be more fluid than the Church is willing to admit and the theological underpinning of gender espoused in this and earlier reports simply will not continue to work.

Sources

The report uses the (then) thirty-year old work of O'Donovan and the more recent *Transsexuality* as the principal source documents. It does not fully consider the other source documents that it quotes. The voices of Kolakowski, Watts and Holder are used as a foil representing a more liberal view of transsexuality.

Some issues in human sexuality does not include the voices of trans people, those who work with them, or any recent peer reviewed journal which may shed light on the causes of transsexuality, or recommendations of pastoral care for trans people and their families. It does not fully utilise the Home Office Report cited. While it could be argued that *Some issues in human sexuality* is a theological work and not a review of the causes of transsexualism this would be disingenuous. The report itself sets out to explain transsexuality and is highly selective in its use of source materials to do so.

One such example is the inclusion of a single medical journal article (Lothstein & Levine 1981). This article describes a therapeutic regimen of what can only be described as reparative therapy. It describes patients being broken down over several months by aggressive psychotherapy and 'electric treatment' until they form a therapeutic alliance (sic). The article reports that these patients frequently feel unsafe and refuse to be left alone with therapists. Refusal of cooperation is labelled 'lack of productivity because they are incapable of fantasy and lacking in mental imagery' (Lothstein & Levine 1981: 927). The article claims an 80 per cent success rate of curing (sic) transsexual people.

The five case studies of healed (sic) individuals show people with severe mental health problems, including bipolar disorder, alcoholism, schizophrenia, and issues arising from the survival of childhood abuse. It should be noted that under the WPATH Standards of Care it is doubtful if these folks would be eligible for GCS as they are presented in this study. It should also be noted that critique around reparative therapies already existed at this time as evidenced by Bennet (2000). This critique is not engaged with on any level. Citing only Lothstein and Levine (1981) is not an adequate discussion of the effectiveness of reparative therapies, although they are embraced in *Some issues in human sexuality* as a cure for transsexuality.

Another problem with the source material used is that there are several unpublished and inaccessible materials, such as the letters from Peter Forster and Catholic theologians Luke Gormally and George Woodall. These were neither published nor peer reviewed and so they cannot be evaluated. Of particular concern is the inclusion of an article from Parakaleo Ministries by Keith Tiller and Mark Dainton. The report cites the testimony of Dainton as evidence. It should be noted that Dainton later publicly severed links with Parakaleo and was living as a trans woman around the time the report was published.

Scripture
Scripture is briefly discussed and it is found that there are no specific biblical injunctions against transsexuality. It rejects Deuteronomy 23:1 as a ban on transsexuality citing, that any prohibition is lifted by Isaiah 56:4-5, Matthew 19:12 and Acts 8:26-9. The report spends longer on Genesis 1:27 reiterating O'Donovan's view of the immutability of sex and gender (2003: 230). Watts' more inclusive view of Genesis 1:27 is neither offered nor discussed.

Advice on Church Practice

Chapter 7 discusses the possibility of Christian marriage for post-operative trans people and raises two objections to it. The first objection is that trans people have deliberately voided their ability to procreate. This is an inconsistent argument because the Church of England does not require fertility testing or declarations of intention to procreate from any couple. Nor does it refuse to marry those beyond child bearing age. The second objection is that a person would be psychologically unfit for marriage because of the psychological cause of transsexuality. This argument is not consistent with expert opinion in this area. A third, implied objection, is that it is gay marriage through the 'backdoor' as inferred by the inclusion of Kolakowski's point about the increasing recognition of same sex unions in civil society.

In Chapter 8, 'Homosexuals, bisexuals and transsexuals in the life of the Church', the report raises the subject of transsexual clergy. It recommends that they should be ineligible for ordination because they are unwholesome (2003: 287) and that they are not psychologically stable (2003: 288).

The report uses a quote from Watts (2002) as evidence for this assertion. Watts begins his discussion by saying he can see no reason for a prohibition on transsexual clergy (2002: 81). He then goes on to explore the objections of others and discounts these. He cites the case of the Revd Carol Stone and the acceptance of her congregation after transition. Misquoting Watts in this way makes it seem as if he only highlights problems rather than also exploring possibilities, thereby altering the original writing.

Reactions by trans people

Tina notes in her critique that none of the voices of professionals who work with transgender people or the voices of trans people of faith are included (2005: 342). She also notes that more favourable reports within the Church of England's tradition that may have balanced the debate, such as the 1989 Osborne Report on Homosexuality, were completely ignored (2005: 339). She also argues that the exclusion of other pertinent materials is not reasonable, and that weight is disproportionately given to tradition and a specific reading of Scripture. She notes that the argument regarding Scripture is circular with the interpretation of Genesis 1:27 as purportedly proving binary gender. She also argues that *Some issues in human sexuality* gives no real context for transsexuality because it does not give information about DSM IV or The Harry Benjamin International Guidelines for the Treatment of Transsexual People. She is also critical of the prominence given to reparative therapies and quotes experts in the field in rebuttal.

Trans people speaking for themselves

The aim of the literature produced by trans people is primarily to tell their stories and explore the way these stories may inform the wider world. Within this literature, the term trans is understood differently from the literature discussed previously. While Church based writers have been preoccupied by biology and medical considerations, the writings of trans people about themselves are primarily about identity. This identity is broader than the narrow categories of transsexuality or those with gender dysphoria. It often includes all those who could be considered gender variant in some way.

This section is limited to only UK trans voices or those quoted in UK church reports. This includes autobiographical stories by Mann (2013) and Ford (2012) and the anthologies *Trans/formations* (2009) and *This is My Body: hearing the theology of transgender Christians* (2016). The many US voices that provided background reading for this book include McCall Tigert and Tirabassi (2004), Mollenkott (2001), Mollenkott & Sheridan (2003), Sheridan (2001), Stryker (2008) and Tanis (2003) and are listed in the further reading section.

Writings of trans people on Scripture/theology
Exploring the eunuchs in Scripture

Both Reay (2009) and Kolakowski (1997a, 1997b and 2007) make the connection between biblical eunuchs and trans people. Reay makes parallels between Jesus' discussion of eunuchs in Matthew 19 and modern trans people (2009:156). He concludes that Jesus' discussion about eunuchs and particularly verse 19:12 is a direct and clear analogy. These identifications offer trans people visible narratives of identity located within the Bible. They also provide a powerful counter narrative to O'Donovan, *Transsexuality* and *Some issues in human sexuality*.

There is a concern that this use of eunuchs plays into a medical model whereby identity becomes located entirely in the physical, and transition becomes a medical process. That approach misses the complex issues of constructing identity, finding the courage to follow one's inner truths despite the obstacles or to challenge the gendered assumptions of society. It also negates the ability to self-name and self-define and cedes the power of self-definition and self-expression to others. It also excludes. It ignores the pre-operative, the gender queer and those happy in their gender expression without surgery or medical intervention. As Stone (2006) argues, to limit the identification of the trans identity to a category of postoperative transsexual people ignores the richness and the variety of the trans experience.

Nor do trans people occupy a similar place in our society to that of the eunuchs. The only demographic study of trans people is Rosser et al. (2007). It shows a population at high risk from HIV, experiencing greater mental health issues than average, and suffering from the threat of violence (2007: 52), more often without family or supporting social structures, and economically poorer than the general population (2007: 59). There is very little in this description that would seem analogous to the elevated social position of the biblical eunuch.

Apophatic Theology

A queer interpretation of the apophatic tradition is represented by two contributions in *Trans/formations*. Cornwall (2009: 34) argues that using apophatic ways of doing theology quashes boundaries of heteronormativity and homonormativity and creates a way through them by claiming that all human imagery is insufficient. This is also echoed in B.K. Hipsher's contribution which explores how a trans image of God can be liberating because it:

> transgresses all our ideas about who and what God is and can be... transports us to new possibilities of how God can incarnate.... transfigures our mental image from limitations... transforms our ideas about our fellow humans..... and transcends all we think we know about God (2009: 99).

Trans woman and Church of England priest Rachel Mann also uses apophatic theology in her memoir/theological reflection *Dazzling Darkness* (2012). As she states in her introduction:

> so much of what I want to say here comes down to the idea that we cannot quite say who God is and as such we must ultimately be left in silence in her presence.... it is only in the creative dynamic between Word and Waiting that we may hope to be our true selves (2012: 16,17).

While apophatic theology has an ancient pedigree and is scarcely the invention of these writers, it can be argued that they bring different and new insight to it. They bring an element of disruptiveness to the idea of a gendered God, either through their own gender journeys, or their theological reflections about the known limits of gender.

Contribution to Liberation theologies

This emphasis on personal histories is the third contribution made to theology. God's identification with the poor and marginalised, the importance of embodied experience and liberation theology's challenge to oppressive structures is also part of this trans liberation theology. Mann (2012) chronicles her struggles with both illness and gender identity and reflects on what she has learnt from her experience. She asserts that because she has experienced 'otherness', failure, loss and brokenness, she has had to deeply ponder her faith. This has led to a richer and deeper faith life in the 'dazzling darkness' rather than in the light of certainty.

Ford's (2013) self-published account of her own experiences and struggles as a transgender Christian contains an identification with a suffering, abandoned Christ (Ford 2013: 86). This is also echoed by Hannah Buchanan's identification with a ridiculed and marginalised Christ (2009: 44).

These accounts provide a direct challenge to those who confidently expound the immutability of gender from their positions of institutional power. I believe it is no accident that the denominational responses on trans people exclude their experiences, otherwise their stories would offer a powerful counter narrative to their assertions.

What can trans people tell us about their pastoral care?

Two different aspects of pastoral care are contained in the writings of UK trans people. The first is a set of pastoral guidelines called *The Transsexual Person is my Neighbour* (2007) written by Tina, some of which has been updated within this book.

The second contribution to pastoral care is the crafting of liturgies designed to celebrate and legitimise trans people's experience. *Trans/formations* contains two such liturgies. In his contribution Himschoot discusses the healing aspects of constructing a liturgy for Transgender Day of Remembrance: He observes:

> Liturgy that addresses the themes of pain and possibility, horror and hope, is not only a work of theological reflection but a work of action, done by a community together (Himschoot 2009: 144).

Playwright John Clifford's contribution can also can be interpreted as a type of liturgy where he has created a monologue articulating his rage and despair at the theologies and images of God that have imprisoned trans people in places of pain and guilt.

These liturgies are not just important for trans people, in order to celebrate their identities, but also enable families, friends and allies to participate in these actions. It can be argued that they also serve an educative purpose. After attending a Transgender Day of Remembrance service it would be impossible not to be aware of the multiple issues of violence, race, class, and economic disadvantage that affect many trans people. Reading Clifford's performance piece articulates the pain and hypocrisy he has felt at the hands of the Church.

General concluding comments

The literature shows that there are two very different viewpoints about trans people in the UK religious landscape. The first view focuses on the need to mitigate the threat posed by trans people to the Church. This viewpoint is expressed in the literature based on O'Donovan (1982) and includes both Evangelical Alliance and Church of England responses. This has become the de facto viewpoint of the UK Church because no other official denominational viewpoints have been proffered.

The second voice is found in the writings of trans people about themselves. These writings are not primarily interested in the physicality of their condition but in what it means to be trans and/ or to live in the Church as a gender variant person. These writings have entirely different preoccupations of identity, justice and spiritual insight. These self-understandings and definitions are broader and more expansive. They often include under their banner many folk that the Church has not even begun to think about.

These two conversations are happening in completely different intellectual, cultural and theological spaces with radically different conceptions of what it is to be a person and the nature of faith. The Church does not appear to hear, understand or want to move out of its comfort zone or its preoccupations, to join this second conversation and explore how the trans experience could enrich the Church rather than threaten it.

Chapter 3

Results of the Transfaith project

Overview of the project

This chapter contains an overview of the methodology and the results from the Transfaith study which Chris conducted as his doctoral research project. It was the first study of its type to attempt to collate the experiences of different individuals to see what similarities and differences had been experienced by trans people within the Church.

What follows is a summary of the research methodology and the results it produced.

Methodology
Ethical Framework Indigenous Knowledge

Trans writer and activist Viviane Namaste (1993) argues that trans people have been studied by researchers in exploitative ways. She draws parallels between the exploitation of trans people and that of indigenous peoples within colonial settings and suggests that researchers should consider using a research method called indigenous knowledge. Indigenous Knowledge (IK) was developed by indigenous peoples in Australia and North America in response to their experience of anthropological studies about themselves (Simpson 2004). Indigenous knowledge can be summarised as:

- The researcher does not impose their knowledge and views on the community.
- The researcher is aware that they cannot hope to learn everything there is to know.
- Knowledge is gathered by observation, experiential learning and apprenticeship.
- The researcher is aware power imbalances exist between academics and native peoples and works to minimise them.
- The researcher understands that some knowledge cannot be taken out of the culture and understood properly.
- The researcher looks for wisdom and learning in stories of life lived.

- Indigenous Knowledge relies on subjective experience of the people being studied and does not attempt to make assumptions beyond its own locality.
- Indigenous knowledge is about taking seriously the thoughts, culture and experience of indigenous people on their own terms.

These values were imbedded into the project. It is also why the copyright of this book and any proceeds it might generate will go to one of the primary organisations that cooperated in this research, in recognition that this project collated knowledge that already existed within the trans community.

Ethical Framework Liberation Theology

In her work Marcella Althaus-Reid makes clear the link between liberation theologies and what she terms sexual stories:

> *The methodology of liberation should always be worked around elements of a passion arousing style. At a community level this has meant that people's starting point has always been their own experiences ….* (Althaus –Reid 2000: 126)

Following this statement, she explicitly links the oppressive religious and economic structures in Latin America to the binary and heterosexual gender structures that also exist to oppress:

> *For centuries they have embarked on the organisation of religious processions, and paying for masses and promises to God and the Virgin Mary. This has been for the forgiveness of the gods, and not the hanging conditions of international trade. Jubilee was requested from the deities, to stop the economic crises that were destroying the lives of the whole communities, but no one thought about organising a Jubilee for the lesser Gods of the International Monetary Fund to cancel external debt … … the same can be applied to the pervasive gender making structures … … it is difficult for people to see the sacred in their lives outside heterosexual parodies, repeated endlessly* (2000: 126).

This ethos is also echoed in other writers:

> *Once transgressive sexual stories are spoken, they become disruptive by challenging the status quo. They will be heard, interpreted, redefined and will present sexual possibilities. The telling of sexual stories is a*

continual process of 'coming out' revealing a (divine) revelation of sexual experience (Simpson 2005: 104).

The ecclesial considerations of homosexuality and other forms of non-normative relations of gender, sex and sexuality, provide an occasion, a moment of rupture, exposing philosophical and meta-physical assumptions that might otherwise be obscured (Hutchins 2001: 11).

If I'd known then what I know now would I have persisted in rekindling my love affair with the Church? But of course I would, it's my Church, my Virgin Mary, my Salve Regina as much as it is theirs (Taylder 2009: 77).

This project is firmly located in this understanding of liberation theology's ability to challenge oppressive systems with the stories of the disenfranchised and oppressed.

The intention of the project was not to simply catalogue suffering of trans people, although there is an element of this in all twelve life stories analysed in this chapter. These stories speak of years of invisibility, fear and oppression which is self-inflicted as well as church inflicted.

But more importantly, these sexual stories disrupt these 'dominant ways and forms of knowing' and challenge assertions of a God ordained binary gender system and understanding of trans people typified by the church-based writings analysed in the Chapter 2. They also attempt to give dignity and voice to folk who have found ways to survive and even thrive despite the difficulties they have faced in trying to remain as part of the Body of Christ.

Recruitment of the interviewees

Recruitment was principally by word of mouth. An invitation to potential interviewees was sent via email. The email explained the project and invited interested trans people to contact Chris via the dedicated email address transfaithproject@gmail.com.

Basic information about the interviewees

The basic information about the interviewees is contained in the table below with accompanying explanation of the categories contained in the table:

Designation Letter	Gender Identity at time of Interview	Description of Church Involvement	Estimated age at time of interview	Geographic location of the interview
A	Female	Member of a church	31-40	Scotland
B	Female	Member of a church	21-30	Scotland
C	Male	Non- attender of a church	31-40	Midlands, England
D	Female	Member of a church	>51	Scotland
E	Male	Clergy	41-50	Scotland
F	Male and Female	Member of a church	>51	SW England
G	Male	Clergy	>51	SW England
H	Female	Exploring Vocation as a nun	>51	Midlands, England
J	Gender Queer	Member of a church	21-30	Midlands, England
K	Female	Accepted as novice in a convent	>51	SE England
L	Female	Exploring Vocation to clergy	41-50	SW England
M	Male and Female	Non attendee of a church	>51	SE England
N	Female	Clergy	41-50	Northern England

Designation letter

One of the central ethical concerns of this project was to protect the privacy of individuals. To this end a letter of the alphabet was randomly assigned to each interviewee. The letter bears no relationship to either their given or family names.

Gender identity at interview

In line with the ethos of this project individuals were invited to self-define their own gender within the interview. As an interviewer Chris did not make an assumption based on the personal presentation of the interviewee at the time of interview.

Age

The age is estimated by Chris or was disclosed within the interview.

Limitations of the sample of interviewees

It is impossible to know how representative the sample is of trans people of Christian faith. For example, the ethnicity of the entire sample is White British. While it was not expected many people with an Asian ethnicity would identify as trans and Christian, there was a reasonable assumption that some of the sample could have been either Afro Caribbean or African trans people. Chris believes it is likely that the ethnic segregation of so many churches within the UK is also mirrored in the networks of Christian trans people. It may also be that trans people of African or Afro Caribbean descent do not wish to belong to networks that identify them as trans and Christian. There has been no research among black Christian trans people in the UK that could prove or disprove this hypothesis.

This study also does not consider those who may have left Christianity. Kidd and Witten (2008), Reinsmith-Jones (2013), Smith and Horne (2007), Schuck and Liddle (2001) and Sullivan-Blum (2008) suggest this may be the most common or at-least-as-common experience. All but one of the interviewees were actively involved in regular Christian worship at the time of the interview and describe themselves as part of a faith community. The focus and concerns of the study were entirely Christian in nature.

The conduct of the interview

The interviews were carried out at times and in places convenient for the interviewee. Prior to the interview commencing the interviewee was given a hard copy of the information sheet they had been emailed when the interview was arranged and was asked to read it. The interviewee was asked to fill out a consent form which also included consent for the interview to be recorded.

The interview questions

In line with the ethos of this project the questions were very broad and open. They were supplied to the interviewees prior to the interview so they would have time to think about the information that they wished to share. The questions were used as an aid to the conversation and to ensure that the interviewees had the opportunity to volunteer similar information. The questions were:

Tell me about yourself...... (Life story as much as is comfortable)

The original aim of this question was to put the interviewee at ease. It soon became apparent that most of the interviewees used this question to relate all the information they felt was relevant, and Chris was repeatedly given a narrative of the interviewee's life with little or no prompting.

Tell me about your image of God. How do you think your image of God has changed because of your gender variance?

The initial reading of the available literature on the subject suggested that most people of Christian faith who undertake a gender journey also undertake a faith journey because much of what was previously believed is re-examined and tested in the process of claiming their identity. This question was asked to see if the interviewee's experience agreed with the literature.

Where are the places in Christianity and particularly in the Bible where you see trans people being included?

Queer theologians such as Kolakowski and Reay suggest that trans people are likely to identify with biblical characters such as eunuchs. This question tested whether there was a general identification with eunuchs or if there were other characters from either the Bible or the Christian tradition that trans people identified with more strongly.

Where do you see yourself excluded?

Both pastoral conversations and friendships had left Chris with the impression that many trans people had had difficult relationships both with communities of faith and the wider Church. He was also interested to test if interviewees had been troubled by the apparent biblical prohibition in Deuteronomy 22:5.

Have you stayed in the Christian Church? If you are still a regular attendee, why?

Most of the networks that Chris accessed were ones based on faith, so many of the interviewees were part of a worshipping community. He wanted to find out the reasons why interviewees had stayed within Christianity rather than leaving it.

Or if you have left why have you left?

This was a reverse of the previous question. The aim of this question was to find out why interviewees had left the Church.

What have been your experiences of Christianity as a trans person?

This open-ended question was designed to allow the interviewees to freely volunteer any experiences that they attributed to being trans within their own congregations or from the wider Church.

What do you think trans people can teach the Church?

This open-ended question was designed to allow the interviewees to volunteer their own insights and opinions about what they felt they could offer the Church.

How do you reconcile your past identity with who you are now? And how do you explain it in spiritual terms?

From personal and pastoral experience, Chris had noticed many of the trans people he knew had abruptly severed contact with people they knew after transition. On several occasions he had walked the gender journey with people as their minister only to find them leaving his church at the point that they transitioned. Colleagues reported similar experiences. When he had previously asked folk they had said that it was all 'too difficult' but had not elaborated further. He wanted to explore why this had happened. The second part of the question was an attempt to see how the interviewees had reconciled their lives if they saw their lives as one continuous narrative.

Recording and transcription

All interviews were recorded digitally and transcribed by Chris. No other person heard the recordings and they will be kept for ten years (until 2022) and then erased. The aim of the transcription was to attempt to capture the conversation as accurately as possible. To achieve this, each time the interviewee paused or took an intake of breath, a new line was initiated to signify breaks in speech. The transcripts were transcribed verbatim in an attempt to capture the individual words and phrasing of each interviewee.

otherwise Approval by the interviewees

Once the interviews were transcribed they were sent via email to the interviewees for approval. The interviewees were given complete freedom to edit, omit or change information. Three made changes to the interview transcript either to omit personal details or clarify a point that they had made. One interviewee withdrew their transcript entirely. Once the interviews were amended, they were then deemed ready for analysis.

Analysis using Nvivo

Once the interviews were transcribed they were loaded into a computer programme called Nvivo 10 for analysis. Using the interview questions, data was grouped by subject. While some of the data was a direct answer to one of the interview questions, other relevant parts of the transcript were also added.

This collated data was reanalysed and concepts and themes were identified from it. These concepts and themes were then cross-referenced by age, gender identity and geography to see what patterns emerged.

The results

The 13 interviews resulted in over 500 pages of transcript that detailed over 20 hours of recorded conversations. During the long hours of transcription and analysis, 13 different life narratives emerged and Chris began to interpret them as parables in the sense described by Graham, Walton and Ward (2005). These authors describe a parable as having the potential to construct meaningful stories out of an individual's life and 'emphasise the mysterious and indefinable aspects of the human experience' (2005: 47). Another theologian, Stephen Crites also calls such stories sacred:

> not so much because gods are commonly celebrated in them, but because men's (sic) sense of self and world is created through them (Crites 1971: 295).

The aim of the rest of this chapter is to begin to interpret these sacred stories and to use the available literature from experts in the fields of medicine, psychology, sociology and theology to help explore what they may mean.

The stories explored
Early years to adolescence

Many of the interviewees remember very early experiences of gender variance. Several (C, G and K) believed that they were their preferred gender rather than their birth gender. Others (A, E, H and N) remember feelings of discomfort around their gender identity from a very early age.

This identification and discomfort played out in several ways. Many of the interviewees report playing with toys designed for their preferred gender. A remembers playing with dolls while G remembers playing with guns and being the male leader in war games. E remembers playing almost entirely with boys, while L loitered around the girls' toilets hoping to be invited in. G also pretended to shave his face as a child.

Clothes also play a major memory in almost all the interviewees. All the trans men (C, E and G) remember protesting against wearing dresses and wishing to wear either boys' or gender neutral clothes. As G recounts:

> *I was staying with one set of grandparents my granny would dress me up in a frock to take me out and then as soon as I got back to their place I would say dress me now granny meaning can you put my proper clothes meaning my trousers normally my tartan trousers (laugh).*

Many of the natal males (A, B, F, K and L) experienced cross-dressing from an early age. They recount secretly dressing up in female clothes while their families were out of the home. As K recounts:

> *Really as far back as I remember I have had issues over gender um*

> *And even at the age of 6 and I know I was 6 because it was in a house that we moved from*

> *I was dressing in a cousin's female clothes and on one occasion I fell asleep in them and got found in the morning when my mother pulled away the bedclothes*

> *And*

> *The identified female and dressing in female clothes continued throughout my childhood and my teens err*

> *When my parents went off in the car and my brothers were out I would*
> *go to my mother's clothes cupboard and dress in her clothes and just*
> *potter around the house or watch television*
>
> *And just feel happy*

From an early age most of the interviewees knew that their feelings
of gender discomfort were a secret that they needed to keep to
themselves. Almost all the interviewees (A, B, C, E, F, G, H, K, L
and N) remember the need to keep their unexplained feelings and
actions away from adults and other children. This secrecy led to
feelings of abnormality and guilt. Several (A, F, H, L and N) consider
these feelings of abnormality led to feelings of inadequacy that have
resulted in their underachievement throughout life.

The research carried out agrees with the interviewees' reported
experience. The early awareness of gender variance recounted by
interviewees also agrees with experts (Grossman and D'Augelli
2006, Conroy 2010, Forcier and Johnson 2013, Kennedy and Hellen
2010, Dietert and Dentice 2013 and Futty 2010). They all state that
consciousness of a gender variant identity and gender variant
behaviours occurs before adolescence. Kennedy and Hellen put the
average age of realization at 8 years (2010: 28) while Grossman and
D'Augelli put awareness of gender variance at 10.6 years (2006: 120).
The very early manifestation of these behaviours argues against any
form of conscious, transgressive choice by an individual. Indeed,
the children in the narratives were aware that their behaviour was
different and learned very early in their lives to hide it.

The narratives also show many of the parents were aware their
children were different in their feelings of gender. Many of the MTF
interviewees (A, B, F, K and L) report being discovered cross-dressing.
As K recounts:

> *My parents knew there were incidents but didn't know it was a*
> *sustained thing going on as far as I know err*
>
> *Um*
>
> *I got sent to a boy's boarding school to toughen up at the age of 7 no*
> *8 err*

In all these cases except B (where this prompted disclosure of being
transgender) this discovered cross-dressing was not addressed

positively. Parents either ignored the behaviour or dealt out punishment to try to change it. Forcier and Johnson as well as Dietert and Dentice note that parents often attempt to redirect the behaviour of the child to more acceptable social expressions of gender (Forcier and Johnson 2013:100, Dietert and Dentice 2013: 35). Grossman and D'Augelli also note that parents often act abusively to 'correct' their child's behaviour (2006: 125). In contrast to the literature and the other interviewees' experience, C recounts his family deliberately creating a gender-neutral childhood that allowed him to feel comfortable at home.

The findings and the literature both argue that gender variant children are vulnerable and are aware that they are different from other children at an early age. It also argues that their gender variant behaviour is not a transgressive choice to be punished. This vulnerability is exacerbated by family members reacting negatively and, at times, abusively to their gender variant behaviours. This raises pastoral issues for churches around the way they treat children who manifest gender variant behaviours and how they engage and counsel families who may come to them for guidance.

Adolescence to Coming Out as trans

This is the time in the lives of the interviewees between puberty and the recognition of their identity as trans. For some of the younger interviewees, such as B and J, this is a relatively short period in their lives. For others such as E, F, H, L and M this was a period of over 40 years.

The interviews show that adolescence brings the reality of birth gender. It forces children (who became C, G and N) to abandon their illusions of being their identified gender. Interviewees (C, E, G, H and N) report extreme trauma around puberty. This is particularly the case for the trans men who recount their horror of the changes to their bodies around menstruation. As E recounts:

> *it was a complete and utter nightmare for me because I was totally totally alien to what I really wanted*
>
> *but it was so confused and I didn't know why*
>
> *I clearly remember*
>
> *Being on holiday and having the most horrendous awful awful period pain and being hardly able to walk about*

> *And it's like that physical pain is so so intense*
>
> *But it was more the kind of emotional pain that went with it*
>
> *But I couldn't make that understood*
>
> *I couldn't really say that the physical pain was*
>
> *I remember being all doubled up but it was the*
>
> *It was like it penetrated all of me and just wanting that to stop and having no idea how this could be possible so it ....*

Many of the interviewees mention self-destructive coping behaviours in this period of their lives. Three of the interviewees (A, E and N) report using drugs and alcohol as ways of coping. Other destructive behaviours include self-harm by cutting (K), suicidal behaviour (K and N) and extreme weight gain (C). Other interviewees (D, F, G, K and L) report depression and mental health issues. Many of the natal males (A, D, F, H, K and L) report continuing to cross-dress in secret.

Compensating behaviours were reported by the interviewees that were hyper-masculine or hyper-feminine. This behaviour is noted by Brown (2006: 537). A joins the air force, B plays football, F indulges in extreme sports, H rides an enormous motorbike, N becomes a 'young male rock god', E becomes a home economics teacher in the conservative south west where he is encouraged to wear feminine clothes and K takes up mountaineering and a 'male job'. As K recounts:

> *But I tried to be male so I tried mountaineering*
>
> *Cross country running but*
>
> *I know they are activities that females do perfectly well but I think I was trying to establish myself*
>
> *Get a foothold in a male world and I think when I became a prison governor that was the same I bought myself a very expensive pin stripe suit and waist coat and*
>
> *And so I was entering a male world (laugh)*
>
> *On whatever terms I could negotiate*

Another pattern that emerged from the narratives was how the interviewees constructed their relationships and sexuality. The older interviewees (D, F, H, K and L) all married and had children (except for H whose wife was unable to have children due to disability). They marry believing that marriage will cure them of their gender dysphoria. The reality is that this does not happen and ready access to women's clothes encourages their cross-dressing. These interviewees come to a realisation that they are trans after they have raised families. Many believed they were the only person with gender dysphoria in the world because of lack of information available in their younger lives. They never identify as gay or lesbian as part of their gender journey.

Those aged between 30 and 55 (A, C, E and G) initially come out as gay or lesbian before coming out as trans. They are aware that they are not heterosexual and conclude they must be gay or lesbian because there is little information about trans people for them to access. As A relates:

> One of the reasons I've finally come around to accepting my transgenderism is the fact that for ten years I have thought that you're gay B except that
>
> 10- 15 years I think
>
> So I had given myself permission to be gay
>
> But it hasn't happened

In the case of two of the trans men (C and E) they were aware that in the United States there was a possibility to transition but discounted the possibility of doing so in the UK. These interviewees (A, C, E and G) attempt relationships with a same sex partner with varying degrees of success. After several years within the LGBT community they recognise their gender dysphoria and begin to transition. The only variation on this theme amongst those between 30 and 55 is N who marries, comes out as trans and then comes out as a lesbian.

It is hard to see this time in the lives of the interviewees as positive. Almost all the interviewees fight feelings of guilt and shame (A, C, D, E, H, K, L and N). Some (A and K) report that they felt dirty and disgusting. Others (A, E and K) describe feelings of fear and confusion. L describes a cycle of buying clothes, then being consumed with guilt and discarding them:

As um

this you can understand the living of a double life

Desperate to live out your female persona

Which completely takes over.

We might trash half a dozen wardrobes of clothes and shoes and bags and things

maybe more

by getting rid of it all and thinking we can pretend it is not an issue

Well it doesn't go away

And it doesn't go away because it is genuine

K poignantly describes a feeling of homesickness for her real identity:

And at the same time I was recognising that it was more painful to me

Because I was homesick for a person that

I wasn't allowing myself to be

During this time all of the interviewees show a responsible face to the world, often holding down responsible jobs, raising families and being key congregants in their churches.

At the end of this period of their lives, interviewees begin to explore their identity and move towards an understanding of who they are. Two of these (J and N) began by researching gender theory and transgenderism within university libraries whilst students. Internet and the media were recognised as powerful tools to help create community and explore identity (E, F, H and K). K for example used internet chat rooms to try out having a feminine identity in cyberspace and makes a friend who hosts her debut as a woman at a house party. After watching the same documentary about transmen on television E and G both recognised themselves for the first time. This led to their decisions to transition.

Coming out

By coming out the individual accepts that they are trans and begins to disclose this identity to others. This period in the life of the interviewees is not necessarily a linear or straightforward process that immediately leads to a transitioning of identity. Several of the interviewees (D, K and N) made initial decisions to stay in their birth gender despite coming out to themselves as trans.

The main reason for coming out is the recognition that this was the only way for the interviewees to find peace. All talked about this time in positive ways, and three commented (D, G and K) that it was the best decision that they ever made. Several of the interviewees (A, F and N) felt this was the only way that they would be able to resolve the guilt and secrecy that had blighted their lives. As F relates:

> *I used to go to hotels to dress before I went out in public and it was really was a major thing to keep it all under wraps I decided this is not honest I can't go on like this*

> *the fear of discovery*

> *It was just getting too much especially the more I went out locally for that very reason*

> *So I said to S I can't go on like this*

> *And we had both reconciled ourselves that this wasn't going to go away*

> *I was much happier when I didn't*

> *I was coming around to the idea that I didn't hate myself*

Most of the MTF interviewees (D, F, H, K, L and N) were in heterosexual relationships prior to transition. There seem to be two different patterns that emerge in the reactions of the partners of MTF interviewees at disclosure. Similar patterns of disclosure are reported by Bischof et al. (2011: 24).

The first pattern is early disclosure. Two of the interviewees (D and F) told their partners very early in their relationships. Both remained with their partners after disclosure but neither completely transitioned to a female identity (D remained with her partner until the partner's death and then transitioned). In both cases there was a series of negotiations that allowed the relationship to continue. Both Chase (2011: 437) and Bischoff et al (2011: 26) identify this pattern in enduring relationships. There is a clear dividing line between the acceptable acting out of gender dysphoria and the unacceptable changing of gender identity. To maintain their marital relationship, F negotiates with her wife about the amount of time she spends in her male identity and how much time she spends in her female identity. D's wife was tolerant of her behaviour but threatened to leave D if she transitioned fully.

The second pattern is those who told their partners much later in the relationship at the point of beginning transition of identity (H, K, L and N). All the interviewees who disclosed their identity after the relationship was established had their relationships break down. In these cases, there was rejection (L and N) or it evolved into a friendship (H and K). Two of the interviewees (K and L) mention that the rejection of a continuing relationship was in part because their wives did not wish to be identified as lesbians. As K relates:

> *But she didn't accept that transsexualism was right and she has a right to her beliefs*

> *She wanted to remain my friend but she felt quite understandably I didn't sign up for this I'm not a lesbian*

> *She was a Christian woman who wanted to be married to a husband*

> *It was really really so sad and so painful.*

There are tremendous issues for the partners of trans people. They need to negotiate a new relationship with their partner or live with the guilt of leaving them at a time of need. They also need to re-evaluate their own identity and sexual orientation (Chase 2011: 444, Bischoff et al 2011: 26 and Pfeffer 2008: 341). The needs of female partners of FTM trans people are often subordinated to the trans partner and they feel guilty about focussing on their own needs. Their vulnerability is a pastoral issue that supportive churches need to be aware of.

Both D and K decided to postpone any action towards gender reassignment because of their family responsibilities. As D relates:

> *But as time went on*

> *I just I couldn't do it*

> *It just became more and more impossible to keep on living as a man*

> *And eventually I got to the stage that I got to S my wife I can't go on living as a man I've got to*

> *I've got to transition and she said*

She was deeply upset she said I can't

(silence)

If you do that it will mean the end of our relationship because I can't deal with that

Which was heavy and I thought well we have been together such a long time and we had been so happy together I am not going to destroy our relationship

And soon after that she fell ill with a brain tumour

D transitions after her wife dies. K waits until her children have left home. It is only after these responsibilities have been fulfilled that either feels free to live into their gender identity.

The pattern was observed to be different with FTM interviewees. All three interviewees were in lesbian relationships before transition. All disclosed to their partner soon after they recognised their gender dysphoria. All relationships have survived. In the cases of C and G the relationship has become notionally heterosexual while E discovered that his partner was also trans and they transitioned together into a gay male couple. There has been little research done into the relationships of trans men and their lesbian partners. An exception is Pfeffer (2010) whose work suggests a complex picture of adjustments and identity changes by the lesbian partners.

In all situations, the responses of family members have been mixed with each interviewee receiving many different responses to their disclosure. Bockting, Knudson and Goldberg (2006) note that family members are not a heterogeneous group and that their reactions are varied (2006: 56). This finding is also echoed by Norwood (2012) who finds that the reaction of family members is a complex process involving grief for something that is akin to death (2012: 84). This is further complicated by dealing with personality changes (2012:85) and balancing the family's needs against the desire to support the trans person. Norwood notes:

> Support-giving was constructed as somewhat problematic in light of religious beliefs, family values, and even lack of cognitive and empathic understanding of TG identity (2012: 89).

Several of the interviewees (B, C, D, F, K, L and N) experienced family acceptance from some members of their family. This is despite two of them (K and L) recounting very difficult family dynamics caused by their struggles with their gender dysphoria and resulting mental health issues in the past. At the same time acceptance was not uniform with several (D, F, K and L) reporting that they were also rejected by family members with religious scruples and three (D, F and L) experienced outright condemnation based on religious belief. Super and Jacobson (2011: 189) identify that families who reject LGBT members also experience a sense of dislocation and pain as they try to navigate multiple loyalties which is damaging to their spirituality. As L relates

Of course, it hurt

I had but my family who profess those Christian values and beliefs

of unconditional love couldn't show it to me

because of this

it became a barrier and became something that was too much for them

I understand that

but it did hurt

Interviewees reported that the reactions of other people were also mixed. In the case of several interviewees (B, F, K, L and N) employers and fellow employees were very supportive. Only K relates discrimination in the job market. As an experienced teacher, she applied to over 100 schools without getting a single interview. E found that many of the gay men he had associated with in the past were confused and threatened by his new identity as a gay man. They were concerned that they may inadvertently pick up a gay man who had a vagina. This made them insecure in their gay identity and worried about how they would deal with this situation. E also experienced confusion from many of his friends as both he and his partner transitioned from a lesbian couple to a gay male couple. Many found the situation inexplicable. This is also reflected in the literature (Raymond 1979, Frazer 2005, Nataf 2006, Morrison 2010) which notes an uneasy relationship between the lesbian and gay community and trans people.

Several (A, E, F, H and K) joined trans support groups where they begin to meet others and become part of an organised trans community. Others (F, H, K and L) began to venture out dressed in their newly claimed gender identity.

Medical intervention and physical transition were identified as important tools in identity confirmation (D, E, G, K and L). Those who wished to confirm their identity completely (G, H, K and L) experienced few problems with the medical establishment. Others who did not necessarily conform to a 'standard outcome' found opposition from medical professionals. D fought with her surgeon about the extent of surgery she required. E was advised not to disclose that he was a gay man because he may not be considered a candidate for surgery. N consciously played a female stereotype to the delight of her doctors and psychiatrists realising that it was necessary to play down the androgyny that is part of her identity.

Life after coming out

Not all the interviewees had completely settled into their confirmation of their identities. A, for example, is at the very beginning of her gender journey and has yet to give herself a new name. C gave the impression of still having some issues around coming out by describing himself as 'not quite right', and L had literally completed her GCS only a few weeks before being interviewed and was waiting to explore her new world.

The transcripts suggest that several of the interviewees experience their lives as a split narrative where there is a disconnection between their previous life and their new lives. Several (H, K and L) refuse to acknowledge their previous names or identities. N described her early years after transition as 'attempting to obliterate the male within her'. Beardsley, O'Brien and Woolley (2012: 268) note that for some trans people there is as much of a closet after transition as there was before.

Integration seems to come with length of time after a settled identity is achieved. Those who have been in their identities the greatest length of time (B, D, E, G and N) seem to come to a place where they reintegrate the narrative of their life into a more coherent whole. In the debrief conversation after interview, N disclosed that she had participated to explore how she could better integrate the two halves of her life story.

Church experience narratives
Experience of clergy

Experiences prior to transition were reported as positive. After transition the picture is more mixed regarding the behaviour of male clergy. Some of the experiences were supportive while others were not. N was supported by both her university chaplain and her evangelical Anglican minister while coming out as trans. K found similar support from a novice monk via the internet who helped her explore meditation and mysticism. K was also welcomed into a conservative evangelical church with the minister thanking her for making him think about the issues she had raised. L was supported and visited by her minister throughout the transition process. She described him as a 'wonderful and loving man'.

Other experiences with male clergy were not so positive. After disclosure B was asked to leave her church by a male minister. H battled with her minister for several years which only ended when the minister transferred to another congregation. This minister objected to H wearing female clothes to church and hid her away from any visible ministry. The most devastating narrative is the story of F who was stripped of all ministry and excluded from participation within the congregation after 40 years of involvement. F's wife was encouraged by her minister to leave the marriage. They were both shunned for a year before finally they decided to leave. As F relates:

> *we negotiated a year with the leadership*
>
> *um to see if they could see things my way and they couldn't*
>
> *And in the end*
>
> *During that time I wasn't allowed to minister in any way*
>
> *Ah I had been leading worship for 30 years our group split up*
>
> *we had a few loyal supporters*
>
> *at the end of the year we said there is no future for us here*
>
> *Which was probably what they were hoping for anyway*

Literature records similar experiences. Beardsley, O'Brien and Woolley (2012) tell a story where a trans person was harassed for 'living unbiblically' (2012: 267). In his memoir, Ford (2013:23) recounts his rejection from the church in which he had grown up. Super and Jacobson (2011) report that religious abuse is a real concern for counsellors working with LGBT folk. They note that these experiences set up a dissonance between the religious and sexual identities which leave the person feeling hopeless, condemned and confused (2011: 181).

In contrast, all the interviewees' experiences of female clergy were positive. When F and her wife were referred to her new church, the female minister intentionally did groundwork with the congregation and leadership to ensure that F and her wife were welcomed into their new church home. H found that her female curate removed transphobic Christian literature from the church when she discovered it. H also recounted the story of two female clergy making sure that she was comfortable, welcomed and supported at a wedding. The female curate in the village where N had grown up supported her mother when she disclosed her gender dysphoria. This helped N's mother to accept her as a daughter instead of a son.

K also recounts a story of welcome and inclusion by female clergy. K was welcomed by several communities of nuns as a female guest. Over the course of several years she visited a number of convents as she openly explored her call to become a nun. She recounts how one of the convents tested her call and finally offered her a place amongst them. The test that K relates is not a test to see if she was female but rather if she was a contemplative and therefore suitable to join the community. Since her interview, H has reported a similar experience as she explores her own vocation as a nun.

While it would be tempting, it is not possible to make the generalisation that female clergy are more tolerant of trans people. It may be there is greater sympathy for minorities from a group of clergy who are minorities themselves. It may be simply chance that all experiences were positive.

People and structures beyond the local church

Kolakowski (2000: 36) states that she does not believe that there is a vast conspiracy to disenfranchise or exclude trans people from the Church, but instead the barriers from social institutions, customs and hierarchical structures are organised in such a way that they are oppressive.

The treatment of the interviewees was mixed. N was accepted into Anglican ordination training as an out trans person. She was shown a confidential discussion document from a committee of Anglican bishops about trans people seeking holy orders that recommended they be treated seriously as candidates provided they had the necessary aptitudes for a life in ministry. Her bishop recognised her disadvantage gaining employment after training and offered her a guaranteed post. In a different Anglican diocese, L was refused training without explanation.

F also received favourable treatment from her bishop when she and her wife went to find an Anglican Church after their traumatic experiences in their previous home church. It was the bishop who directed them to their current church and presumably briefed the new vicar on what he had done. F has also had positive experiences in her search for a spiritual director, being assured that most spiritual directors would have little problem with her as a trans woman.

In complete contrast D and others were engaged in a piece of performance art about faith and being trans and became the focus of a demonstration coordinated by the Church leadership of the town. It was picketed by protestors screaming abuse at both cast and the theatre patrons. In her interview she recounted the wild rumours circulated about the play:

> *And we got relayed some of the fantasies some of the stories they were telling about what happened on stage like you know*

> *Oh God really obscene stuff*

> *That was going to be naked people*

> *the cross was pissed on*

> *Nuns dressed in bondage gear and just kind of horrible horrible horrible sexual fantasies these people were circulating as if they were true*

> *Where did they hear them from (interviewer)*

> *You do wonder where they hear them from*

> *you mean you just go my God*

> *(silence)*

> *Gosh and I mean I could spend the rest of my life trying to investigate all this but*

> *(laugh)*

> *There are far better things to do*

Congregational reactions

As an Anglican priest N recognises that the treatment of trans people within congregations is very varied. It is entirely dependent on the leadership of the clergy person and the reactions of the congregation.

The interviewees (A, B, D, E, F, G, H, J, K, L and N) have found a place within congregations if they wished to remain within a worshipping community. This may not have been their initial congregation. F was hounded out of her original church but found another church in the same denomination. F related that even with the general condemnation from the congregation, several people supported them. As an act of defiance, her old worship co-leader continues to use the worship songs that F wrote as a reminder that she was there. Another (B) was asked to leave when she disclosed she was trans. She moved to another denomination. Ford (2013: 89) notes in his biography the hypocrisy of the congregation who excluded him as a sinner while acknowledging that they were sinners themselves.

Several of the interviewees have joined a monthly mission project of an existing denomination set up to serve trans people (A, B, D and E) and attend regular church services weekly. G leads a church originally set up by E to welcome LGBT people. J's primary church community is a group of young radical Christians who explore faith and spirituality together. Others have found churches in mainstream denominations. Whilst the interviewees have found worshipping communities, it has not been without difficulties.

One of the major issues that came out of the interviews was the difference between toleration and celebration. The interviewees who attend the mission project (A, B, D and E) feel that their monthly worship celebrates trans people in ways that more traditional churches do not. They criticise the silence on LGBT issues generally and note that inclusion often means silence on difference rather than celebration and exploration of it. As A relates:

> *So few ministers are standing up and saying including*

> *They are talking about the poor and disadvantaged and stuff but really I never hear the word transgenderism or homosexuality mentioned so I think because I think you are being excluded because you are not deliberately being included*

> *And so we are not having it mentioned knowing that some of the congregation was struggling with it*

It is the elephant in the room you know

The minister was saying we should all be you know open to everybody but it seemed to be looking around the congregation tended to be white

And I hate to say this white and middle class

And rarely did I ever hear a minister turn around and acknowledge that transgenders homosexuals or lesbians in any way shape or form so you know I think

I felt a sense of being excluded because I wasn't actively included

Accounts of those worshipping in mainstream denominations confirm this. Shottwell and Sangrey (2009) note that the burden falls disproportionately on the trans person who must micromanage their behaviour to fit in and not offend (2009:57). This seems particularly true in the case of F who has been welcomed into her new church but feels that she is there on toleration. While she attends social occasions as a female she is careful to dress in male clothing for regular worship. She is also concerned that an impending interregnum may make her less welcome without a supportive cleric. L also wonders if there are some people within her congregation who are less supportive of her than they appear. H attributes any reserve to a prickly personality rather than any lingering transphobia. H also feels that her problems with the previous minister have led her to isolate herself rather than others avoiding her.

Others recount mixed messages by church communities. This is often around the utilisation of their gifts and skills. H was allowed to continue at the mixing desk during worship because there were few with that expertise and the role was not visible, however, she was excluded from other ministry. L was church secretary but felt that the acceptance was conditional on her being quiet about her identity as a trans woman. N is aware that she is often praised for her intellectual gifts but feels that lingering unease exists about her as a trans woman:

I get told all the time by those in authority

You're a gift and have so much to offer

And you catch a glance or

You hear a story …

Experiences of homophobia and assumptions of transphobia

Many of the interviewees mentioned homophobia within the Church (A, C, E, F, G, H, J, L and N). This has formed their assumptions about how they would be treated. For example, C felt he was rejected by the Catholic Church as a lesbian. Because of this previous rejection, he felt that the Catholic Church would also reject him as a trans person. He specifically mentions the Catholic pastoral letter against gay marriage read out in every pulpit in the UK in 2012:

Where do you see yourself excluded in the Church (interviewer)

My views

As I said my mum still goes to church every Sunday

And she recently became quite kind of

Nonplussed by this whole letter they got from the bishop about gay marriage

She couldn't understand why people have such a problem and so really for me the viewpoints I have ......

There are so many things I disagree with

That

The church seems so kind of irrelevant really

Cornwall notes (2010: 141) that Church concerns about being trans are often reduced to an anxiety about whether it is really allowing homosexuality by another name. A reading of the Evangelical Alliance and the Church of England reports would seem to confirm this. One of their primary motivations in establishing if one's gender can be 'changed' (as they conceptualise it) is the perceived threat to heterosexual marriage were that to occur. This would mean they would be performing 'gay marriage by stealth' by marrying two people of the same gender.

J has not brought up her gender queer identity in her worshipping congregation because she feels that she would be humoured and dismissed rather than engaged with. B hid her identity because she felt that she would have been disowned. L left her Anglican congregation after witnessing their poor behaviour towards an openly gay curate, assuming this would also happen to her as a trans woman.

Such assumptions are not always true. N found that her evangelical church was very supportive of her as a trans woman. She believes this is because being trans gave her church a medical narrative in which she had a condition that was being treated. Jasper (2005) notes that most of the population sees gender reassignment as a medical process that brings the body in alignment with gender identity without questioning assumptions about the God given nature of binary gender (2005: 46). Cornwall agrees that gender confirmation surgery may affirm the existing binaries and make it more difficult for those who are either intersex or gender queer (2010: 151).

For N the difficulty came when her congregation perceived that she had made a choice to 'become a lesbian'. H also considers that being gay or lesbian would 'push the envelope' in her church while she believes her own situation has been accepted. In her interview, F admitted that while she had accepted her own identity she struggled to do the same in regards to gay or lesbian people. It was only with much thought and prayer that she changed her previous convictions that being gay or lesbian was sinful.

Reasons for staying or leaving a congregation

At the time of interview C is the only person who was not actively involved in a faith community. His disaffection started prior to his coming out as trans when he identified as a lesbian. This exclusion led him to question the validity of the Church's stand on homosexuality and, later, transgender people. Subsequently this expanded to questioning the validity of it at all. Later he began to wonder if God was real. He reasoned that an all-powerful all-knowing God could not make mistakes such as gender dysphoria or permit a Church that perpetrated homophobia. Therefore, God could not exist and C decided that he was an atheist.

Other interviewees recount times in their lives when they left the Church and later came back. N left the Church because her prayers about being made a girl were not answered. B left the Church after being rejected for being trans. D also left the Church after serving on the PCC and observing the unloving behaviour of the committee towards each other and the vicar she liked and respected. This was further exacerbated by the conflicted relationship with her mother-in-law who declares her love for her 'son in law' and calls her an abomination simultaneously.

For many of the interviewees there was 'no option' but to stay (E, F, G, H and L) within the Church. The interviewees gave several reasons. One of the main reasons was community. Schuck and Liddle (2001: 73) confirm that this is a reason why many LGB folk stay in churches and it is likely this is the case with trans people as well. J values the small close-knit group of Christians that she meets with to explore their faith and their doubts. Others (A, B, D, G and N) also mentioned community. N believes that the Church is full of extraordinary saints and that it mirrors both the best and worst of humanity within it. As she recounts:

So I discovered that you know

The Church is full of extraordinary saints ....

But you know the Church

Has the best and the worst because it's a human institution because that's how it should be but some of my friends

Colleagues

Friends like X are inspirational who make

Not only the Church but the world a better place

Another reason to remain in church was service (A, B, D, E, F, G, H, L and N). This service may be a specific outreach to trans people or LGBT folk (A, B, D, E, G) or the ability to make a difference in some other way (E, F, G, L and N). It may be the alleviation of the suffering of others (E) or the ability to speak out as a person of faith (G and N). G believes that it is his mission to expand other people's theology, while N believes she is called to be a holy maverick. For several (B, G, E, H and N) it was the need to contribute to the community that they were part of. This is also found in the literature (Bockting & Cesaretti 2001: 297).

Many of the interviewees (D, E, F, G, K, L and N) have pivotal roles within their churches. They all feel a call to work with the excluded and the vulnerable. Both G and N consider that their clergy status allows them to speak with authority on behalf of others and to be able to influence society in positive ways. K is about to enter a convent. H and L are exploring their call to ordained ministry. D works as a playwright and a poet on religious themes. F intends to spend her time after retirement campaigning for evangelical churches to accept LGBT people.

The main issue for the interviewees was finding a place where they could worship with integrity as trans people. For H this meant remaining within her existing congregation and fighting for acceptance from both congregation and clergy. For many others (A, B, D, F, J, K and L) this meant finding a congregation that would accept them as openly transgender members. This has been either within a mainstream denomination or in a church that was created to welcome LGBT folk. Several of the interviewees (F, J, K, L and N) also found local congregations within mainstream denominations that welcomed or tolerated them. Others (A, B, D and E) joined a mainstream church with a specific mission to trans people. Only G remained within the LGBT friendly church that he previously pastored as a lesbian.

There was disagreement between the interviewees' views about congregations that focussed specifically on LGBT issues. All of those worshipping regularly in these types of congregations (A, B, D, E and G) saw them as providing a safe place to celebrate their identity. Some of the others (H and L) saw such churches as ghettoes and considered they were not places that were attractive to them.

Teachings on gender

There was very little response to the question about Church teachings on gender. Conroy (2010: 301) notes that binary gender is presented in churches as a fact rather than a belief, despite evidence to the contrary. She also notes that this belief comes from a literal reading of Genesis 1 and 2, and that other religious cultures are much more accommodating (2010: 308).

Many of the interviewees had received these traditional teachings on gender (A, C, F, G, L and N) where the differentiation of male and female and separate gender roles was preached as being biblically ordained. There was no mention of gender variance from the pulpit and gender was always presented as a binary. Even J, who had a liberal feminist upbringing did not hear any mention of the idea of gender variance.

Several of the interviewees (A, D, G, J, L and N) were highly critical of the patriarchal nature of the Church and considered that it privileged men while oppressing women. They identified that patriarchy does this by excluding women from roles of responsibility. Several cited the arguments within the Anglican Church around women bishops. As A relates:

Overall general view of Christianity is that it gives such a crappy deal to women

Churches argue about women bishops and stuff you know

I think of the centuries the male power and control and authority

My personal view is that it has side-lined women's authority and

And led them away from the Church

Three of the interviewees (A, D and N) believed that the Church was inherently patriarchal and did spiritual and emotional violence to those who did not agree with and/or did not conform to its teachings on gender and gender roles. Sheridan (2001) echoes this in this observation about what is truly taught to trans people about the challenges they pose regarding gender:

> *We wish you were invisible, we don't accept you. We wish you would simply go away and we will pretend that you don't exist. We will ostracise and marginalize you. We will deny you any rights because you are different and we hate you (2001:52).*

Theological insights and gifts that trans people bring
Spiritual journeys of interviewees

There was a strong sense among many of the interviewees (A, E, H, K, L and K) that God affirmed their gender journeys. Several (H, K, L and N) felt that their gender variance and the struggle to become themselves had been an important part of their spiritual journey. It had led them to spiritual places they would not have found without the struggles they had experienced and the questions they had to answer.

The literature surveyed echoes this. Tanis writes that there was an important sense of following God's will into a new and unexpected direction (2003: 43) in his gender journey. Wilcox (2002) notes that God was real and present in the coming out journeys of LGBT folk (2002:507). Reinsmith-Jones (2013: 83) notes that three out of four of their interviewees felt loved and closer to God for embarking on their gender journey.

All the interviewees had experienced shifts within their beliefs. This often involved moving from legalistic types of Christianity to more open interpretations on matters of faith (F, H, K and L). As K recounts

> *but this switch of view theologically was like coming out of the woods in to a wide meadowland*
>
> *a sunlit meadowland where there was wide open space*
>
> *because suddenly*
>
> *I didn't worry if someone was a Baptist or a Catholic or whatever*
>
> *I didn't worry if someone was a Muslim or you know whatever even an atheist or agnostic*
>
> *I just saw the sunlight of the love of God and God was always this person I could run down the field towards and know that I would get embraced*
>
> *and this coming together of my theology occurred at the same time as coming together of my body and mind with the hormones*
>
> *it didn't build up before that*
>
> *what I found is a psychological happening*
>
> *Spiritually and religiously as well as my gender*

This is also reflected in the general literature about LGBT folk reconciling faith and their lived experience. Sullivan-Blum (2008: 199), in her study of drag queens reconciling their sexuality / identity with their faith, recognised that in order to navigate the conflict between conservative faith and life experience there is a reconfiguration of beliefs to accommodate their reality. Schuck and Liddle (2001) and Levy and Lo (2013) found similar shifts in their studies.

These changes in faith were marked by more generosity towards themselves and others. As a conservative Christian, K had believed her father was in hell because he was not a believer; she now does not believe this. F originally believed that being gay or lesbian was sinful but her own journey led her to a place where she could accept her lesbian daughter when she came out to her.

Hattie and Began (2013) believe that the reconfiguration of personal theology incorporates concepts like goodness (2013: 259). Beardsley, O'Brien and Woolley note that the network of trans

Christians who are known as the Sibyls meet to pursue 'value, meaning and transcendence' (2012: 262). Wilcox (2002) adds that these reconfigurations of belief are often marked by a deeper trust in God because when God was turned to in crisis, God did not abandon even when others did (2002: 510).

These changes also led to a spiritual practice of forgiveness amongst many of the interviewees (B, D, E, F, H, K, L and N). F is remarkably forgiving of her former congregation and defends them despite the treatment she received at their hands:

And I quite carefully tried not to trash that church

and when people outside the Church ask how do those people call themselves Christians I say well I say you have to see it from their point of view and I am spending the rest of my life defending what they did

not agreeing with it but understanding the reasoning was and why they were doing it

K is gracious about how she was effectively shut out of teaching when she transitioned and how people rejected her.

I think you are remarkably forgiving anyway (interviewer)

It's more survival you have to take what things are

D is very forgiving of the crowds that protested despite the fact that the situation was hurtful.

I mean I think about it now and I think God these are Christian people

Mmm (sad)

Why do you think that they were like this (interviewer)

(silence)

(silence)

Well now that's a good question

I mean I think they were

They are not bad people really and they are very genuine

D is also forgiving and loving when she talks about her mother-in-law's refusal to accept her transition and continues to regularly visit her. L is gracious about the comments, stares and mutterings she receives on the high street, believing that by meeting these behaviours with cheerfulness and love, hearts and minds will change eventually. B forgives a friend for rejecting him and hopes to be reunited one day. E forgives the treatment of those in a supposedly trans affirming denomination who found it hard to accept the transition of himself and his partner. He forgives the 'heteropanic' that his transition engendered amongst his gay male friends.

Forgiveness is also evident in the writings of trans people about themselves. Mollenkott and Sheridan (2003: 73) write that forgiving yourself and others is the key to personal emancipation. For Tanis forgiveness causes the healing of both body and spirit (2003: 107). Sheridan calls for trans people to forgive those in the Church who have wronged them because broken relationships cannot be healed with hatred (2001: 117). Reinsmith-Jones (2013: 82) writes about a process in which the body changes to self-love and by extension self-forgiveness. A study by Greene and Brittan (2013) shows that forgiveness is positively linked to an increase in self-esteem and a decrease in shame amongst LGBTQ folk (2013: 201).

Many of the interviewees disclosed a mystical experience (G, H, L and N) involving feelings of knowledge, intense love and praying aloud. These experiences often came at times of deep despair and confusion. They frequently included some elements of the natural world such as wind (K), fog (G), fire (K) and water (L). G relates his experience

> *Woke up and there was smoke or fog in my bedroom*

> *Now you know a scientist would say that you are halfway between being awake and asleep in that funny stage*

> *But*

> *Because I thought it was smoke I woke myself up thinking shit what the hell is going on so I know what I'd seen*

> *And I know it didn't smell so*

> *Like just a really warm feeling*

> *So I had seen something supernatural if you like*

That had no explanation there was nothing in the house where it could have come from

Umm so that had to be God

So even though I find it hard to define what God is that has to have been for me

I think it was part of the healing but also part of God saying to me

However you perceive me

Or don't or can't perceive me

Somehow I'm here

The work of Hay and Nye report that this is not a surprising statistic. They quote from the Gallup Omnibus surveys which state that 76 per cent of people said they had some form of mystical experience when they were asked in 2000 (Hay and Nye 2006: 28).

Images of God

Justin Tanis argues that the images of God presented by the Church are constricting and unbiblical (2003: 137). Reinsmith-Jones reports trans people interviewees with images of a God who is neither male nor female (2013: 84). Wilcox argues this shift to a more personalised vision of God is a coping strategy to deal with the negative religious images and messages that bombard LGBT folk (2002: 501). Like the literature on the subject, many of the interviewees (A, D, E, F, G, H, J, K, L and N) have rejected the traditional patriarchal image of God. As K recounts:

in my understanding of God I know I no longer have to think of God as an old man with a beard who ordered ethnic cleansing of the Canaanites because they were outside of the plan for Israel

I still regard God as one of my understandings as being an amazing caring and loving father because I had an amazing caring and loving father

But

I now totally believe that God fully understands

Fully understands and knows what it feels

And means to fully express as a male

And knows what it means and knows what it is to fully express what it is to be female

That God's own nature and being male and female he created them in his image

And it's part of God's image and template to take the mythical

I mean archetypical genesis is actually the God in person fully embraces and acknowledges male and female.

This rejection of a patriarchal God did not mean that the interviewees had dismissed the idea that God could be represented in a human image. They had expanded their imagery to include many different images of God such as a reproductive female or mother (A, F, K and N), a 'normal person' (B), a being that transcends gender (K), daddy (K) and a child (K, L and N). As N states:

God is disabled for me

God is a lesbian

Gods is trans (Silence)

B.K. Hipsher (2009: 99) argues that the image of a trans God is very attractive and deeply unsettling at the same time because it shows God in all the possible manifestations of humanity while being deeply transgressive to traditional images of God.

Many of the interviewees now see God as an attribute or value. E and J see God as human connectedness, while H and L see God as a comforter and rescuer. Both L and H see God as shattering love, while K sees God as gentle and playful. Several of the interviewees also offered natural imagery when they described God as water (J and N), wind (G and K), fire and blossom (K).

Many of the interviewees had an apophatic view of God (B, D, E, G, H, K and N). They did not necessarily use the term (or were aware of it) but many of them described a God that did not conform to human imagery or exist within human boundaries. Others talked about what God was not - such as someone not interested in ethnic cleansing. This is also reflected in the literature. Mollenkott and Sheridan describe what God is not as anything that creates a 'theology of rage and hate' (2003: 85). The participants in the study carried out by Wilcox (2002: 506) also describe God as 'not judgemental'. Many found their image of God was too large to be constricted into a single image. They attributed their growing understanding of God in this way to their growing understanding of their own identities.

Jesus is an important figure in the theology of many of the interviewees. Their Jesus is seen as radically inclusive (E, G, H and N), incarnational (H) bearing the wounds of his suffering in heaven in a very similar way to the marks and scars of humanity (N). As E and K state:

> I think I can identify with that sense of God's spirit and Jesus you know as God's presence being displayed through the actions of Jesus and how radical his actions were and how very much Jesus' life and ministry were about including those who had been excluded and making a stand for those who had been treated badly and when that was just so against the norm of that society
>
> That is my sense of seeing God today in the world and God in my life (E)
>
> What I relate far more to is Jesus
>
> who was basically God come down to have a look
>
> 'did it' 'got the t shirt'
>
> I do not look on Jesus Christ the son of God
>
> not so much as come down to live among us here
>
> but come down here because the only way he could do it was to experience it
>
> Even the creator of the universe
>
> has got to be here and feel it and
>
> Live the life and that
>
> That is the heart of my gospel (K)

The literature written by trans people also echoes this. Sheridan (2001: 22) sees Jesus as a liberative figure. Tanis notes that Jesus 'challenged in ways that shocked challenged and transformed' (2003: 141).

Queer theologian Bob Goss sees Jesus as a gender liminal figure who transgresses gender boundaries (1993: 81-82).

Engaging with the Bible

Mollenkott believes that the Bible is an extremely trans friendly document (Mollenkott 2001: 146). She lists many transsexual images, such as women being called brothers, men called Brides of Christ, Jesus and Paul depicted as mothers and the Church depicted as having a female body with a male head (John 16:21, 17:1, Galatians 4:19 and Ephesians 4:15). In contrast, none of the interviewees in Reinsmith-Jones (2013: 82) saw themselves reflected in the Bible.

This mixed picture was replicated in the interviews. The Bible was seen by some of the interviewees as having value (A,G,K and N), but they were clear that it needed to be read with a critical eye and caution should be exercised about reading it literally as a template for modern life. Some identified with biblical characters. Others (A, C, G and K) saw the Bible as a distant document that was compiled for and by people in a different age. As G comments:

> *It's not*
>
> *It's not my history*
>
> *It's the history of other people*
>
> *And their relationship with God so whether there is*
>
> *A lot I have no idea because I have never really read it for a long time.*

The only scriptural passage that the interviewees identified as being anti-trans was Deuteronomy 22:5 which is a prohibition against cross-dressing. Two of the interviewees (F and H) had struggled with the passage but both had resolved the issue for themselves and now considered it irrelevant to their lives. Some of the interviewees (A, C, F, G, H, L and N) saw the passage as a weapon of spiritual violence used against trans people by conservative Christians. As A recounts:

> *And is it Deuteronomy when it talks about males not wearing females' clothes*
>
> *Yes (interviewer)*
>
> *Again that is a really pathetic use*

That some people use it as a stick

Fundamentalists use to

Beat people who they choose to

Because you know culturally it wasn't that long ago that woman were not allowed to wear trousers because it was considered

That was considered cross-dressing so truly we are

Um talks in the Bible about not wearing you know

Clothing of mixed fibres and that slavery is acceptable

And stoning adulterous women is OK then I think

I think this is all rather pathetic and extreme

Fundamentalists will say anything.

Mollenkott and Sheridan (2003: 119) discuss this passage and conclude that it was a decree for certain times and places and was specifically around cultic cross-dressing. They also argue that the only way for trans people to deal with negative interpretations of Scripture is to become biblically literate and learn to discern the difference between the words of the Law and spirit of the Law. They also call for a hermeneutic arising from the trans experience that is informed by the struggles of trans people in their fight for liberation. Wilcox notes a common strategy of modified literalism is used by LGBT folk to deal with unhelpful Scripture. This is a process where unhelpful Scripture is placed within its historical context and then evaluated for relevance to contemporary life (2002: 509).

The places in the Bible where interviewees saw themselves varied. The most common biblical character mentioned was the eunuch (discussed at length in Chapter 5). Galatians 3:28 was also identified as explicitly endorsing trans people. Others included Psalm 139 (G) and Joseph from Genesis (H). Most touchingly N speaks of the woman in Luke 8:42-48 saying:

when I encountered that woman who touches the hem of Christ and is healed it spoke profoundly to me on

Who felt

Maybe still in some respects feels unlovely and unlovable

And maybe

Still wonders or wishes that I were other than I am

Wishes I had just been born a woman

Had been born female

But felt within that story me who was skirting around in the shadows and had been laughed at and abused

(silence)

Could still be (very emotional)

Loved and (very emotional)

Healed in some sense (very emotional)

But I didn't even need (very emotional)

To speak to God to touch the hem of his garment is enough (very emotional)

And as you can see it still gets me and to discover that I didn't

Didn't have to produce this magic trick and turn this boy

Somehow genetically into a girl and you know somehow had to change reality in some sense is that me

Who felt on the edges of society could reach out and be good enough to meet this person face to face (very emotional)

That somehow my faith in him was enough (very emotional)

To save me

It's that

It still gets me

Gifts and theological insights

When asked what unique gifts and insights they feel they had gained, the most common response was the insights gained by moving from a faith position that created pain and confusion to a faith position that allowed self-acceptance and peace (A, D, E, H, J and N).

While other groups such as LGB, disabled people and women question assumptions the Church makes about sexuality, gender, embodiment and identity, trans people pose these multiple questions simultaneously. The interviewees have had to question almost everything they believed about themselves and God through the lens of their experience. Beardsley, O'Brien and Woolley (2012: 277) see this as a process of self-discovery and self-awareness in which unhealthy coping strategies are overcome. Gender and sexuality come to be seen as a gift rather than a curse. Tanis (2003: 145) writes that God delights in diversity. What we learn from trans people is that when we suppress this diversity, spiritual and psychological suffering are created. He also writes that the gender journey is an invitation to set out on a journey of body, mind and spirit (2003: 147).

Interviewees attributed their gender journey to radical changes in their beliefs about gender, sexual orientation, embodiment and biblical interpretation. As K relates:

I think it can probably deepen our understanding of God

Um

Not necessarily put us on a pedestal

I'd never dream of doing that

but I think we can relate to so much of what it is to be human

So much of human experience

if you are a genetic female

you may not necessarily understand

and if you are a genetic male you might not necessarily understand

We somehow have this fusion of both

which has caused the situation sometimes referred to as gender confusion

Um

And

I think that has

(silence)

It has been a problem in my life in the early stages because I had to work out for myself what was going on

But through all the loss

All the personal heartache

The difficulties of working my way through

to the point where I am now absolutely 100 per cent female .....

I am totally at peace with peace with that and I know that God is at peace with me over it too

and as a result of it I am

a much stronger person not just physically but emotionally

Hutchins (2001: 21) sees one of the gifts that trans people bring is encouraging the Church to stop channelling its energies into illusions of theological simplicity and instead release and use those same energies to liberate. Several other writers make this same point. Ford (2013: 81) notes that 'pink and blue can make a pleasing purple'. Tanis (2003: 181) writes that churches assume that societal norms are part of the Gospel when they are not. Trans people remind us that God's standards are not ours. Sheridan echoes this, saying that being trans confronts the issue of being other in a culture that demands uniformity (2001: 10). Mollenkott and Sheridan (2003: 151) argue that learning to live with ambiguity means living with the Spirit rather than living with forms of religious certainty.

The interviewees echo these sentiments. Several (E, G, J and N) mention one of the major gifts trans people bring is the ability to live with ambiguity. To live with uncertainty and without rigid categories means living with multiple layers of meaning, identity and complexity without attempting to classify, regulate or simplify, but rather allowing life and faith to be experienced and reflected upon. Several of the interviewees also identified that many churches have issues with dealing with ambiguity and often seek simple answers to complex questions. They also suggest that the energies the Church spends on theological definition, patrolling and enforcing could be better expended on adapting itself to the current age. As J relates:

> *I think like that err*
>
> *(pause)*
>
> *That the boundaries of things don't need to be*
>
> *so rigidly defended*
>
> *mmmm*
>
> *like um*
>
> *you know um*
>
> *like I think the Church is defensive about a lot of things*
>
> *and um*
>
> *(pause)*
>
> *Um*
>
> *(pause)*
>
> *it's not going to*
>
> *it's not going to*
>
> *undermine the Church to be more open to um*
>
> *to actually*
>
> *listen to other people's experiences and um*
>
> *accept that's who they understand themselves and the world*
>
> *and think that would make it stronger not weaker.*

Both N and L consider that a deeper relationship with God can be found in the place of bewilderment they experienced. Ford echoes these sentiments by calling his gender transition his Gethsemane (2013: 87). As a congregation grapples with the fact that gender is not as rigid as they previously believed, it may also begin to question other assumptions it has held. McCall Tigert and Tirabassi (2004: 14) identify this process as finding and losing as part of the journey. Tanis also describes this as learning to live with revelations that we don't want (2003: 45). This questioning may lead to re-evaluating previous beliefs and seeking new ways of being a Christian. Spiritual honesty may not be found in places of comfort and power (Tanis 2003:181). Trans folk have already experienced this and can offer their experience and wisdom gained from their journey.

This also leads to the concept of evaluating what is theologically important (E, F and N). Many of the interviewees start in a place of rigidity and literalism but through their experiences change their attitudes. F's experience of exclusion from being a white middle class pillar of a church community to one shunned and on the edges, has profoundly changed how she views the message of the Gospel. As she relates:

> *and I have learnt so much it has softened my heart it has given me a sort of understanding of what people go through that are different and in some ways marginalized people and that is so true to the Scriptures*
>
> *I mean what my church was thinking about really you know*
>
> *marginalized people in society are being marginalized by the Church*
>
> *and the Church should be an example not to marginalize people. (F)*

One of the other insights expressed by the interviewees (D, E, J, L and N) is the costliness of honesty and following your intuition. Mollenkott and Sheridan describe these gifts as honesty and integrity (2003: 87) and coming out as an act of faith (2003: 133). Reinsmith-Jones describes this as needing to live in authenticity (2013: 80). The interviewees were aware of the potential cost to their careers, families, relationships and life chances. They were aware that the road that they had embarked upon was difficult and heart-breaking. But this did not deter them from embarking on it because to do otherwise would not allow them to honestly express who they were. As K relates:

> *The psalmist says um*
>
> *When I take away your breath you die and go back to the earth um*
>
> *When I send my spirit you are created I renew the face of the earth and there is a sense that the amazing creator God*

In all eternity knows who we are

A bit like my gender journey

It has become a journey of trying to

Really acknowledge and be and become who I am

And

So in terms of vocation it is a journey of starting to recognise myself and let God call me into deeper being with that.

Concluding comments

Given the richness of the narratives it is hard to summarise in a few sentences what they contain. These sacred stories powerfully speak of an atypical gender experience that is full of discovery, faith and redemption. They speak of a costly co-creative relationship between God and humanity and the power of faith to heal.

But these stories also speak of the harm that is done to individuals in the name of gender conformity and religion. They speak of pain, fear and alienation. They speak of damage wittingly and unwittingly done. This damage is to trans people themselves, the people they love and the communities that they are part of.

But mostly these narratives speak of silence. They speak of years of silence in which people have held secrets believing that silence was more acceptable than truth and struggle and heartache carefully masked by an exterior of Christian conformity. Good people have suffered needlessly and grievously because the Church and society did not want to listen to their truth. Chapter 6 is a response to these narratives. It is a series of pastoral reflections that arose from interaction with the narratives.

Chapter 4

Reuniting the Earth Creature

Introduction

This chapter deals with two of the theological objections often levied against trans people. The first objection is that the biblical account of Genesis tells us all we need to know about gender. This objection states that God made male and female as part of a divinely inspired plan and the people who disrupt this system are somehow guilty of a terrible sin. The second objection is that trans people violate Natural Law. This is currently the view of many inside the Catholic Church.[1]

This chapter attempts to deal with these objections seriously by exploring the Creation accounts contained within Genesis Chapters 1, 2 and 3. It will seek to explore and disentangle our own assumptions from the account of creation by looking closely at what the text actually says. We will also seek to explore alternative viewpoints arising from a close reading of the text from a trans positive perspective.

This chapter will then proceed to explain the concepts of Natural Law and examine why objections to trans people have been made using Natural Law as an argument. This chapter will then seek to evaluate the objections and attempt to evaluate the validity of these arguments.

Genesis Explored

Many people forget there are two differing accounts of the origins of humanity in the Bible. The first is a lyrical version in the first chapter of Genesis that speaks of a majestic creation when God spoke the Word and everything came out of nothing. It is a familiar sequence that looks like this:

Day 1 - God created light and darkness

Day 2 - God separated the water from above from the water below and calls one sky.

---

1   (Pope Francis: It's 'terrible' children taught they can choose gender) Catholic Herald posted Wednesday, 3 August 2016 on website

Day 3 - God created dry ground and gathered the waters into seas. God also created vegetation (plants and trees).

Day 4 - God created the sun, moon, and the stars.

Day 5 - God created every living thing that fills the waters and the sky with life.

Day 6 - God created the animals to fill the earth. God also created men and women in God's own image.

Day 7 - God had finished the work of creation and rested on the seventh day, declaring it holy.

This story is so part of our Christian heritage we rarely question it. It is the stuff of school assemblies and Sunday school and tales around the camp fire at church camps. We rarely read the account in the Bible because we feel that we already know the story so well. We often overlook that there are two stories and they are not the same. They do not follow the same sequence nor do they describe the same mechanisms of human creation – they cannot be reconciled as the second adding more detail to the first. The difference between the first and second narrative is that in the first both genders seem to be created simultaneously. There is no implied hierarchy or discussion about who these created people were or their natures. There is no Adam or Eve named and there are no numbers of created people mentioned but the account gives the impression that men and women are plural. There is no story of one creature divided which we encounter in the second creation story – only a command to reproduce to populate the earth and to be good stewards of it.

The second creation story contained in Genesis 2:4-20 is a more matter of fact version of the creation story which sets up the creation of the Garden of Eden and the Tree of the Knowledge of Good and Evil. It begins with a created earth that is watered by a mist and an earth creature called Adam who was placed in the Garden of Eden, a garden to till and look after. The account takes pains to locate the garden at the convergence of the Pishon, Gihon, Tigris and Euphrates rivers.

The story does not indicate that there is an intention for the creature to reproduce, indeed it seems to be a unique creation designed to look after the Garden of Eden. The original creature is not designated as male or female and it is our assumption that the creature is male – gender is designated when it is later divided into man and woman later. Up until then it is called Adam which means 'Ruddy or Earth' (Metzger & Coogan 1993: 10).

It is only when God realises that the creature is lonely that God seeks to find a companion for it. To find a helper-companion God creates animals and birds. We are told that none of these creatures was deemed a suitable helper for the creature in the garden. It is only after this exploration of alternative helpers that God divides the creature in two calling one part 'man' and one part 'woman'. The solution of dividing the creature into two different people is only arrived at once all the other options to find a companion have failed.

It can be argued that the creation of the two creatures in the second story has little to do with the creation of gender but rather is a solution to the lonely state of the original creature. If this is the case, then it is important to see that the original intention of dividing the creature was to banish loneliness rather than create gender.

The accounts in the Transfaith project spoke powerfully about isolation and loneliness caused by the teachings and actions of the Church. If we take the concept that God's original intention was to alleviate loneliness, then the actions of some parts of the teachings and actions towards trans people have directly contravened God's original intention for humanity.

In many Christians' minds, the two stories become fused into one. We skip from the seven-day creation story and move onto Adam and Eve in the garden without paying attention to Genesis 2:4-20 in which the second narrative is located. It creates a muddled understanding of the Genesis stories in which the original intention of God is to create a binary gender and heteronormative gender roles. A close reading of both creation accounts cannot support those assumptions. Given that there are only two creatures it is inevitable that they represent a binary in the story. It is an assumption that a binary gender is somehow God's will. There can only be two expressions of gender because there are only two humans and there are as many gender expressions of humanity as there are people. This is no basis for assuming that male and female exhausts the possibilities of human gender identity and that God's intention is that there are only two genders. The story is silent on the idea that if other humans arrive that they might have different genders.

What we have done is to map our own assumptions based on our binary gender system onto this story. At this stage, there are caretakers in a garden who have as many gender expressions as there are humans and there is no indication that they have even considered their gender or the possibility of sex. They seem to exist in a state of innocence because they do not even recognise their nakedness or the erotic possibilities that nakedness might afford them.

The story changes when the serpent tricks the woman into eating the fruit of the Tree of Knowledge. It is here the shame and sexuality enter the story - the man and the woman are suddenly aware of their nakedness and try to cover themselves and hide before God finds out what has happened. Once God finds out that they have eaten from the Tree of Knowledge they are punished. The woman is cursed to bear children in pain and she is visited with sexual desire. She is told that she will experience desire and because of that desire she will be ruled over by the man. It is not God but Adam who names her Eve 'Mother' because she will be the bearer of his children. This the first mention of sex or reproduction in the second account.

It should also be noted that this is Adam's first act. Up until this time he has been a passive figure who follows the urgings of the woman. In his punishment he is not visited with desire but forced to work hard and return to the dust from which he is created.

It would be mischievous and unhelpful to describe Eve's punishment as a curse of heterosexuality. Both Tina and Chris understand human sexuality in all its forms as a gift from God. Eve desires the only other human that exists. It should be noted that Adam has yet to take any action or initiative, while Eve has shown herself to be the active agent in the partnership up until this time. Indeed, a plausible alternative reading of the curse placed on Eve is that 'stupid will be in charge now'.

There is also little to assume that we as their descendants would be bound by this punishment. There is no mention that this pattern of behaviour is to be followed by us as their descendants. We are simply not mentioned or considered. The only mention of our legacy from their disobedience is a hatred of snakes.

Adam and Eve are then expelled from the garden because God fears that they will eat from the Tree of Life and will unwittingly become like God themselves. An angel with a flaming sword is stationed at the entrance of the garden so that they can never return.

It is important to recognise that this second Genesis tale is a story about the origin of the first two humans. But it is an enormous assumption that Adam and Eve are meant to encompass the entire permitted gender expression or sexuality. Indeed, even at the end of the story Adam's desires are ambiguous - it is Eve who is visited by desire for Adam. We have no way of knowing if this is reciprocated as it is simply not mentioned within the story. It is the reading of this story from a heteronormative perspective that inserts many assumptions that are not contained within the text itself.

Natural Law

While the ancient Greek philosopher Aristotle came up with the original concept of Natural Law, we are mostly likely to associate it with the religious philosopher Thomas Aquinas (1224-74). Aquinas believed that human beings are naturally inclined towards goodness and that the certain principles are inherent in all human beings. Aquinas believed that these principles are hardwired into us and that when we follow them we are rewarded with happiness. This happiness occurs because we instinctively understand that we are doing what is right. Aquinas considered these principles to be

- Preservation of human life
- Continuing humanity through reproducing
- Educating our offspring
- To live in society
- To want to know God.

Aquinas helpfully makes the distinction between intention and effect. He believed that the important thing was intent. He argued that if we decide to help someone it should not be because of the positive comment that we might gain from others but we are helping the person because it is an inherently good thing.

He goes further and argues that reason is an important aspect of Natural Law. Using reason, we take these five basic principles and create laws that support them. For example, the law against murder happens because it violates the principle of the preservation of human life. We make laws that are designed to stop us killing people by action and inaction (such as Health and Safety Laws) because we recognise one of the highest goods we can achieve is the preservation of human life.

Implicit in this championing of reason is the underlying assumption that we need to have all the information possible to ensure that we are supporting these basic principles. One of the problems with Natural Law is that it can become static unless we are always seeking new information and revisiting our laws to make sure that they are the best expression of protecting our five principles. A good example is the use of arsenic in wallpaper during Victorian times. It created a brilliant green wall paper that was pleasing to the eye and helped to create the impression of a beautiful home to raise and educate children in. But as more information about the effects of arsenic became known it became clear that those bright green rooms made children ill and sometimes killed them. One of the concerns about much that has been written about trans people by the Church is that the authors have not tried to formulate an opinion based on the experiences of the trans community, nor those who support them, but have tried to formulate an opinion in an intellectual vacuum without all of the information they need for a rounded argument.

Chapter 2 explored the literature produced by the Church and found that there was a distinct lack of consultation with people who could rightly be considered experts. The voices of the very people who were being discussed were not considered to have anything to add. People's lives were being discussed in an ivory tower that had little to do with the realities that people were living. Similarly, there was a reluctance to engage with expert opinion. What had been produced by authors of Church reports was an attempt to reach a conclusion to fit a predetermined position. Any information that did not fit this position was either proof texted or discarded.

Aquinas also recognises that sometimes what seems good on the surface is not always good for us. For Natural Law to work it requires a reasonable evaluation of the consequences of any action to be sure whether or not it is good. Much of the Church writing seems written in defence of traditional gender roles and marriage. To achieve this some very harsh things are said For example, *Some issues in human sexuality* describes trans people as unwholesome and psychologically unstable (House of Bishops 2003: 287).

While on the surface the defence of orthodoxy may seem to be an initial good to those who feel Church teaching on gender and human sexuality is under attack, the coarsening of compassion and the sacrifice of a marginalised and misunderstood group of people on the altar of orthodoxy seems a price too high to pay. Trans people should not be ignored or vilified by people who refuse to engage with them, or experts within that area, in order to prop up a gender system that is under challenge as not fit for purpose for our twenty-first-century society on many fronts.

Natural Law is also not without problems. The most famous objection to the Natural Law Theory was described by the Scottish philosopher David Hume in his 'is/ought' fallacy. He argues that we tend to believe what is pre-existing is natural and that our tendency is to classify what we see and experience as its natural state. He also argues that there is inertia in our desire to change things and that we tend to believe that if something has not already occurred then it probably should not.

Chris believes that the Church is caught up with this is/ought fallacy about gender in general and trans people in particular. We tend to see the systems of gender we live in as natural. We think we know what men are and what women are and that this is a universal principle for all humanity. But there is nothing inherently natural about a male/female gender system. Most other cultures have come up with at least one intermediate gender. The Berdache, Hijras, Sworn Virgins of Bulgaria, Fa'afafine, Xanith, Muxe are all examples of variant genders in different societies all over the world.

The problem is that many of us have never heard of these cultures nor these different gender systems because we inhabit a dominant culture that has pushed these other cultures and those who live in them to the margins. For example, the Hijras (a recognised third gender in India) served as priestesses in temples before British colonial rule, but are now some of the most deprived people in Indian society often living by begging and prostitution.

Natural Law cannot be static. If we are to use reason to derive secondary precepts then we must continue to seek out more and more information to be able to discern what is the most sensible thing to do.

Looking at the five primary precepts in relation to trans people

Natural Law has been used as an objection about trans people. As a result, it is important to consider whether this argument has validity. This next section explores each precept to consider if trans people are in contravention of the precept. This section also asks if trans people may be following the concepts of Natural Law rather than being in contravention of them.

Self-preservation

The Transfaith project uncovered stories of deep unhappiness and desperation told by the interviewees about their inability to resolve the conflicts between their feelings of discomfort with their gender identity and their faith. As a result, many of them had lived difficult lives prior to coming out as trans. The interviews recounted broken relationships, secrecy, guilt, internalised anger and emotional pain that frequently made people consider taking their own life.

It is therefore not surprising that the suicide and self-harming rate is much higher than average amongst the transgender population. On its website in 2017 the UK campaigning group Stonewall has sobering statistics on the prevalence of suicidal feelings and self-harm for young trans people:

> Nearly half (48 per cent) of trans people under 26 said they had attempted suicide, and 30 per cent said they had done so in the past year, while 59 per cent said they had at least considered doing so.

More than four in five trans young people have self-harmed, as have three in five lesbians, gay and bi young people who aren't trans.

These statistics are shocking. But it is not surprising that these statistics are high when tales are told of transphobic bullying and religious denunciation so that shame and guilt have been part of people's lives. As has been mentioned previously, the experts believe that gender dysphoria manifests itself sometime in early childhood and from that time the child has had to keep a secret and be mindful of their actions so that their secret is not exposed and they are punished.

Older interviewees recount that they felt that they were the only people on earth who felt the way they did. Behaviours that released the pressure of living such as secret dressing simply added to the shame they felt.

There is a high rate of satisfaction once gender issues had been resolved. The report produced by the Audit, Information and Analysis Unit for Kent, Surrey, Sussex, Essex, Bedfordshire and Hertfordshire for 2008 shows a 98 per cent satisfaction rate with surgical interventions. It also cautions one of the problems that trans people experience is the waiting times for initial treatment and the consequences to health if people resort to unregulated medical interventions such as buying hormones over the internet because they are eager to begin their gender journey.

The primary reason the Transfaith project found that people come out was for reasons of self-preservation. They were not attempting to overturn a binary gender system or to disrupt the Church's interpretation of Genesis; they are doing so to be able to live at peace with themselves and in some cases so they could survive.

Coming out as trans is not an act of rebellion but a desire to be able to live a life that is happy and free from trauma. All of the interviewees of the Transfaith project felt that they were happier after they had accepted their transgender identity and had taken steps to confirm their gender through whatever procedures (whether they were medical or not) that allowed them to manifest their true identity.

It is genuinely difficult to consider how the existence of trans people could threaten the self-preservation of other people. While Oliver O' Donovan considers that there may be deception this is far more likely to occur in an environment where trans people are not allowed to discover themselves or have been subjected to a regime of fear and shame so that they feel they must remain hidden.

Therefore, it is hard to see how trans people can be said to be in contravention of the first principle of Natural Law. It is much easier to argue that the actions of coming out and embracing the potentialities of happiness, wholeness and healing that occurs when people can name who they are and align their identity, gender expression and their bodies is an act of self-preservation.

Reproduction

One of the objections about transgender people listed in *Some issues in human sexuality* is that they have deliberately voided the ability to procreate (House of Bishops 2003: 235). This shows a misunderstanding of the lives of many trans people. Some of the interviewees of the project for example transitioned well after childbearing age, others opted for non-surgical interventions that manifested their identity. Some may not have been able to have children for many reasons. While it cannot be denied that some people may be unable to have children due to medical procedures used to confirm identity this was not universal.

It is hard to use this argument against trans people if they are infertile or have passed childbearing age. But it would also be outrageous to insist on theological grounds that each trans person was asked to wait for medical interventions until they had passed fertility. It would also be outrageous to insist on fertility testing people whose gender journey may compromise their ability to procreate. This would be as intrusive as applying fertility testing to prospective married couples and refusing them marriage on the grounds that marriage is solely for the purpose of procreation.

Up until the miracle of modern medicine there was a need for many people to have children as there was a high infant mortality rate and societal structures meant the family was the main source of support in illness or old age. The advent of the welfare state meant that people no longer needed to have children as some form of social security. We live in a very different world from Aquinas.

In our society, many people decide not to have children. For some this is a conscious choice where they wish to concentrate on other aspects of their lives such as careers or they may simply decide that they would prefer not to parent. For others, this is a less conscious choice but happens because of circumstance such as the inability to find a suitable partner, lack of economic resources or simply that time marches on and they find that their fertility is waning without deciding.

The Church also encourages the practice of celibacy if a person is unmarried and some Church traditions actively encourage lifelong celibate religious vocations. It is difficult to insist that one group has a duty to procreate when it is either silent in other circumstances or actively promotes the idea that some people are called by God not to procreate. The Church cannot have it both ways.

It would then be disingenuous of the Church to apply this concept of Natural Law solely to transgender people when it teaches something else or remains quiet about the other life choices that people make. As such it would seem difficult to object to trans people on the grounds of this second principle of Natural Law.

The Education of Children

It has already been stated several times that feelings of gender dysphoria manifest themselves at an early age. One of the reasons this is important is that it shows that this is not the product of fevered imagination or a desire to transgress. These are feelings that children have from an early age.

It therefore seems reasonable that children are taught to name their feelings. This will save some of the anguish of being unable to explain why they are feeling the way they do and also will help them to be able to seek help earlier so that they can grow up with as little trauma as possible.

The second reason that it is important to educate children is to stop bullying. Many of us, whether trans or not, have some unhappy memories of being bullied at school for being different. Indeed, the statistics on bullying in the Stonewall report show bullying is rife in our schools:

- 64 per cent of trans pupils are bullied for being LGBT in Britain's schools.

- Seven in ten LGBT pupils report that their school says that homophobic and bi-phobic bullying is wrong, however, just two in five LGBT pupils report that their schools say that transphobic bullying is wrong
- More than four in five trans young people have self-harmed
- More than two in five trans young people have attempted to take their own life.

Teaching children that being transgender is wrong will do little to alleviate this situation. Instead, we need to educate children to either embrace themselves or to learn to be tolerant of difference. Theological positions that marginalise young trans people and other people who are different metaphorically have blood on them because they encourage bullying, shame, suicide, secrecy and guilt.

If we are to serve the precepts of protecting life and educating our children, it is hard to see how not teaching our children about the feelings that they may be having, or the need to learn to be tolerant of others, serves any greater good.

To live in society

In 2016 *The Independent* newspaper reported an astonishing rise of 170 per cent increase in hate crime against the trans community. Most of this hate crime is perpetrated by men but a third was perpetrated by women. These crimes were anything from physical abuse, verbal abuse, name calling or being mocked. Victims did not feel that they were able to stand up for themselves for fear of escalating the situations.

It is hard to account for the spike - it may be the first time that hate incidents are being reported because victims feel they will be taken seriously or the increase in visibility and confidence means that trans people are more likely to be visible in public rather than attempting to camouflage themselves to avoid abuse. Or it could be reasons currently unknown.

But these actions come from the idea that somehow trans people are neither normal nor are they innocent. It comes from the idea that somehow, they are destroying our gender system and people feel that they have the right to defend themselves and punish perpetrators. The lack of a positive voice from the Church means that this violence is being sanctified. It is hard to decry violence against people when you have pronounced them unnatural.

If we are to pursue this precept that it is good to live in society then we must accept difference unless it is harmful. It is difficult to see how a trans person manifesting their own identity has a negative impact on the identity of others. If people are secure in their gender identity then they should be untroubled by people offering alternatives and if they are insecure then the acceptance of gender variance will embolden them to make explorations on their own.

The only damage to society is the breakdown of cisgender privilege; the idea that being comfortable in your natal gender is superior to having to explore and take steps to confirm identity. This seems suspiciously like selling cheap grace: telling people that they are more blessed than others for no other reason than an accident of birth. Indeed, cis people could be at a disadvantage because they have never had to ponder matters of gender and identity as deeply as someone who has experienced gender dissonance. Often cisgender people have no reason to question the gender system they live in which means that everything about gender has been accepted uncritically. One of the gifts that trans people give society is a new lens to examine the human condition.

To worship God

One of the surprising findings of the Transfaith project was that the gender journey had deepened the faith of the interviewees. While they had all struggled with their faith at different times they had come to embrace a much more loving, forgiving and laughing God.

It is highly probable that many trans people have fled the Church after hearing transphobia, and experiencing discrimination or abuse at the hands of the Church. It is hard to quantify this number as there is no research done to date in the UK. But it would be highly likely that some people have been driven away from worshipping God. Reports like *Transsexuality* give trans people a stark choice: either conform to our gender teaching or leave. If this is the case, the actions of the Church have violated the last precept of Natural Law by discouraging people from worshipping God.

If we are to encourage trans people to worship then we need to reframe our theology. Chris has written several liturgies (see Chapter 9) that speak to some of the needs of trans people looking to sanctify the rites of passage they may experience as part of their gender journey. It is not an exhaustive resource but it is a start.

It is difficult to see how an open trans person would stop others worshipping God. The project showed that trans people were keen to blend in to worship and not draw attention to themselves. While people may be initially surprised, it is just as likely that a visible trans person may signal to newcomers that all are truly welcome in the Lord's house and to feel that the sign out the front that says 'all are welcome' is for once speaking the truth.

In Conclusion

This chapter has attempted to look at the theological objections often used against trans people and found little to support them. Read as they are written, the Genesis creation stories contain little about a God ordained binary gender system beyond telling people to multiply. Natural Law also offers little objection and indeed, the act of coming out as trans is more likely to honour Natural Law principles than violate them. This prompts the question then why are they used?

Perhaps the answer lies in the power that the Church gains from being custodians of the founding gender story of our society. While much of our intellectual capital is gone and science is now the test of proof in our society rather than theological beliefs, we can still point to the fact that our understanding of our creation stories influences the way that people see gender in Western society. It may also be that some Christians have painted themselves into a corner on the subject and find it difficult to admit that what has been written was wrong and hurtful to no good end.

If this is the case, the reason that some parts of the Church have found the acceptance of trans people problematic is much more about guarding privilege and pride. The objections to their full inclusion may not be so much theological as institutional and personal arrogance.

Chapter 5

What does the Bible Say?

Introduction

This chapter explores two different ways to find places of inspiration and affirmation for trans people in the Bible. The first section considers how the biblical eunuch has been used to claim a place for trans people within the biblical text. The second way opens up a conversation between the transcripts and the biblical figure of Job. By comparing the experiences of the interviewees with the story of Job, we argue that the resonances between the two work at a deeply meaningful level.

Exploring the eunuchs as transcestors
What trans theologians say

Lewis Reay considers biblical eunuchs to be his 'transcestors' (Reay 2009: 150). As he writes:

> Let me introduce you to some of my spiritual transcestors ... Mehuman, the faithful, Hegai, the Eunuch .... Harbona, the ass driver and Biztha, the booty, all eunuchs of King Xerxes... (Reay, 2009: 150)

He defines the term transcestor as:

> the elision of trans and ancestor to signify those transgender characters and people who provide a history and prove we have always been there (Reay 2009: 149).

Tanis (2003), Mollenkott (2001), Reay (2009) and Kolakowski (1997) all make this connection between biblical eunuchs and trans people. Each of them uses scripture to make their point. Tanis (2003: 72), Reay (2009: 156) and Mollenkott (2001: 136) all make parallels between Jesus' discussion of eunuchs in Matthew 19 and modern trans people. They all conclude Jesus' discussion about eunuchs, and particularly verse 19:12 (where Jesus mentions eunuchs who are made by others), is a direct and clear analogy to themselves. The affirmation they find in the words of Jesus is clear within their writings.

Kolakowski further explores the implications of welcome for trans people within the story of the Ethiopian Eunuch (1997a: 24).

Her discussion of the Ethiopian Eunuch concludes that the radical act of inclusion of a transcestor counters any biblically based objection against the inclusion and welcome of trans people. Her discussion about Queen Jezebel's eunuchs (2000) is a biblical analogy exploring tensions between some parts of feminism and trans people. Kolakowski concludes the anxiety is that trans people will act in ways that will destroy the women's movement, just as the eunuchs betrayed the strong and proud Jezebel to her conquerors and caused her death.

It would seem these are two good reasons to accept the analogy. It provides both affirmation and a place for theological reflection about matters that confront trans people today.

Affirmation

There is a human need to be able to find our historical roots. This is particularly important to people who have been made invisible, appropriated by others, or ignored in history. The eunuch offers a visible and identifiable transcestor located within the Bible. As Reay proudly claims:

> *I am from those powerful gender variant souls whose line stretches throughout history (Reay 2009: 151).*

The eunuch allows trans people the ability to claim a place in Scripture that recognises and legitimises their existence and identity. It places them within the larger Christian story, reminds the wider Church of their existence and their right to a place within Christianity. Stories such as the Ethiopian Eunuch in Acts 8, Jesus' discussion of the eunuch in Matthew 19 and the blessing of Isaiah 56 offer legitimacy, a history and an identity for trans people within the biblical narrative.

These stories also provide a powerful counter narrative to the negative theology that uses the Creation stories of Genesis 1 and 2 to set up a binary, birth defined, and essentialist gender system as God ordained. It also counters the prohibition against cross-dressing in Deuteronomy 22:5 which is the most frequently used text against trans people mentioned by many of the interviewees (A, C, F, G, H, L and N).

Acceptance

Kolakowski (1997b) uses the eunuch to make a plea for tolerance from the broader Church. Her argument is that if eunuchs are blessed in scriptures, such as Isaiah 56, then God approves of eunuchs. If trans people are the heirs to the eunuchs, then God approves of them also. The logical conclusion of this argument is that if trans people are approved in Scripture, then there are no grounds for modern Christians to exclude or persecute them. Taken to its logical conclusion, the role of the modern Church should be to welcome and affirm trans people.

The logic of this position is simple and elegant. For those who take Scripture seriously and make the same links as Kolakowski, the inclusion of trans people in the wider church community becomes a biblical principle to be followed. This may persuade the doubtful to allow their church to offer welcome, affirmation and support to a community at the margins of the Christian experience.

Limitations of the analogy. Buying into a medical model

The eunuch=trans analogy plays into a medicalised model of trans identity where surgical intervention is required to correct a physical problem. This medical model does not focus on gender identity but upon the state of a person's genitals, secondary sexual characteristics and any other medical interventions that may have occurred. Identity becomes located entirely in the physical. Transition becomes a mechanistic medical process with a predetermined outcome where a person moves from one side of the gender binary to the other.

This model entirely misses the complex issues surrounding identity that the transcripts of the interviews uncovered. It does not consider the difficulties of constructing identity, the courage of following one's inner truths despite the obstacles, challenging the gendered assumptions of society or the psychological and spiritual challenges that are part of the gender journey. By doing so it misses the point of what the research uncovered: that the journey that trans people undertake is primarily a social, spiritual and psychological one, and while the physical changes are important milestones they are only one aspect of a complex journey.

More concerning, this model only includes those who have been diagnosed with gender dysphoria by psychiatric assessment and have submitted themselves to medical interventions that have physically changed their gender. This negates the ability to self-name and self-define. It is the ceding of the power of self-definition and self-expression to others. It ignores the pre-operative, the gender queer and those happy in their gender expression without surgery or medical intervention.

As Stone (2006) comments, in the seminal article 'The Empire Strikes Back', to limit trans identity to a medicalised category of post-operative transsexuals ignores the richness and the variety of the trans experience:

> *Concomittant with the dubious achievement of a diagnostic category is the inevitable blurring of boundaries as a vast heteroglossic account of difference, heretofore invisible to the 'legitimate' professions, suddenly achieves canonization and simultaneously becomes homogenized to satisfy the constraints of the category ... Emergent polyvocalities of lived experience, never represented in the discourse but present at least in potential, disappear; the berdache and the stripper, the tweedy housewife and the mujerado, the mah'u and the rock star, are still the same story after all, if we only try hard enough (Stone 2006: 229).*

Following Stone's argument, the richness of the spiritual experience and the challenge and insights that trans people offer the Church would also be significantly reduced by a focus on the physical and medical changes of those transitioning. Vital insights from the spiritual journeys of trans people could be lost if the eunuch was considered the best and only transcestor.

So who exactly were eunuchs?

Stone (2006: 248) argues that our understanding of the word *saris* (eunuch) is incomplete. There is no definitive proof that all eunuchs were castrated and it may have been a general term for 'servant'. Their role was certainly more than court officials and guardians of harems. They were officers in charge of armies and explorers as well. While it does seem eunuchs were in some way gender liminal characters, there is no clear understanding of the social or biological mechanisms that created their situation. Claiming eunuchs as transcestors without completely understanding the societies they came from and the roles they played within them is problematic. It is impossible to be sure how far the analogy between trans people and eunuchs can be taken, or if it is accurate at all, because we know too little about the eunuchs of biblical times to be certain.

The analogy also ignores the different societal contexts in which biblical eunuchs and modern transsexual people live. Directly comparing trans people of the 21st century with Near-Eastern court officials in biblical times is a difficult comparison to justify. As Guest notes:

> *... while tracing a transsexual or a trans ancestry to ancient times might be understandably popular and have strategic advantages, the*

> *very different constructions of gender and sexuality in different places and times seriously undermine such ventures (Guest 2006: 134).*

The place that both groups occupy in their societies is radically different. The *saris* are portrayed as royal court officials. They are people of great power and influence within their society. Trans people do not occupy a similar place in our society. The only attempt at a demographic study of trans people is Rosser et al. (2007). The study used the internet to attempt to capture demographic information about trans people across the United States. While this may be slightly different in the United Kingdom there is no similar UK study, so the data gives us the best approximation available. The findings from the study paint a picture of disadvantage. The demographic data collated shows a population at high risk from HIV, experiencing greater mental health issues than average, and suffering from the threat of violence (2007: 52). Trans people are more often without family or supporting social structures, and are economically poorer than the general population (2007: 59). There is very little in this description that would seem analogous to the elevated social position of the biblical *saris*.

Biblical eunuchs were not always inspirational characters in the Bible. As mentioned by Kolakowski, Queen Jezebel's eunuchs are traitors to their queen and murderers. They throw their queen out of the window to try to preserve their own lives when she is conquered by Jehu and Elijah. Similarly, the eunuchs in the book of Esther connive and scheme to bring down their rival Haman. These are not necessarily transcestors one would wish to claim.

The eunuch analogy is also limited to MTF trans people and may not be inclusive of FTM folk since the biblical eunuchs are always presented as natal males. This has the potential to exclude the experiences of the FTM and the gender queer.

Job as a transcestor

The story of Job appears in the Old Testament. Job is part of the type of literature that we call Wisdom literature. Jews divided the collection of their holy books into three major divisions: The Law (Pentateuch), the Prophets (Major and Minor) and the Wisdom literature. Wisdom Literature includes Psalms, love poetry in the Song of Songs and discussions about life such as Job, Proverbs and Ecclesiastes.

Job is included in the part of Wisdom literature that is normally seen as the product of the sages. They were different from the priesthood or prophets in that they were not interested in theological issues but practical guidelines for living, such as the maxims of Proverbs, and the challenges of how to live in a world that is full of ambiguity and inconsistency, as in Ecclesiastes and Job.

Job is not a history in our modern understanding. There was no person called Job who was inflicted with the calamities by a vindictive god. Instead the book is an allegory in which fictional characters are used to explore universal truths about the human condition. Job examines many 'big' themes, including suffering, loss, faith, truth, reality and integrity.

The story of Job is deceptively simple. God and Satan are having a conversation about what an upstanding person Job is. Satan claims Job is pious only because his life is blessed by fortune. God and Satan engage in a wager on whether Job will maintain his faith in the face of catastrophe to see who is right. Job first loses his family and then his fortune. When he still refuses to curse God, he is afflicted with boils and made an outcast from the society in which he was formerly held in such high esteem Even then, Job still does not curse God but instead he curses the day of his birth.

Eliphaz, Bildad, and Zophar are friends, who come to comfort him in his distress. In a misguided attempt to help they urge him to confess whatever transgression he has committed to merit this punishment. Their lengthy statements about the reason for Job's sufferings use their society's conventional wisdom. This wisdom argues the only possible reason for Job's misfortune and fall from grace is a hidden sin he refuses to acknowledge. Even as they utter their arguments they are exposed as foolish because we as the reader are aware that the real reason for Job's predicament has nothing to do with their theological sandcastles, but a wager between God and Satan unrelated to anything that Job has done.

Throughout his trials and tribulations, Job stoutly maintains his innocence. He refuses to bow down to the received 'wisdom' of those who claim to know better about his situation than he does himself.

At the end of the allegory, God appears to the characters and puts things right. God rebukes Job's pompous friends for their lack of piety, and tells them to go and sacrifice valuable property while Job prays for them. God gives Job a new family of seven strong sons and three beautiful daughters, and an even greater fortune as a reward for his piety. Job lives a long and happy life seeing his descendants unto the fourth generation and is never tested again.

The Book of Job and suffering

The Book of Job is traditionally linked with the issue of suffering. As Alexander notes:

> *The story of Job revolves around the issue of suffering and how we are to understand it. It is a conversation piece between the sufferer, Job - a good man - and his well-meaning but small minded friends, until at last God speaks.... (Alexander 1999: 349).*

Job's suffering has been used to explore many different facets of human suffering. For example, Jesurathnam (2011) explores the issues of social justice, oppression and poverty through the lens of Job in relation to the Dalit Community in India. West and Zengele (2004) use Job to explore the prevailing prejudice against HIV positive people in the South African Church. Magdalegne (1996) discusses how Job's wife is viewed as a negative stereotype of women and has helped justify prejudice against women in the Church.

Job has already been discovered by Queer Theology. As Stone (2006) explains, Job has much to offer Queer people:

> *Of course lesbians, gay men, bisexuals and trans persons are only too familiar with a certain amount of 'incongruity' between 'lived experience' and particular core claims of religious tradition; but are often unaware of the parts of the Bible that give voice to that 'incongruity'. Thus, the speeches of Job and similar texts have much to offer a 'queer reading (Stone 2006: 293).*

Why Job is a particularly good transcestor

The uses of Job discussed above are all valid and useful ways to explore the meanings of Job in a contemporary world. The themes of disadvantage, gender oppression, being a minority and shunned because of perceived wrongdoing or moral failing, are present in the trans experience. But we also believe that there is another layer of similarities between the story of Job and trans people that goes beyond the identifications already discussed. Matching excerpts from the transcripts from the Transfaith project, and/or literature produced by churches, with Bible passages from the Book of Job, we will attempt to show how the allegory contained within the book of Job could help to reach a scriptural way of understanding trans people and their gender journeys.

Extreme Loss

The Job story starts with extreme loss. In Job 1:13-22, Job suffers a catastrophic loss. He loses his oxen and camels to raiders, his sheep and servants to fire, and his children to the collapse of the house where they were gathered for a celebration.

> *One day when Job's sons and daughters were feasting and drinking wine at the oldest brother's house, a messenger came to Job and said, 'The oxen were plowing and the donkeys were grazing nearby, and the Sabeans attacked and made off with them. They put the servants to the sword, and I am the only one who has escaped to tell you!'*
>
> *While he was still speaking, another messenger came and said, 'The fire of God fell from the heavens and burned up the sheep and the servants, and I am the only one who has escaped to tell you!'*
>
> *While he was still speaking, another messenger came and said, 'The Chaldeans formed three raiding parties and swept down on your camels and made off with them. They put the servants to the sword, and I am the only one who has escaped to tell you!'*
>
> *While he was still speaking, yet another messenger came and said, 'Your sons and daughters were feasting and drinking wine at the oldest brother's house, when suddenly a mighty wind swept in from the desert and struck the four corners of the house. It collapsed on them and they are dead, and I am the only one who has escaped to tell you!'*
> *Job 1:13-19 New International Version (NIV)*

This theme of extreme loss is present within the interviews conducted. Almost all respondents recounted stories of the loss of contact with friends, family, jobs, marriages and even children. This loss was prompted entirely by their decision to tell people of their gender dysphoria and their decisions to begin a journey that would confirm their identity. One of the interviewees (L) makes a direct connection between their story and the story of Job:

> *Job had lost everything*
>
> *His family wiped out*
>
> *His farm his animals his livelihood*
>
> *Everything*

And in a twentieth century sense that is what happened to me

I have nothing left from the marriage and I still struggle to make ends meet

Others (D and F) recount similar losses:

I've got to transition and she said

She was deeply upset she said I can't

(silence)

If you do that it will mean the end of our relationship because I can't deal with that

Which was heavy and I thought well we have been together such a long time and we had been so happy together I am not going to destroy our relationship (D)

And they (F's Family) are telling me to go back in again so there was that brief period when I told them and they never saw me dress and they never wanted to and I don't know how much they appreciate that that's painful for me

Because they don't want to talk about it

So it's a catch 22

I said to S after four years silence I'd like to talk about it but I'd have to ask their permission

They are just very uncomfortable about this kind of

I'm an embarrassment to the family that's what it is (F)

This loss is extreme, sudden at the point of revelation and devastating. In the case of L, it involved the loss of home, family, wife and job. For D it involved a loss of identity with the decision to keep her marriage going at the cost of herself. In other transcripts, as typified by F, the loss is one of intimacy. While on the surface family members sympathise, like Job's friends there is a severing of the intimacy of the family relationship. While families may stay in contact, there is no desire to know the real person revealed to them. These losses appear to mirror the catastrophic losses that Job experiences - home, family and social position are all lost.

Being other because of appearance

In some narratives trans women mentioned they felt immediately identifiable as trans and treated as outsiders as a result. As Bettcher (2007) notes, being trans places people outside the margins and protections of 'normal society'. Violence is often the result if they try to pass according to their gender identity.

Similarly, in Job Chapter 2, Job is afflicted with physically identifiable sores that place him outside the realms of his normal society.

> *Skin for skin!' Satan replied. 'A man will give all he has for his own life. But now stretch out your hand and strike his flesh and bones, and he will surely curse you to your face.'*

> *The Lord said to Satan, 'Very well, then, he is in your hands; but you must spare his life.'*

> *So Satan went out from the presence of the Lord and afflicted Job with painful sores from the soles of his feet to the crown of his head. Then Job took a piece of broken pottery and scraped himself with it as he sat among the ashes.*

Leviticus 13:12 decrees that those with the types of skin condition described in Job would be unclean. Leviticus 13:45 adds that they must wear torn clothes with their hair unbound, cry 'unclean, unclean' on the approach of others, and live outside human settlement. While we cannot be sure Job did this, Job 2:8 tells us that he sat in ashes scraping himself with broken pottery. Job is easily identifiable as an outcast. This sense of being an outcast is echoed by L:

> *because I can project myself with confidence wherever I go*

> *and eventually people are coming around and becoming more chatty*

> *When originally they were standoffish to start off with because they don't know what they are dealing with*

> *They don't know if I am some*

> *crazy Martian that's landed*

that is just a little bit off from the rest of the world

They don't know if I'm going to harm them

You know when you are confronted with something you don't understand

Something you don't know

L knows that she is treated as an outcast by society because of her appearance. She is a very tall woman with rugged features and very broad shoulders. While she may not be wearing torn clothes, wild hair and screaming 'unclean'; her initial attempts at passing proclaim her as much of an alien to our society as Job was to his.

Perceived wisdom versus lived experience
Job is accused of being a great sinner by his friends because they believe a great sin has created Job's misfortune. This is the conventional wisdom of their society. When Job refuses to accept his guilt, he is accused of believing he knows better than God. He is taunted by Eliphaz in Job 4:

As I have observed, those who plow evil

and those who sow trouble reap it.

At the breath of God they perish;

at the blast of his anger they are no more.

And later in the chapter:

Can a mortal be more righteous than God?

Can even a strong man be more pure than his Maker?

If God places no trust in his servants,

if he charges his angels with error,

how much more those who live in houses of clay,

whose foundations are in the dust,

who are crushed more readily than a moth!

Between dawn and dusk they are broken to pieces;

unnoticed, they perish forever.

Are not the cords of their tent pulled up,

so that they die without wisdom?

The Evangelical Alliance report did not include the voices of the people it was researching or discussing. The entire report speaks about trans people but makes no attempt to understand them or their point of view. There is no evidence the compilers of the report had ever met a trans person or had attempted to try to understand a different wisdom than the one they claimed. The report's tone is negative and dismissive of trans people and blames them for their situation. Here is an example from the report:

> *A difficulty with transsexuality is that it is largely concerned with a state of mind – a person's desires and psychological identification – rather than any concrete set of facts (Evangelical Alliance 2000: 38).*

> *Much of the experience of sex alienation seems rooted in gender perception. Whilst alienation is undoubtedly bad, we believe the grounds of reconciliation ought to be the truth, i.e. the truth of a person's sex, and not false gender beliefs (Evangelical Alliance, 2000: 65).*

The words of this report echo the blame and abuse Job is subjected to by his friends. They blame what they do not understand and are suspicious of what lies beyond their own theological comfort zones. This feeling was also echoed in the interviews. For example, J and A observe

> *I don't know it just sometimes feels like that because of the debates around*

> *gender and mainstream church are so like*

> *male and female and you when they talk about gender issues they mean women and are women are all right*

> *Rather than kind of exploring gender in any way or ah*

> *questioning binary gender seems like*

> *a big step um (J)*

We don't like you people

Deuteronomy I think

It is Deuteronomy that some people struggle with yeah

And is it Deuteronomy when it talks about males not wearing females' clothes

Again that is a really pathetic use

That some people use it as a stick

Fundamentalists use to

Beat people who they choose to (A)

The transcripts show the tension between the perceived wisdom of the Church and the experience of the interviewees, which is also evident in the quotes from Job 2. The interviewees' quotes show a Church unwilling to move from their own theological comfort zones to explore anything other than its already received wisdom.

The experiences and the truths the interviewees have laboured to find are subordinated to the needs of their congregations who wish to stay safe within their own assumptions and prejudices. The mechanisms of denial that congregations show in these quotes are reminiscent of the behaviour of Job's friends Eliphaz, Bildad and Zophar as they ignore Job's cries and protestations of innocence and stay safely within their own prejudices and assumptions.

Blame and accusation

Beyond the denial of lived experience is the blame and accusation heaped on the unrepentant Job because he refuses to bow to the perceived wisdom of his friends.

In Job 15 his friend Eliphaz scolds Job for his denial:

Would a wise person answer with empty notions

or fill their belly with the hot east wind?

Would they argue with useless words,

with speeches that have no value?

But you even undermine piety

and hinder devotion to God.

Your sin prompts your mouth;

you adopt the tongue of the crafty.

Your own mouth condemns you, not mine;

your own lips testify against you.

The mechanism that Eliphaz is employing is often known as 'if you throw enough mud some of it will stick'. Blaming your opponent's character rather than dealing with the presenting facts is a time-honoured way to try to win an argument when there are few facts that you can command to support your argument. Parakaleo Ministries are engaged in a similar activity towards trans people. They support an ex-trans ministry that has the same aims as the now discredited ex-gay movement. In one of the reports written by Keith Tiller and published on the Parakaleo Ministries website they assert:

> *Trans people are deeply wounded people, regardless of how mature they can outwardly seem. Wounded people have a deep sense of shame. Addictive behaviours have roots into shame. Trans behaviour is addictive and fuelled by shame. Fantasy is an indicator of the level of addiction. Acting out the fantasy by hopefully depositing oneself into a different body with a pain-free existence, can create immense distress (Tiller 2010).*

Abuse was experienced by one of the interviewees first-hand when she was involved in a play that explored transsexuality and religion. The performance of the play provoked the fury of some local Catholic and Evangelical churches who set up a noisy street protest in response:

> *And of course the audience had all had to go past these people who had all been haranguing them with words of hatred so they were all on our side*

> *(laugh)*

> *So that was great and that got us through*

> *But when I discovered some of the things they were saying*

> *What were they saying?*

(interviewer)

Well one of them had a placard that says God says my son is not a pervert

God says that

(silence)

And then someone says you don't know this play is so evil

And they said you don't have to go near a sewer to know that it stinks

(sigh)

(silence)

I mean I think about it now and I think God these are Christian people (D)

This is the fury of Job's three friends. They are unable to find proof of his wrongdoing and have run out of arguments to dissuade Job from his protestations of innocence. Therefore, they attempt to discredit Job as a person. A similar mechanism can be seen in the work of Parakaleo ministries who are unable to provide evidence to back up their accusations of wounded-ness and dysfunction. It is also the reaction of the local churches confronted with a play exploring trans issues and Christianity. They attack it as offensive and sacrilegious without attempting to see, read or understand the play or what it may be trying to say. They merely denounce it, rather than attempt to explore the possibility the beliefs they hold are mistaken or that there may be other valid viewpoints.

Experiences of pain and isolation

Many of the interviews chronicled times of deep despair. They found the conventional wisdom of the Church was not only lacking in its ability to explain their condition, but the Church was unable to give any hope of help, comfort or support. In Chapter 30 Job gives voice to a similar despair:

And now my life ebbs away;

days of suffering grip me.

Night pierces my bones;

my gnawing pains never rest.

In his great power God becomes like clothing to me;

he binds me like the neck of my garment.

He throws me into the mud,

and I am reduced to dust and ashes.

'I cry out to you, God, but you do not answer;

I stand up, but you merely look at me.

You turn on me ruthlessly;

with the might of your hand you attack me.

You snatch me up and drive me before the wind;

you toss me about in the storm.

Many of the interviewees recounted this sense of isolation and alienation. They discussed how they had always felt different from those around them and that this impacted upon their relationship with others. As L notes, her earliest feelings isolated her from her school friends:

From that moment on it was always a part of my life

And um

err

It is sometimes difficult to describe it

But a sense of consistent alienation

Not belonging

and the other boys strangely knowing or perceiving you as different

And you can't understand why that is either and then you start thinking that

Of course it must be me

there is something wrong with me

This sense of being different and being isolated was compounded by the secrecy surrounding their transgender feelings. The need to keep these feelings secret meant that the interviewees were unable to seek support, comfort, or guidance, and were left to struggle on their own. This became a vicious cycle leading to even greater feelings of isolation and abandonment as described by Bockting et al. (2006: 59). As H recounts:

I never wanted this (vehemently)

I DID NOT WANT THIS (emphasis)

I never wanted this

I do not need this I am a man and I hate it

and I didn't know where I could go or anything I just thought

this is who I am and I hate it (H)

The despair of Job mirrors the despair the interviewees recounted. Being able to legitimise these types of feelings in Scripture may be helpful to trans people seeking the solace and wisdom most churches seem unable to offer them. To be able to identify a transcestor who experiences such feelings of desolation, and yet is vindicated and rewarded for their faithfulness to their truth, is very important. It is a powerful biblical promise that there is a way forward for isolated and struggling trans people.

Reconciliation and restitution

At the end of the Book of Job there is a sense of restitution and completeness. Job is vindicated by God; his friends are exposed as fools. Job is rewarded with a new and better life than he had before. One of the themes in the narratives was the sense of peace and joy that accompanied the positive resolution of the gender journey. Interviewees who resolved their gender issues recounted a deep sense of peace and reconciliation within themselves. This allowed them to find a greater sense of spirituality (H, K, L and N). It manifested as a journey out of the pain of religious certainty into a place of limitless spiritual experience and allowed them to find a deeper, more loving vision of God. As K recounts:

This very rigid faith started to (sigh) fragment

But my faith didn't God was still there

That was the weird thing with the view that I had held previously that when I abandoned my loyalty to the literalness to the Bible and I guess I felt pretty noble about in one sense and that God would abandon me to my wretchedness but it was the other way

And actually I found God was faithful and changing and my faith deepened

In the act of discarding certainties that had hampered their acceptance of themselves as trans people, the interviewees also discarded many of the rigid beliefs they had previously held about Christian faith in general. By accepting themselves and embracing their own ambiguity, they learned to embrace religious ambiguity and a larger, more expansive vision of God. As L, K and E recount:

but yes my image of God now is undoubtedly one of unconditional love

and I have long since reconciled the fact

that you know

how I was born isn't an issue (L)

So I sometimes see God as a father who I can run to and he picks me up

Like a girl and he holds me and that feels pretty safe

I sometimes see God as a mother and I can suckle at her breast

And feel safe forever at my mother's breast

I also see God as a playful mischievous girl on a May day when I am out in the woods will jump out from the bushes err

Amid all the blossom and be playful because you look at God (K)

Is that you know I see God in the connections in the connections people have with each other and the sense of fairness and compassion that folk have and a sense of justice

That can be you know demonstrated in all sorts of actions of care and love and compassion and activism and political lobbying and social um just kinda social actions that led to helping people become inclusive of each other

And being with folk at their most vulnerable

Being with people at their most vulnerable and at the times when people really need you to be there (E)

This sense of reconciliation and restitution is a very strong reason to embrace Job as a transcestor. There are significant parallels between Job and trans people - the story of the righteous sufferer who refuses to renounce their inner truth despite persecution from conventional religious wisdom. The sufferer whose faithfulness is vindicated and his accusers are shown to be fools. This is a powerful and inspirational story for trans people to embrace.

And beyond vindication comes reward. Those interviewees who had completed their gender journey not only freed themselves of the pain they experienced in their former lives, but were also able to embrace a God of love and justice. A punishing, capricious God was stripped away and the narrowness and arbitrariness of their former religious views replaced by a much more expansive Christianity and a more loving God. Like Job, these stories have a happier ending than might have been expected.

Why is this important?

While it is easy to dismiss the story of Job as a piece of Old Testament Wisdom Literature that explores suffering, this ignores much of the meaning within the story. Analogies between Job and trans people create new and deeper meanings for the reader exploring the Book of Job. Trans people will be able to claim a biblical transcestor who experiences extreme loss, denial of lived experience, blame and accusation, pain and isolation, and finally, restitution and reconciliation. This mirroring of their own narrative may give the sense of pride that Reay speaks about when he claims those powerful gender variant eunuchs of the Bible.

In addition, the Christian reader of Job unfamiliar with the lived experiences and spiritual journeys of trans people may gain an insight and understanding into their experiences. It is difficult to empathise with a life experience that seems unfamiliar or even alien. The Book of Job offers a familiar frame of reference; it can lead to greater understanding and acceptance of the difficulties, gifts and insights trans people may bring, and provides the rationale for welcome that Kolakowski writes about.

This analogy also makes the Book of Job painfully relevant to a modern Church which is often deeply conflicted about how to deal with gender variant individuals. Our own preference for resting on conventional wisdom and unwillingness to be challenged leaves us as exposed as Job's friends and accusers. Using Job as a lens to explore the mechanisms we use to protect ourselves against what we don't understand gives an additional relevance and edge to the text.

This trans reading of Job offers a new perspective that removes Job from the enclosed safety of the Old Testament, and makes his predicament and the responses of his friends something that confronts the modern reader. It makes the Book of Job a painfully raw text. We are no longer talking about a distant patriarch infected with boils in the historical Middle East. We are talking about the person who doesn't quite pass; who is sitting bravely in our congregation; hoping for welcome amidst gossip and speculation. It makes Job painfully relevant, exposing our own pretended omnipotence and confronting us with our own prejudices as modern Christians.

Concluding comments

The aim of this chapter is not to denigrate the writers who have found inspiration in the analogy between biblical eunuchs and modern trans people. That analogy is useful because it allows both a readily identifiable transcestor, and also a biblical precedent for those who wish to counter biblical objections to the inclusion of trans people within their congregations.

But we would argue that the analogy between Job and trans people works on another, deeper level. It does not rely on a physical analogy. The reader does not need to explore the social location of the eunuch in biblical times, or even understand the society in which the story of Job is placed, to understand the similarities between Job and modern trans people.

The analogy arises from the narrative of a person persecuted, blamed and excluded, in order to allow people to remain in their theological comfort zones. The analogy goes even deeper as the story unfolds to reveal a figure who experiences extreme loss, social isolation, slander, despair and yet retains a faith in themselves and God. The vindication and reward for this faithfulness contained within the narrative of the Book of Job also find an echo and a promise in the peace and wisdom contained in the narratives of the interviewees who had completed their gender journeys.

This reading of Job allows trans people to claim a transcestor who operates on a deeper level of analogy. It also gives cisgender readers both a frame of reference that can help them understand the experience of trans Christians and a raw, painful insight into the mechanisms that can be used in order to remain comfortable within unchallenged theological 'wisdom'.

Chapter 6

Reflecting Pastorally

Introduction

This chapter explores how the findings from the Transfaith project can inform pastoral practice. It is not intended as an authoritative or exhaustive guide to every pastoral situation. Instead it offers some background thinking about issues that may arise. These thoughts are organised into thirteen insights that are not ranked in any order of importance.

There are three assumptions in this chapter. The first is that trans people should be encouraged to embrace their gender journey in a positive manner. The second is that it is important to support family and friends because they are also affected and they have their own pastoral needs. The third is that strategies such as denial, deliverance or conversion therapy are always inappropriate pastoral responses. We concur with the literature and the British psychiatric and counselling bodies that enormous damage is done to trans people by attempting these unethical and ineffective strategies.

Insight 1: Gender dysphoria happens very early in the life of a child

The project concluded trans children know they have atypical gender feelings long before they understand what these feelings mean. This agrees with the literature on the subject. There are several implications arising from this. The first is that being trans is an inherent part of personhood and is not a transgressive choice. If there is no choice in being trans, then 'pastoral' strategies such as blame, guilt, punishment or heavy shepherding back to gender conformity will not work because they rely on the assumption that people can choose to be trans or not.

A second implication is that trans children face an immense burden from a very young age. Many of the project interviewees were aware of their difference to other children very early in their lives. They knew they needed to hide their difference even when they did not understand why. Some of the project interviewees believed this burden and the strategies used to hide and survive had created difficulties later in their adult lives. These difficulties included mental health issues and social insecurity. This belief has also been reported in the literature researching the link between being trans and mental health.

When caring for trans people you may find yourself working with people bearing deep emotional scars. These scars may be there long after they have completed any medical interventions to alter their bodies. It is important for you to recognise it may take much longer for the soul to heal.

A third implication is that children with gender dysphoria are very vulnerable and likely to be hidden. Both the project results and literature show that parents are often aware that their children are displaying atypical gender behaviours and that they punish them to try to correct (sic) them. This reinforces the child's awareness that they need to hide their gender dysphoria, which is further reinforced and rewarded by a cessation of parental disapproval. When working with any group of children you may be unknowingly meeting children who are hiding atypical gender feelings and behaviours. You can make their lives easier by being approachable and non-judgemental in your dealings with them, being aware of how you model and represent gender and also being cautious about enforcing gendered rules, roles and behaviours on children.

You may also be the person to whom a parent confides their worries about their child's atypical gender behaviour. If this happens it is important to reassure parents and refer them to support services which can help them and their child to deal positively with the struggles that they face. While it is important to provide ongoing support and encouragement to the child and family, it is vital that parents access the medical and psychological expertise needed to help their child. In accessing such services they will meet other parents who completely understand their situation because they are also experiencing it.

Insight 2: Adolescents with atypical gender feelings are particularly vulnerable

The project showed adolescence was a particularly difficult time for young trans people. At adolescence they were confronted with the physical reality of their birth gender by either menstruation or the acquisition of secondary sex characteristics. This physical change stripped away coping strategies such as believing that you will develop in line with your gender identity, denial of birth gender, or pretending to be who they had hoped to become. It is also the time when society begins to rigidly enforce gender roles and rules which add to an already difficult situation.

Project interviewees reported that they engaged in many destructive coping behaviours such as self-harm, alcohol abuse and extreme weight gain in adolescence. They also reported secretive and shame-filled behaviours such as secretly cross-dressing, stealing clothes from washing lines and hiding them in their bedrooms. Surprisingly, they also reported hyper-gendered behaviours, such as extreme sports or wearing birth gender specific clothing. We believe this is an attempt to prove to themselves and to the world that they were comfortable in their birth gender.

The literature on young trans people shows that depression, low self-esteem, social anxiety and suicidal tendencies are common experiences. Reports by organisations such as Gendered Intelligence (2012) indicate that bullying is a major concern for young trans people today. Behaviours listed in the report include cyber stalking, outing, harassment, refusal to use the person's preferred gender pronoun or name and physical attack. Given the secrecy in which many young trans people live, this means that young trans people may be experiencing bullying as well as suffering their gender difficulties in silence.

When working with a young person you suspect could be trans, it is important not to jump to conclusions or try to give them an identity they do not claim. There are many reasons why they may be withdrawn, secretive, silent, self-harming or indulging in behaviours such as drinking or drugs. There could be many reasons why they are exhibiting hyper-masculine or hyper-feminine behaviours. What you should be alert to is bullying, social isolation or self-destructive behaviours. Be open, approachable and prepared in case they approach you seeking help, reassurance and support.

Insight 3: Trans people who are not out are likely to be suffering in silence and may not even be able to name the issue that haunts them. Their families are also suffering in silence too

The saddest and most difficult parts of the life stories recorded by the project were the times between childhood and coming out as trans. These times were often catalogues of confusion, pain and suffering for both the interviewees and the people who loved them. Their suffering occurred in silence with people struggling with shame-filled behaviours and secret longings. The interviews hinted at difficult family relationships and friendships, where emotional withdrawal and/or struggles with mental health had damaged relationships. Yet the image that the project interviewees often presented to the world was one of a successful Christian who was in Church leadership. On that shiny surface was little to indicate their private struggles.

This brings three observations. First, there may be people in your church who are struggling in silence. It may be a trans person who has learnt the lessons of their childhood only too well, or a parent, spouse, child or friend who is affected by the gender variance of someone they know. Any of these people may feel these experiences are an occasion for sin, a reason for blame and/or the basis for immense guilt. Making congregations aware of gender dysphoria in a positive way may help ease these negative feelings and encourage affected people in your congregations to come to you to seek support and help.

Facilitating an open discussion about trans people may name a situation that was previously unnameable for someone. The older interviewees who participated in the project had neither the concepts nor the identity to understand themselves in the earlier parts of their lives. They often believed that they were the only person like them in the world. Their lives might have been very different if they had access to words and ideas that would have allowed them to name their feelings. Educating congregations about trans people may provide someone with the tools they need to begin their gender journey.

Thirdly, congregations may react in shock and may feel betrayed if someone comes out as trans. They may blame the trans person for keeping this secret and feel that they have been wilfully deceived. Tanya Bettcher (2007) writes that trans people are often accused of deception. While she is mainly writing about the extreme violence done to many trans men and women who are killed or raped around the world each year, churches do indulge in other behaviours such as name-calling, refusing to acknowledge a new name or gender, not giving permission to use appropriately gendered toilets (or being made to use the accessible one), socially isolating the person or removing them from Church ministry.

If congregations understand the likely difficulties experienced before someone's coming out, and the bravery required to make the announcement, they may feel very differently about the situation. By being open with the congregation the trans person is saying 'I love you enough to tell you. I am telling you because I want to stay in relationship with you even though it would have been much easier to go away.' Ideally, once this is understood, the congregation can join in celebrating that this difficult situation is being resolved, and they can rejoice that clarity has been finally found.

Insight 4: The life journeys of trans people are specific to an individual but there may be some common patterns

The project hinted at patterns in the participants' life experience depending on age. Older interviewees tended to have had married, often they had children and came out as trans later in life. Middle-aged participants tended to come out as gay or lesbian and then subsequently came out as trans, while the youngest interviewees came out as trans or gender queer at an early age .

Even if this age-related pattern is not exactly replicated by further research, it does seem to indicate several different possible life trajectories. Working with older and/or previously married trans people involves the possibility of working pastorally with former or current partners who may vary in their degree of acceptance. This is discussed in more detail in insight 5 below.

Issues may also be complex for the children of trans people. There may be many years of difficult behaviours to forgive while the parent struggled with gender dysphoria and perhaps mental health issues. There may also be difficulty in establishing a relationship with the 'new' parent and grief at the seeming loss of the 'old' one. While some of the interviewees had experienced acceptance and relationships with their children, others found that their children rejected them. Trans people who were parents sometimes felt guilt for taking away a beloved parent by the decision to transition identity. They may need help in establishing a new relationship with children or the opportunity to deal with complex emotions if their child rejects them. Equally, the child may need to deal with the complexities a parent coming out as trans poses them.

The second group who came out in middle age and/or transition having previously identified as gay or lesbian also had unique challenges. One of the participants found his LGB friends reacted negatively when his transition altered his sexual orientation from lesbian to gay man and he needed to find new places to find friendship, support and affirmation. Several of the FTM interviewees continued relationships with their female partners after transition. These relationships became notionally heterosexual – or in one case, a gay male relationship – rather than lesbian relationships. Family and friends found the situation confusing and confronting.

Those who came out as trans initially have different challenges. Young trans people may find their parents have difficulty accepting the announcement and express the hope that they will grow out of it. Parents may feel the plans and dreams they had for their child are no longer applicable. Parents may grieve for the child they have 'lost' and struggle to accept the child they now have.

Given the huge advances in medical interventions and greater knowledge of gender dysphoria, one might expect that younger trans people and their families would have an easier set of issues to face. But increasing medical options and knowledge mean that more decisions have to be made. Parents may need support while they decide whether they should consent to artificially delay their child's puberty. They may need reassurance when the child wishes to present and be referred to in keeping with their gender identity, with a name the parents did not choose.

By acting as advocate you can ensure that they are not fighting this battle on their own. You can ease their burdens by helping the congregation to understand and normalise the child's gender journey so that the family can be given the most nurturing church home possible. You may also help by explaining to the church youth group leader that a child has changed name and gender. You may need to calm the anxieties of other parents who have a very limited understanding of what has happened and yet wish to withdraw their child from church youth provision.

Insight 5: The partners of trans people have specific pastoral needs that can be forgotten in the excitement of transition

The narratives show cisgender partners are deeply affected by the coming out of their trans partners. Partners need to adapt their relationship to fit in with new and unchosen realities. This new situation may not be one that meets their own emotional needs. In many respects partners are presented with an ultimatum – they must decide to stay with their partner throughout their gender journey or leave. If they stay, they face questioning of their own sexual orientation or risk divorce if they decide to leave. Whatever the decision, they experience the loss of a partner that is a bereavement.

There is almost no research into the needs of partners of trans people. There are only two peer reviewed articles published about female partners. They show that they are likely to struggle with feelings of anger, shame and inadequacy. The articles also indicate that self-esteem, identity and body image are adversely affected and that women often put their own needs on hold while they prioritise their family and partner. This means they delay dealing with their own adjustments and concerns. In addition, they may be stigmatised by their partner's decision to transition, both within churches and the wider community, and they often face the loss of financial security if the relationship ends in divorce or the transitioning partner loses their job.

Some of these issues are likely to be true of partners of either gender. Spouses may need support to negotiate a new relationship or to divorce. They may need to be reassured it was not any behaviour on their part or their lack of sexual attractiveness that caused their partner's gender dysphoria. They may need support as they reflect on their own sexual orientation. They may need help to model loving and forgiving behaviour for their children, family, church and community if they decide to leave the relationship. They may also need help to arrive at a theological understanding that permits them to see their partner is not mired in sin but has chosen a difficult and costly response to a complex problem. They may simply need you to allow them space to deal with the situation themselves.

Insight 6: Families and friends of trans people have complex reactions to a person's gender journey

Literature also shows that a gender journey is difficult for the family and friends. There is also likely to be a grieving process. It can be a disorientating situation where the person they knew and loved has in many ways gone and yet someone with the same memories, shared experiences and a physical resemblance has taken their place. Families may also struggle to accept this new person because of religious beliefs or because they have little understanding about what has happened. They may have difficulty in understanding why the person felt the need to transition and blame them consciously or unconsciously for disrupting existing relationships. There may be blame, recrimination, confusion, divided loyalties and unease.

These dynamics can also be played out in Church families. Congregants may have problems accepting the 'new' member and feel that they want to mourn the old. They may experience divided loyalties if a marital relationship ends. They may believe that being transgender is sinful and could struggle to accept what has happened. Pastoral care may be required to help folk come to terms with their own reactions to a loved one's gender journey. You may need to clarify concerns; to help people reflect on their reactions, or refer others to appropriate support services. You may have to lay the groundwork so that a congregation is prepared to be able to genuinely welcome folk who are trans.

Insight 7: If undertaken, GCS is a tool for constructing identity and not an end in itself

It is easy to assume the gender journey ends when someone has transitioned physically. The project interviews and the work of Canadian psychologist Anton Devor (2004) seem to indicate this is not the case. Both show that the psychological and spiritual aspects of the gender journey continue long after transition. If people undertake gender confirmation surgeries it is a tool to establish an identity they have already claimed. This means that while GCS and other medical procedures used to alter the body are an important step, they should be seen as a rite of passage rather than the completion of the gender journey.

As previously explained, many of the project interviewees had lived from an early age with feelings of abnormality, shame and guilt. They had learned to hide from themselves and others. Several had spoken of mental health issues they blamed on the pressure of trying to live heteronormatively. These psychological issues are unlikely to be cured by medical interventions or resolved overnight. You may find yourself supporting someone who transitioned several years ago but still needs help to heal spiritually and psychologically.

One of the most puzzling things Chris has found working pastorally with trans people is that at a certain stage of their gender journey many of them seem to disappear. At other times someone had shown up late in their journey and confided they had transitioned but did not want anyone else to know. Both of these situations appear to occur because of the split narrative observed in the interviews with folk who had recently transitioned. These transcripts show that in the early years after transition the newly emerged trans person begins to move away from the friendships, support networks and pastoral relationships that were important to them in their gender journey. They abruptly sever relationships and their previous lives become a closed file. Several project interviewees refused to acknowledge their former names. One described her first few years after surgery as an 'attempt to obliterate the male in her'.

This can be deeply upsetting for those working pastorally with trans people. It may leave you wondering what you did wrong, or feeling that you have been discarded because you are no longer needed. It is important to see this as a pastoral success. The energy previously directed into transitioning can now be directed into creating a new life. With this new life comes new relationships and new opportunities. If this new life is to be embraced, it is necessary to leave part of the old and often painful life behind. This may include people who have shared deeply in their lives prior to or during transition.

Pastoral workers may encounter trans people who are living this split narrative. They may be the only person who is aware that the person who has just joined their church had a different birth gender to their gender identity and current expression. They are unlikely to wish their history to be known by the wider community. Care must be taken to ensure that the person's confidentiality is respected.

The project interviews also showed that some trans people reintegrate their pre and post transition identity into a coherent whole after several years. This seems to come as part of a continuing physiological and spiritual healing process that happens when the body is finally congruent with the soul. This reintegration may prompt them to share their stories with others, or they may wish to continue to keep their personal history private. In either case this is a decision to be respected and supported.

Insight 8: There is a marked difference between celebration and toleration of trans identity

The interviewees in mainstream churches reported they were expected to moderate their behaviour and appearance to avoid causing offence to other people in their churches. They often micromanaged their behaviours because they felt acceptance was conditional on not drawing attention to themselves.

While this is clearly much better than condemnation, it is not the most nurturing environment for people who have spent most of their lives hiding. While the polite ignoring of difference may initially lead to less friction, it also invalidates. It also leaves difference as a permanent unresolved issue on the margins of the congregation's awareness.

Celebration includes talking about what is unique about people and their lives. It is referring to, and addressing, their specific concerns and life experiences as part of worship and church life. It involves discussion of difference, perhaps being uncomfortable with it and dealing with it honestly. In the specific case of trans people it is the validating of life experiences by providing rites of passage.

Another aspect of celebration is the open acknowledgement of the gifts, insights and experiences that are brought into Christian service. Interviewees stayed in their existing church homes when they were allowed to use their gifts and skills. If a church is seeking to reintegrate an existing member who has transitioned it needs to allow them to retain their ministry. Churches looking to attract trans people need to allow equal access to all areas of ministry available to other congregation members. This equal access is a powerful symbol of equality and acceptance.

Insight 9: Clergy have tremendous power to hurt or heal. A deliberate and considered response is essential

The life narratives from the project confirm that the behaviour of clergy was key to whether trans people felt welcome in congregations. Some show clergy at their worst. In some cases clergy took the initiative by directly asking the person to leave or they created an environment that was unwelcoming and hostile in the hope that the person would eventually become disheartened and leave.

The narratives also show clergy at their best, with enormous power to heal. The project interviews illustrate several healing roles that clergy played:

    i)   Advocate. One project interviewee told how a young curate was able to support and encourage her mother to embrace her as a daughter. A church official encouraged a transwoman's application to commence ministerial training by showing her a confidential document that reassured her that she would be taken seriously, and her transition was no impediment to ordination.

    ii)   Facilitator and educator. Prior to the arrival of a trans woman and her wife, their new minister did intentional work with the congregation to make sure that they would feel welcome after their previous traumatic church experience.

    iii)   As a pastoral worker. Another person described her minister as a wonderful man. He had actively supported her in her gender journey. An example of this was that he was present in her home at the time of the project interview to ensure that she was able to debrief with him if she was upset by her interview.

All these roles show a deliberate and planned response by clergy. We believe that the first step in formulating a response is honest self-assessment. The pastoral worker needs to be honest about their doubts and fears and work to resolve them. Even those who believe that they have no issue with trans people may find a lingering unease. This unease may be theological in nature, or it may be about practical concerns such as the use of pronouns or toilet facilities. There may also be fears that other congregants will leave if this person is encouraged and welcomed.

We believe that if this unease cannot be resolved satisfactorily you should have the courage to be kind to your own feelings. If this unease is likely to create an unwelcoming or unsafe environment it may be more positive to signpost to another church. While we do not think this is desirable or to be encouraged as a first response, it does limit the spiritual violence done to someone who is otherwise left without support in a potentially hostile and degrading spiritual environment.

You may also need to do intentional work with church leadership and/or other pastoral staff. They may also have reservations that hinder them being able to offer an honest welcome. They may need additional learning so that they have a clear understanding of the types of words and actions that are required to allow trans people to find a safe spiritual home in their community.

Insight 10: Our language and understandings of words that describe sexual orientation and gender identity are often inadequate

The Church has often mistakenly framed its response to trans people by conflating sexual orientation and gender identity. There is a concern that a seemingly heterosexual relationship between a trans woman or trans man with a person of the (now) opposite gender could be a Trojan Horse for gay marriage. This train of thought starts in the 1980s with Oliver O'Donovan's *Transsexualism & Christian Marriage*, and is carried into the more recent present by the Evangelical Alliance's *Transsexuality* and the Church of England's *Some issues in human sexuality*.

It is important to separate these issues. Gender identity (how we describe our own gender) and sexual orientation (who we are attracted to sexually and emotionally) are independent of each other. While both issues do create sexual minorities they are not the same issue or the same minorities.

Currently we do not have the concepts and terms to describe the complexities that arise when considering trans people and their sexual/emotional relationships. Language around sexual orientation and trans people is inadequate and incomplete. While it is possible to remain bisexual (orientated to both genders), all other sexual orientations necessitate a fixed gender point as a reference. When this reference point changes, our current understandings of sexual orientation tell us that there has been a change in sexual orientation even if the same relationship continues. An example of this is when a project interviewee moved from being a lesbian to a heterosexual trans man while remaining in the same relationship. This arbitrary reclassification of an existing relationship feels inauthentic and inadequate. It also makes the false assumption the trans person fully inhabited their birth gender without any atypical experience of it.

If we accept that trans people do not experience their birth gender as cisgender folk experience their gender, then we must accept that knowingly or unknowingly trans people occupy a different gender space before coming out. We have neither the language nor the concepts to describe this space beyond the clinical phrase 'gender dysphoria'. Unable to name this space we lack the terms to classify the sexual orientation of previous relationships.

This does not even take into account the experiences of gender queer people or those who inhabit both male and female gender spaces in different parts of their lives. When somebody born male lives at home with a female partner as a trans woman but goes to paid employment presenting as a male but socialises as both male and transwoman, do they become a lesbian when consciously female and heterosexual when consciously male? At the moment we have no words to adequately describe these situations except the all-purpose label of gender queer.

This can leave one completely confused and reduced to using clumsy words that misrepresent the situation. Pastorally it is important to allow folk to self-identify and not to attempt to enforce simplistic and limited understandings onto complex situations simply because we do not have the language or concepts to adequately describe them.

Insight 11: It is not possible to predict sexual orientation by looking at previous relationship history

The project interviews showed that it was not possible to predict how trans people may identify their sexual orientation once they have completed their gender journey. Some retained their original sexual orientation to a specific gender while others changed their orientation. This means you cannot make assumptions about the future sexual orientation of a trans person based on their previous life story. Our need to name may drive us to attempt to categorise people in ways that simply do not fit when working with people with an emerging gender identity.

Insight 12: Testimony is a powerful and healing tool

As an interviewer Chris constantly recognised a sense of joy and liberation in the interviews. All of the project volunteers were very eager to tell their life stories. As an interviewer Chris was sometimes so profoundly affected by these interviews he needed to sit and reflect on the truths that he had been told before he could travel home.

As we write elsewhere in this book we believe these life stories should be interpreted as parables. They contain deep truth about the way God has worked in the lives of people with gender dysphoria. After hearing these stories it would be hard to dismiss the raw holiness they contain. We believe it is no accident that the negative Church responses do not contain the voices of the people that they wish to condemn. By silencing the voices of trans people, the truth that is inherent in their stories can be obscured and denied. By allowing trans people to tell their stories of joy and struggle we hear of their faith and resilience. We do not hear arguments about gay marriage or Gnosticism but how faith in God saved them when all else was falling apart.

These stories can serve several pastoral functions. First, they help to construct a personal narrative for the trans person. This may help them to make sense of all that has happened. Many of the project interviewees had never sat and told their stories in one sitting before. They were often stunned when they put all the pieces of their life together.

Secondly, such testimony serves to educate others. The narratives are educative without analysis and interpretation. Trans people telling their stories to cisgender people allows them to gain insight into the lives of those who struggle with something that most of our society takes for granted. These life stories throw into sharp relief assumptions and unthoughtful prejudices about gender and being transgender.

Thirdly, it allows the trans person to validate their own experience after years of silence. The very act of telling their stories and being heard was immensely empowering and validating for the interviewees. This is particularly so if these are stories told after years of silence.

Insight 13: An active forgiveness must be sought by all parties

Forgiveness was one of the surprising themes of the interviews. Most of the project interviewees were not bitter about the difficult situations they had survived, and remained remarkably forgiving of those who had hurt them. They also frequently have tried to reconcile with people they believe they had hurt.

Pastoral writers have several perspectives on forgiveness that may be helpful to consider. Komesaroff et al. (2011) note that the binaries of perpetrator and victim, good and evil, are not conducive to healing, but rather allow room for recrimination and bitterness to remain. Healing begins when wounded parties move to a place that encompasses the perspectives of all involved. They note that this process often involves pain, learning and a shared sense of vulnerability and loss.

Several of the project interviews provided examples of this. One trans woman spoke about the guilt she experienced when she realised that she would be taking her children's father away by transitioning. She deeply regretted her emotional withdrawal from her family while she struggled with her gender dysphoria. She also spoke of her guilt about the dissolution of her relationship because her wife 'didn't want to be a lesbian'. In a similar way another recounted how her increasing androgyny had resulted in the breakdown of her marriage.

In both cases the interviewees were able to forgive themselves by understanding that they were people who had struggled with gender dysphoria and that this had created an impossible situation for everyone concerned. They did not assign blame to themselves, or condemn the reactions of their families, but spoke of a difficult situation, recognising its sadness, brokenness and pain. Both have managed to negotiate a relationship with their former spouses based in friendship and one has come to a rapprochement with her children.

In contrast Schweitzer (2010) offers a cautionary note on this wholesale embrace of forgiveness. He argues while there is ample evidence forgiveness is a healthy psychological tool to release anger, rejection and bitterness, it sets up a forced expectation of forgiveness for someone not ready to extend it. Also a forgiver could experience further hurt if forgiveness is not acknowledged or rejected. This is evident in the narratives. While it may be psychologically healthy to forgive abusive treatment at the hands of a former church, it is unlikely to change the opinions or behaviour of the congregation or minister. This act of forgiveness can only ever be one sided and incomplete because there is no recognition of the injustice by the perpetrators.

Schweitzer also maintains forgiveness is something we participate in rather than do. In one narrative an interviewee spoke about being completely estranged from the majority of her family and their refusal to acknowledge her. The family's refusal precludes her participation in a forgiveness process. Any attempt on her part to seek forgiveness for the past is likely to result in her experiencing further pain by either being rejected or ignored.

John Roth (2007) offers another helpful pastoral approach. He explores the Mennonite perspective of right remembering – a commitment to remembering accurately what has happened, rethinking our perspectives on events and considering how this can enhance Christian discipleship through forgiveness. If family relationships do break down it may be pastorally more helpful to encourage those affected to look at their family situation objectively and rethink their own part in it. By taking into account their struggles and attempts to remain in relationship they can conclude they are not inherently evil. If there is no likelihood of reconciliation or restitution it may be helpful to urge people to apply these lessons to other relationships that have been strained.

It is important to realise that there may be no neat solution. Reconciliation needs both parties to be actively involved. That may not be a viable option in all pastoral situations involving trans people.

A concluding comment

We hope that you have recognised that there are common themes running through this chapter. The first is the need to suspend judgment. Secondly, that there are no easy answers. Thirdly, that some of what may be heard is uncomfortably challenging. Fourthly, that pastoral workers who have built strong relationships with folk during their gender journey may have to realise, regretfully, that their role is to wish the now strong traveller Godspeed. While pastoral work with trans people may sometimes feel difficult and challenging, it is a privileged opportunity to witness God's co-creative redemption at work in a most profound way.

Chapter 7

Transgender People in the United States by Justin Tanis, PhD

In the United States, transgender and gender variant people are experiencing greater visibility and acceptance while simultaneously seeing the rise of discriminatory laws and a backlash against them. Levels of discrimination and violence remain outrageously high and yet people continue to come out as transgender. Advocacy organizations are growing and their public profile is increasing. Well-known celebrities, like Laverne Cox, Caitlyn Jenner and Chaz Bono, have told their stories to many millions of Americans, increasing the average person's awareness and knowledge of transgender issues. The vocabulary of gender identity is now a familiar one to many people.

Most importantly, the number of Americans who report personally knowing a transgender person has grown dramatically in recent years. The research organization PRRI (Public Religion Research Institute) reports that between 2011 and 2017 the number of Americans who report having a close friend or family member who is transgender has risen, almost doubling from 11 per cent to 21 per cent (Piacenza & Jones, 2017). That is a significant increase in a very short period of time and this human connection is having an impact on attitudes. Those who know a transgender person have much more tolerant views than those for whom this is just a theoretical idea.

There are several factors that create a unique environment for transgender people in the United States. First is the vast diversity of cultures that make up the country, from the range of native born and immigrant peoples to the strong regional differences in culture and attitudes. There is also a big difference between the experiences of those who live in cities and those in more rural areas. This means that the conditions in which a person lives – both their social experiences as well as the laws and regulations that impact their lives – can vary drastically from one part of the country to another. There are a number of problems with this, since not only can it create confusion about issues like health care coverage and whether or not overt discrimination is legal, but it can also inhibit people's abilities to move around the country, since people are less likely to want to and be able to live in areas where discrimination is higher. Efforts to pass national legislation to address this have not been successful so far.

Second, the United States does not yet have universal health care coverage. This has a significant impact on the health of transgender and gender variant people. This applies not only to those who seek transition related care but impacts everyone's ability to access medical and mental health services. Some transgender people in the United States are fully covered by health insurance, including genital and facial reconstruction/confirmation surgeries and hormone therapy, while others have policies which completely exclude any and all treatment related to gender transition.

Finally, racism remains a powerful force in the United States, creating a climate of violence and intolerance. The negative impact of this on American life is profound and important to understand. Transgender people of colour face pervasive discrimination and extraordinarily high levels of harassment, assault and murder because of both racism and anti-transgender prejudice. Studies show that transgender people of colour experience unemployment, homelessness, poverty and other challenges at even higher levels than white transgender people. The US Trans Survey, for example, shows this throughout its report.[1] Racism impacts every aspect of life and makes the experiences of transphobia and prejudice far worse.

While racism has been present throughout US history, there are many who believe that we are in a period of particularly overt expressions of it. White police officers kill unarmed African-Americans with impunity on a regular basis. Donald Trump, both as a candidate and as President, has played on false stereotypes of Mexicans as rapists and criminals and increased the rhetoric of intolerance and xenophobia. Open marches of neo-Nazis and members of the Ku Klux Klan and other white supremacists have taken place, although fortunately they have often been far outnumbered by thousands of counter-demonstrators objecting to their messages of hate.

For all of these complex reasons, it is important to recognize that the situation of transgender and gender variant people in the United States includes many different realities and experiences. Some people are able to transition or live in a third gender identity, for example, with little difficulty and without experiencing overt prejudice, while

---

1   See the US Trans Survey report, http://www.ustranssurvey.org/.

others (and this is more common) face repeated physical, emotional, and religious attacks and rampant discrimination. Economics, race, education, location and other factors play complicated roles in this situation. Let's consider some of these issues in greater detail.

Transgender Presence and Visibility

According to recent studies (Flores et al. 2016a: 2), approximately 0.6per cent of adults in the United States identify as transgender, which means there are approximately 1.4 million transgender adults. There are some considerable variations by state and region, ranging from a low of 0.3 per cent in North Dakota to a high of 0.8 per cent in Hawaii, although researchers are not certain about the reasons for these differences. Cultural variations probably contribute to this. Young people are much more likely to identify as transgender than older adults.

Interestingly, there is also quite a bit of difference by race, with people of colour more likely to identify as transgender than the white population. The Williams Institute estimates that while 66 per cent of the US population is white, only 55 per cent of the transgender community is white; among African Americans, who comprise 12 per cent of the general population, 16 per cent of transgender adults are African American while among Latin@s,[2] who are 15per cent of the adult population, 21 per cent of transgender adults identify as Hispanic/Latino. Among other races, the numbers are equivalent at 8per cent between transgender and non-transgender adults (Flores et al. 2016a: 2). There are similar patterns seen in the gay, lesbian, and bisexual communities in the US.

There has certainly been a significant increase in visibility of transgender people, with mixed results. While there have been ground-breaking and positive news programs and storylines, the media advocacy group GLAAD found in an analysis of ten years of television programs in the United States, the majority (54 per cent) of the coverage remains negative or biased about transgender people.[3] Many times, as the report's title suggests, transgender people are often shown as either victims of violent crimes or as murderous

---

2   Gender neutral shorthand for Latino/Latina people of Latin American descent.
3   See GLAAD, 'Victims or Villains: Examining Ten Years of Transgender Images on Television,' https://www.glaad.org/publications/victims-or-villains-examining-ten-years-transgender-images-television.

villains, with too few media offerings that portray transgender people accurately.

Still, there have been fictional programs from soap operas to sitcoms, as well as news broadcasts and interviews that have shown a more functional and positive picture of transgender people. Laverne Cox, a transgender actress, has been visible and very articulate in interviews, and Caitlyn Jenner's transition was featured on a reality show that included a variety of other transgender women. Transgender children have been profiled on several high profile news and interview programs, increasing viewers' knowledge of these young people.

Most significant, however, is the visibility of transgender people in everyday life. As mentioned earlier, more and more Americans have a personal knowledge of the issue, with a close friend or family member who is transgender. This also increases significantly among young people who are much more likely to say they know about transgender issues and are favourable about transgender rights.[4] Many teens report knowing someone in their school, church, or social circle who is transgender. As with other differences among people, personally knowing someone breaks down stereotypes and negative attitudes.

Health and Wellbeing

Transgender people in the United States face significant health challenges brought about by overt discrimination within medical settings, lack of insurance coverage for transition related care, and a tendency to delay or avoid care because of the costs or legitimate fears of discrimination. Advocates have made some significant inroads in addressing these situations, with more medical facilities training their staff to provide appropriate care. In addition, the Affordable Care Act, which greatly increased Americans access to health insurance, included a non-discrimination provision which covered gender identity. Sadly, however, that portion of the law was blocked by a federal court in December 2016 and has yet to take effect so there are no federal protections for transgender people against discrimination in health care.

---

4   See results from a February 17 - 20, 2015 YouGov/Huffinington Post poll: https://today.yougov.com/news/2015/02/20/poll-results-transgender/?belbo on=031b3908984b04d39400589a,4711850,subid=38395X1559468X615c84243ef05a6 18776d96a40db48a7&pdl.rlid=203577

Over the past several decades, many more physicians and medical facilities have come to offer knowledgeable care for transgender patients. Often information about helpful doctors is spread by word of mouth from patient to patient, especially in more isolated areas. Still, physician inexperience or lack of reliable information remains a problem and patients may have to educate their doctors about necessary treatments. Every major professional health care organization, including the American Medical Association, publically supports equal access for people of all gender identities through policy statements.

Many insurance companies in the United States specifically exclude transition related care from coverage, meaning that all expenses must be paid by the patient out of their own pockets. This creates a huge, and sometimes insurmountable, barrier to treatment. It certainly limits the options available to most people given the very high costs of health care in the United States. However, more insurance companies are recognizing that transition related care is medically necessary and covering hormone therapy, and, increasingly, surgeries. According to the US Trans Survey (James et al. 2016:95), however, more than half of patients requesting transition related care were denied by their insurance companies. To access benefits, even those you are entitled to, can take a massive effort.

There is an interesting side effect, however, from this uneven system of health care. Some countries which cover hormones and gender confirmation surgeries under national health plans have very clear processes of gender transition, often following the WPATH guidelines. In these cases, there can be (or has been in the past) a strict set of procedures for patients to follow and a linear path to transition from one gender to another. In the United States, however, patients have essentially been left to make their own choices in negotiation with their physicians and surgeons. This has meant that while most medical professionals utilize the WPATH guidelines, a few do not. For example, a plastic surgeon who performs breast augmentation on non-transgender patients may see it as unnecessary to require a transgender woman seeking the identical surgery to obtain a letter from a mental health professional. All of the patients, in this case, would then be treated equally when seeking the same surgery. Other doctors do want to ensure that their patients have been evaluated by a therapist or other mental health care worker. It varies from doctor to doctor, and hospital to hospital.

In this system, patients have greater freedom, provided they can afford the treatments, to make decisions about the extent and direction of their medical transition. Thus, a patient may choose to have chest or genital surgery without taking hormones, for example, or decide not to have some or any genital changes, while still legally and socially transitioning. If there is an upside to a lack of medical coverage, it is the greater latitude that transgender and gender variant people have to make decisions about their own bodies. Thus, a patient can determine the set of treatments that are best suited to them individually, rather than feeling compelled to follow a model that may not feel as comfortable. Some will argue that ideally these decisions should be made in dialogue with mental health and medical professionals but the lack of access means that this ideal is not always possible.

Some transgender people in the United States are unable to afford treatment from a licensed medical provider or may fear discrimination from them. This can lead people to seek care through alternative means, sometimes using medications obtained from other countries, like Mexico or Canada. In addition, some people offer injection services that use oils, plastics, or silicone to sculpt the body and face. This is extremely dangerous as medical grade materials are not always used and has led to serious illnesses and deaths. But in a system that denies transition related care to so many, people do what they feel they must do in order to feel comfortable in their bodies.

Transgender people who are undocumented immigrants in the United States are also systematically excluded from health insurance, including many of the public health safety nets, like Medicare, as a result of their immigration status.

Transgender health is also impacted by a variety of factors, including discrimination. The US Trans Survey reports that 8 per cent of its respondents had been refused medical care within the past year because of their gender identity. People often avoid going to the doctor because they don't want to be treated poorly or face discrimination. This means they put off preventive or other routine health care or wait until they are very sick to seek treatment, making recovery much more difficult. Several well-known transgender people have died of cancer which could have been treated if it had been caught earlier.

But prejudice takes other, indirect tolls on our health as well. Surveys of transgender and gender variant people report high levels of homelessness, substance use to cope with discrimination, depression, HIV and other indices of threats to their wellbeing. Several studies have found that approximately 41 per cent of transgender people have attempted suicide in their lifetimes, an astonishingly high rate. The US Trans Survey shows significantly higher rates of psychological distress among those who had experienced violence or overt discrimination, such as being fired because of gender identity, within the past year.

There is positive news, however. Psychological distress is much less pronounced among older generations and among those who transitioned some time ago. The report states,

> Respondents who had transitioned ten or more years prior to participating in the survey (24 per cent) were substantially less likely to be currently experiencing serious psychological distress, in contrast to those who had transitioned within the past year (41 per cent) .... While psychological distress was higher among those early in their transition, it was higher yet among those who have not transitioned but wanted to. Nearly half (49 per cent) of those who have not transitioned but wanted to were currently experiencing serious psychological distress, compared with 36 per cent of those who had transitioned at any time prior to taking the survey.[5]

In addition, those who experienced family support were in much less distress than those whose families were not supportive. This shows the incredible value of positive networks around transgender people.

Discrimination

Reports like the US Trans Survey and its predecessor, the National Transgender Discrimination Survey, paint a vivid picture of the rampant levels of discrimination faced by transgender and gender variant people in the United States. This situation is even worse – often dramatically so – within communities of colour. Discrimination impacts all areas of life – housing, employment, medical care, religious life, public accommodation, schooling and so on. And sadly, much of it remains completely legal.

While there are no federal laws in the United States that protect people from discrimination based on gender identity (or sexual orientation for that matter), there has been a steady increase in state and local ordinances to address this situation. However, in recent years some of these have been rolled back.

---

5   US Trans Survey, p. 107.

A spate of new legislation has arisen in recent years that attempts to bar transgender and gender non-conforming people from using public restrooms according to their gender identity. Under these laws, people have to use the restroom or locker room which conforms to the gender on their birth certificate, regardless of their lived identity or appearance. Often legislators try to justify these bills as public safety measures designed to protect women and girls from assault in the restroom; however, women's advocacy groups and law enforcement officials agree that this is not a problem. In May 2016, *Time* magazine published an article that summed up many of the arguments noting that many think that these bans are simply a cover up for discrimination (Steinmetz 2016). However, when surveyed, more Americans than not say that transgender people should be allowed to use a restroom according to their gender identity, not their birth certificate (Flores et a. 2016b: 6). The same survey showed that a substantial majority of Americans, 71.5 per cent, agreed (strongly or somewhat) that transgender people should be protected from discrimination, compared to 20.1 per cent who disagreed and 8.5 per cent who didn't know (Flores et al. 2016b: 14).

Transgender people face an unemployment rate three times higher than the rate for the general population in the United States. Almost a third live in poverty, which is twice the poverty rate for the country as a whole. According to the US Trans Survey, 16 per cent of the respondents who had had a job had been fired at some point in their careers simply for being transgender. The survey also found that a staggering 30 per cent of those in the survey who had a job in the last year had been fired, denied a promotion, or mistreated at work because of their gender identity.[6]

Violence

Violence and harassment remain significant problems for transgender people in the United States. A survey of existing research showed that about half of all trans people reported experiencing 'unwanted sexual activity' (surveys range from 10-66 per cent), with some variations (Stotzer 2009: 172). A number of reports also show that sexual assault or coercion started at a young age, in the early teens or before. The prevalence of sexual violence declines with age. Perpetrators of these attacks were often other students, partners, or family members;

---

6   US Trans Survey, p. 13.

victims reported that they felt homophobia or transphobia were the causes of many of the incidents.

One of the painful and shocking findings is how many assaults and acts of harassment were committed by those in the helping professions, such as teachers, police officers, social workers and health care workers. In a study by the advocacy group FORGE, 11 per cent of assailants were helping professionals, such as police, healthcare or service providers. The report of the National Transgender Discrimination Survey found similar results. Those who were the targets of these attacks showed even higher rates of suicide attempt and other symptoms of emotional distress. Being victimized by someone who is supposed to protect and help you has long lasting, dangerous consequences.

Studies have also shown that victims are likely to experience multiple incidents. About a third of those who attack transgender people on the street are strangers, according to studies; the rest are family or friends, or others known to the victim, such as a landlord (Stotzer 2009: 174).

In 2009, the Matthew Shepard and James Byrd, Jr. Hate Crimes Prevention Act was passed. This law expanded existing statues to include gender and gender identity, and mandated that the federal government begin tracking these crimes. It also allowed the federal government to offer assistance to local law enforcement when a hate crime occurred in their jurisdictions and included funding for prevention efforts.

Religion

The experiences of transgender people within the religious communities of the United States is quite varied. Conservative, Reform and Reconstructionist Jewish denominations, for example, all have statements of explicit welcome and inclusion of transgender people (Zauzmer 2016). Several Christian denominations share that position or are silent on the matter and leave the issue up to individual pastors. Others, however, like the Southern Baptist Convention and the Roman Catholic Church have specific statements that exclude or condemn gender transition and frame gender identity within the language of sinfulness, a sign of the fall of humanity. By and large, conservative Christians have, in the last twenty years, come to think negatively about transgender people, while progressive Christians have come to a place of greater welcome.

Several groups, most notably the Unitarian Universalist Association, the United Church of Christ, and the Metropolitan Community Churches openly welcome and affirm transgender people. There are transgender and gender variant clergy in these churches and in others, including some of the larger denominations in the United States, such as the United Methodist Church, the Evangelical Lutheran Church in America, the Presbyterian Church (USA) and the Episcopal Church. These denominations also have a number of transgender and gender queer seminarians in the ordination process.

The US Trans Survey asked respondents about their experiences in communities of faith, the first to provide statistic data about transgender people's religious lives. Of those active in a faith community, 39 per cent reported that they had left because they feared not being accepted, while 19 per cent were actually rejected from congregations. On a more positive note, among those who were rejected, 43 per cent found a new, welcoming religious home, and among people who were in faith communities that are aware that they are transgender, 96 per cent reported receiving at least one positive religious message about gender identity.[7]

Respondents who are people of colour reported higher rates of having to leave faith communities, but American Indian and Black respondents also had the highest rates of finding a more welcoming community. While the rejection of nearly 1 in 5 of those who were religiously active is appalling, these numbers also show that transgender people are often able to locate affirming communities where they are receiving positive messages about both their gender identity and their faith.

Much of the energy opposing transgender rights comes from religious groups and individuals, particularly Christians. There are efforts to expand the understanding of 'religious liberty' in the United States to mean that an individual or business can legally discriminate against a person based on their gender identity or sexual orientation, refusing to offer services in a shop or business, for example, to those they do not approve of. However, Christian, Unitarian and Jewish clergy and members are also visible in support of transgender inclusion and protections.

---

7   US Trans Survey, pp. 77-78.

Conclusion

There is considerable hardship that many transgender people continue to face on an almost daily basis in the United States. Just leaving the house to go to work or the store can expose a person to harassment, sexual abuse, assault or even murder. Transgender and gender variant people are much more likely to be poor, homeless, or experience other kinds of social vulnerability. Acts of discrimination in housing, employment, public accommodation and other issues remain legal in many parts of the country, although advocates are working hard to change that and are making steady progress on a state and local level.

At the same time, there are considerable forces within some state legislatures who are actively working to turn back the clock, removing legal protections from transgender people and making it harder for them to use public restrooms. The most notorious of these actions was in North Carolina, which also used their 'bathroom bill' as a vehicle for other issues, such as preventing local jurisdictions from passing increases to the minimum wage and making it more difficult to sue on the basis of racial discrimination. These 'bathroom bills' would restrict transgender and gender variant people who can be identified by others from being able to participate freely in public life, since their ability to use a public restroom would be seriously impacted. Transgender people who are not identifiable as trans by others would still be in violation of the law when they went to a public restroom that corresponds with their gender identity; to follow the law would put many people at risk. A trans woman in the men's room faces harassment and violence; a trans man in the women's restroom would make women very uncomfortable and also exposed to harassment and violence. These restrictions on participation in public life have a chilling effect on people's freedom to participate in society at the same level as everyone else.

The prevalent racism in the United States is a key aspect of the oppression that transgender people face. Not only are transgender people more likely to be people of colour, they also face the compounding effects of racism and transphobia working together. This makes it even more challenging to find a job, maintain housing, obtain health care, and be safe from violence. In every aspect of life, racism makes it even more challenging for transgender people to survive and thrive.

Yet in spite of this, communities across the country are growing. Transgender people are working as doctors, academics, construction workers, case managers, lawyers and in virtually every other aspect of the economy. People are coming out in large cities and small towns, forming networks of support and connection. Transgender communities are showcasing their artists and musicians, and coming together for transgender pride celebrations. There are both online and in person support groups that people can join.

Transgender advocacy groups are using the law, lobbying, and education to change attitudes and legal protections. For example, activists have succeeded in changing US policy to allow people to change their federal documents, including passports and social security cards, without needing proof of surgery. This opens up a whole world to many transgender people and prevents them from being outed – and potentially put in danger – with employers, border agents and others. All of the major LGBTQ rights organizations, to varying degrees, include transgender rights on their agendas.

Chapter 8

Bible Studies

Introduction

Participants in the Transfaith project varied in their reactions to the Bible (Chapter 3). Some were unable to relate to it, or were bruised by the misuse of Deuteronomy 22:5 as a weapon against them. Others found affirmation in gender variant biblical characters like Joseph in the Book of Genesis and the eunuchs, or the sense of being deeply known and loved by God expressed in Psalm 139, and in Galatians 3:28 where gender distinctions, like those of race and class, are of no consequence within the Christian community. Some of these passages form the basis of these Bible studies. Others, like the eunuchs and Job, have been explored already (Chapter 5) and will not be discussed in detail in this chapter.

Use and abuse of the Bible

For a biblical verse to appear 'a weapon of spiritual violence', which is how participants experienced Deuteronomy 22:5 when handled by fellow Christians, sounds like abuse of the Bible. It is true that Hebrews 4:12 describes 'the Word of God as alive and active' and as 'sharper than any double-edge sword' judging 'the thoughts and attitudes of the heart.' The 'Word of God' here, however, does not refer to passages or individual verses of the Bible. By locating the verse in its context in the Letter to the Hebrews, which quotes Psalm 95:7 'Today, if you hear his voice', it becomes apparent that it is referring to Christ, the living Word of God, to whom the words of the Bible point.

There are three crucial steps that help us to avoid misusing the Bible. First, one needs to know the context of the verse or passage under consideration. Here context means both the biblical book where the verse or passage can be found, and the historical era and culture in which the book was written. The Bible is a collection of writings, of different types, spanning more than twelve centuries, and the various genres often require specific interpretation. Second, one needs to reflect on how the verse or passage relates to the unifying message of Scripture, which for Christians, is bound up with the coming of the Kingdom of God in Jesus Christ. The New Testament expresses this in religious terms such as believing that Jesus is the Son of God, or the believer's relationship with the Lord whose death and resurrection have ushered in a new age. Third, there is the influence of our own context and how the assumptions that we bring to a text or passage may be distorting or illuminating its interpretation.

Although the Bible is frequently quoted in Christian discussions of transgender people, even a relatively conservative document like *Some issues in human sexuality* concedes that 'there is general acceptance that there are no biblical texts that can be seen as addressing transsexualism as such' (House of Bishops 2003: 228). Nevertheless, the following two texts are often cited.

Genesis 1:26-27

Conservative church statements and documents about trans people (see Chapter 2) often focus on the creation accounts in Genesis, as if they offered a self-evident paradigm for the relations between the sexes today. This is especially true of the much-quoted Genesis 1:27: '*So God created mankind in his own image, in the image of God he created them; male and female he created them.*' Yet looking at these verses in context there is a remarkable consensus that Genesis 1:27 refers, not to two individuals, male and female, but to the original androgyny of *ha-adam*, the adam, or earth creature, prior to their division into male and female at Genesis 2:21-23, when Eve emerges from Adam's side as if the earthling has been split in two. As might be expected, this interpretation is favoured by inclusive scholars such as Renato Lings (2013: 25) and Kalina Wojciechowska (2016) and also by Calum Carmichael (2010), writing from the perspective of comparative literature. Yet 'the original androgynous unity of the first created being' (Brownson 2013: 26) also features in the so-called 'traditionalist' argument for gender complementarity espoused by Robert Gagnon and John Stott. This unexpected convergence about a specific and important textual detail, demonstrates the potential of narrative to assert itself, regardless of the divergent theological perspectives of the interpreters.

Perhaps it is the preceding dualistic account of creation which misleads those who invoke Genesis 1:26,27 to argue that trans people are infringing the gender binary, but in so doing they are taking this passage out of context. They are also unduly influenced by their own context. These verses tell us nothing about differences between men and women, or masculine and feminine, but rather that to be human is to reflect God's image. For Christians to interpret Genesis as if it stood alone, apart from the light of Christ, is alien to the New Testament paradigm that is the subject of the first Bible study.

Deuteronomy 22:5

This verse states that 'A woman must not wear men's clothing, nor a man wear women's clothing, for the Lord your God detests anyone who does this.' The Book of Deuteronomy presents itself as a reiteration of the law in the new circumstances that await the nation as it takes possession of the land of Canaan. This particular prescription is directed first at female assumption of masculine attire and may include a reference to armour. It is widely understood as an attempt to distance Israel from its pagan neighbours, particularly the cross dressing associated with Canaanite temple rituals. Note here the link between cross-gender clothes and the sacred which appears to be a feature of the Joseph narrative from Genesis considered below. This verse is the single prescription of such behaviour in the Bible, and Jennings (2005: 193) notes the tendency to exaggerate the significance of Old Testament law and to devalue narrative, like the Joseph story, where cross-dressing appears not to be transgressive.

In terms of context, later verses (9-11) specify not mingling seeds, animals or types of fabric, but the immediately adjacent verses are about the care of animals. In this Israelite law code, the detestable nature of cross-dressing – rendered 'abomination' by earlier translations – simply means that it is taboo, and this could be a possible point of connection with modern contexts, though the differences would need elaborating. Christians who wish to apply Deuteronomy 22:5 to gender variant people would also need to consider the New Testament understanding of Old Testament law. Not to do so would be an abuse of the text. In any case this verse is about nonconformity of gender 'expression' rather than gender 'identity'. One cannot assume that the latter did not underlie the former, but there is nothing in the text to indicate that, and it would be unwise to press the point by suggesting otherwise.

Owning our context

Much biblical scholarship generates ongoing argument and disagreement, and some controversies are noted here, but the main aim in this chapter is to allow a selected number of biblical passages to speak to us, noting any questions that Scriptures pose to our understanding of gender, and what it means to be gender nonconforming or transgender in particular.

Some biblical scholars and theologians have begun to explore the reality of gender variance in the biblical texts (Guest et al. 2006; Jennings 2005), an aspect that has often been obscured by cisgender readings of these passages. The following Bible studies are indebted to these trans and queer interpretations. The text used is the New International Version (NIV).

Outline

The remainder of the chapter is in four sections, comprising four Bible studies:

1. Reading humanity forwards rather than backwards – New Testament teaching about Christ as the new Adam: Romans 5:12-21 (see also 1 Corinthians 15: 22, 45).
2. Rejection and misfortune, dreams, transformation and forgiveness: the Joseph story from the Book of Genesis 37-50.
3. Formed in our mother's womb: Psalm 139.
4. Trapped within but then set free – the raising of Lazarus: John 11.

1: Reading Humanity forwards rather than backwards – New Testament teaching about Christ as the new Adam: Romans 5:12-21 (see also 1 Corinthians 15: 22, 45)

It is puzzling, when gender is under discussion, to find some Christian interpreters turning to the Old Testament, especially Genesis 1:26,27, rather than to a New Testament passage. For Jesus and the first Christians, the Hebrew Bible was their scriptures, and they interpret its texts in the light of the coming kingdom initiated by Jesus' ministry. In so doing they look forward as well as backwards, re-interpreting the earlier message in terms of the new age that has already dawned.

Responding to a question about divorce (Mark 10-2-11; Matthew 19:3-9), for example, Jesus recalls several verses from Genesis, including Genesis 1.27, but he is also orientated to the future. His reference to the 'hardness of heart' that prompted Moses to sanction a man to divorce his wife, may hint at the Messianic age foreseen by Ezekiel (36:26) when God will replace stony hearts with hearts of flesh. Jesus' teaching also departs from the Old Testament in claiming that adultery can be committed against a woman as well as against a man. Present 'in the beginning', the equality of women and men is also the present and future.

Frequently, but unfairly dismissed as misogynistic, a similar dynamic can be seen at work in Paul's writings. This is true even of a passage like 1 Corinthians 11, where he is keenest to reinforce gender differences and hierarchy. Yet because he reads Genesis chapter 2 in the light of Christ (Browne 2007 Chapter 3), mutuality and equality shine through: 'Nevertheless, in the Lord woman is not independent of man nor man of woman; for as woman was made from man, so man is now born of woman. And all things are from God' (1 Cor. 11:11-12)

In two passages, Romans 5 and 1 Corinthians 15, where Paul contrasts Adam and Christ, the Genesis narrative is interpreted within an emerging Christian anthropology, and hence the decision to begin these Bible studies with a New Testament passage about Christ as the new Adam:

Romans 5:12-17

[12] *Therefore just as sin entered the world through one man* [ανθρωπου], *and death through sin, and in this way death came to all people* [ανθρωπους] *because all sinned –* [13] *To be sure, sin was in the world before the law was given, but sin is not charged against anyone's account where there is no law.* [14] *Nevertheless, death reigned from the time of Adam to the time of Moses, even over those who did not sin by breaking a command, as did Adam, who is a pattern of the one to come.* [15] *But the gift is not like the trespass. For if the many died by the trespass of the one man* [ενος] *trespass, how much more did God's grace and the gift that came by the grace of the one man* [ανθρωπου], *Jesus Christ, overflow to the many!* [16] *Nor can the gift of God be compared with the result of one man's* [ενος] *sin: The judgement followed one sin and brought condemnation, but the gift followed many trespasses and brought justification.* [17] *For if, by the trespass of the one man* [ενος], *death reigned through that one man* [ενος], *how much more will those who receive God's abundant provision of grace and the gift of righteousness reign in life through the one man* [ενος], *Jesus Christ!*

Inclusive language is not a new-fangled dictate required by 'political correctness'. It is deeply Christ-centred and has been characteristic of Christianity from the very start. In this passage, where Paul contrasts the old Adam with Christ, the new Adam, he uses the Greek word ανθρωποσ which means human being, rather than the Greek word for male, which would be ανδροσ. Paul is outlining the grand narrative of human disobedience and its redemption through the divine humanity of Jesus Christ. He is reflecting on Genesis chapter 2, but human sinfulness isn't blamed on Eve (as it is in other Pauline texts like 2 Corinthians 11:3 or 1 Timothy 2:14), and by implication on womankind. Sin is a human phenomenon that brings death and condemnation. Its antidote is the overflowing grace of God released by Jesus Christ which brings about justification and a new relationship with God.

Human sinfulness and God's salvation are held together in this passage, but in preaching and practice the two are often sundered. The nineteenth century theologian F.D. Maurice noticed that many of his contemporaries were prone to dwell on the sinfulness of human beings and the fall of Adam, whereas for him, 'Mankind stands not in Adam but in Christ' (quoted in Vidler 1966: 43). Regarding someone primarily as a sinner rather than as a brother or sister redeemed by Christ is bound to distort one's relationship with them.

Writing to his religiously and ethnically diverse congregations, Paul's focus is the corporate humanity of Christ: Christians are members of a body of which Christ is the Head. His is a single body, made up of people of different races and social backgrounds, men and women; a body fed and nourished by Christ in whom everyone who has been 'incorporated' is maturing, growing up into their full humanity measured by nothing less than Christ himself (Ephesians 4:13). This incorporation is effected by baptism, the pattern of Christ's dying and rising and entry point into a totally new quality of life where former hierarchies and distinctions, even gendered ones, fall away. 'For all of you who were baptised into Christ have clothed yourselves with Christ. There is neither Jew nor Gentile, neither slave nor free, nor is there male and female, for you are all one in Christ Jesus' (Galatians 3:27,28). In this much loved text too there appears to be an echo of Genesis (Browne, 2010: 11): 'male and female' recalling Genesis 1:27 and 'one in Christ Jesus' the 'one flesh' of Genesis 2.24, but here reconceived as a relationship, no longer based on flesh and blood connections, but on union with Christ.

Discussion points:

- There are a few gender specific instructions in the New Testament, such as 1 Corinthians 11, but when God's plan is outlined the language used is gender neutral and inclusive. Why might that be and how does it make you feel?
- Paul shares various common assumptions of his day about how men and women should behave, but also finds them being destabilised by his life in Christ. Is this your experience too?
- Paul contrasts the judgement and condemnation that once marked humanity with the freedom and grace of life in

Christ. Why then do you think that trans people so often
feel judged and condemned by their churches? What needs
to happen to change that?

- Some Christians regard gender variance as a consequence of
the Fall (Yarhouse 2015: 39ff) but are unable to cite specific
passages to support this. Thinking about how Paul uses
scripture in the light of Christ, how might you help them to
appreciate that being trans is not a sin?

- Equality before God comes across strongly in Jesus' teaching
and in Paul's understanding of the Christian community as
a body united to Christ. How might the Church today stay
true to this vision?

2: Rejection and misfortune overcome – dreams, transformation and forgiveness: the Joseph story from the Book of Genesis 37-50.

The story of Joseph, Jacob's son, is very familiar in the English
speaking world thanks to the popular musical *Joseph and the Amazing
Technicolour Dreamcoat* by Tim Rice and Andrew Lloyd Webber. That
the garment bestowed on Joseph by his doting father Jacob was a coat
of many colours derives from the Septuagint, the influential Greek
version of the Old Testament, parts of which date from the third
century BCE. Michael Carden, in *The Queer Bible Commentary* (Guest
et al. 2006: 52), finds this coloured robe evocative of the rainbow,
bridging earth and heaven, and notes that heavenly, or Uranian, lies
behind the terms urning/urnind coined by the nineteenth-century
sexologist Karl Ulrichs (see Chapter 1 above) to describe gay men
and lesbians. The connection seems strained but Carden appears to
be making two distinct points.

First, he claims that this symbolism points to a well-established
queer reading of the Joseph narrative in Jewish interpretation. As
Ostriker (quoted in Guest et al. 2006: 53) writes:

'Joseph is the darling, a pretty boy ... his father's pet ... the rabbis
say he painted his eyes and walked with mincing step. Showing
off the coat of many colours which old Jacob made him. Twirling,
hugging himself. No wonder his brothers hated him.'

Joseph's ravishing beauty is explicit in the Targums, the Aramaic
translations of the Hebrew Scriptures which elaborate the text. In
a homo-erotic addition, Potiphar buys Joseph at the slave market
'because he saw that he was handsome, [and] that he might practise
sodomy with him' (Bowker 1969: 244) but is immediately punished by

the withering of his testes. This strange vignette may be a parable to illustrate that the word for court official (as Potiphar was and Joseph would become) and eunuch were synonymous, though not all court officials were surgically altered. Hetero-erotic additions to the text also convey Joseph's physical allure. In one, the women throw gold rings at Joseph's chariot to gain his attention 'so that they could see his handsome figure' (Bowker 1969: 291). In another, the Egyptian women visiting Potiphar's wife are 'so much captivated with Joseph's beauty' that they cut their hands when peeling their fruit snack. A version of this story also appears in the *Qur'an* (sura 12, 4:31).

Secondly, Carden's approach emphasises Joseph's connection with the sacred world, symbolised by the rainbow coat, and developed as the story unfolds in his facility as an interpreter of dreams. It thus highlights the link between gender variance and the sacred in traditional cultures. Joseph's robe, his insight into the dream world and gender nonconformity are all hallmarks of the shaman. In the Midrash, ancient commentary on the Hebrew scriptures, Joseph's coat is said to be the garment made by God for Adam and Eve; handed down through the generations it becomes part of the high priestly vesture.

Joseph's gender nonconformity is even more pronounced in the queer reading of the text proposed by Theodore Jennings (2005: 179ff). The Hebrew for Joseph's coat, *k'tonet passim*, is highly distinctive and only appears in one other place in the Old Testament, in the story of Tamar, the daughter of King David (2 Samuel 13:18). There it is described as 'the kind of garment the virgin daughters of the king wore.' As Peterson Toscano wryly observes in *Transfigurations*, his stunning performance of biblical characters who transcend or transgress gender norms: Joseph was wearing a princess dress!

Why might Jacob feminise his son? Jennings suggests that the narrative counterpoints Reuben, eldest son of Jacob's first wife Leah, and Joseph, eldest son of Rachel, his second wife. The feminisation of Joseph situates him in the family hierarchy. A parallel would be Philippe Duc d'Orleans (1640-1701), younger brother of Louis XIV, who was brought up 'as though he were a princess' (Gilbert 1926: 95) but nevertheless gained distinction as a soldier. In macro terms, however, Joseph's dependence on a higher status male (Jacob, Potiphar, Pharaoh) could also be a parable of Israel's relationship with stronger nations and empires. Did this experience, one wonders, provide the origin of the pattern of God's preference for the younger sibling, which recurs throughout the Old Testament?

Women's significance in the patriarchal narratives is increasingly recognised. Rebekah's subversion of primogeniture by promoting her younger son, Jacob (Genesis 27:5ff) and the grab at sacred power by Rachel, the younger sister, when she steals her father's household gods (Genesis 31: 19, 34-5) are two examples. Following Jennings's homo-erotic reading of the Old Testament, masculinity is the focus in this Bible study but the construction of femininity should not be overlooked. Peterson Toscano has Joseph's butch uncle Esau tell Joseph's story, which starts with the contrast between the 'hairy' alpha male Esau, and his 'smooth' beta male twin brother Jacob. This reading suggests a reason for Jacob's affinity with his feminine younger son Joseph, rather than with his tough older brothers, and the favouritism behind his gift of a special garment, a cross-gendered yet sacred robe.

Sophisticated Egypt, where he is banished by his brothers, is a place where Joseph will eventually thrive, being raised from the prison to become Pharaoh's second in command. Being a court official (or eunuch) was a mediating role, and Joseph would have looked both exotic and unrecognisable to his brothers. Powerful in Egypt, Joseph does not exact revenge on his brothers, as a 'real man' might be expected to do, but forgives them, in a tearful reconciliation scene. Like the story of Job, the Joseph narrative is Wisdom literature, which typically depicts a reversal of misfortune leading to others being blessed.

Esau's monologue in Peterson's *Transfigurations* is a highly creative summary of the Joseph narrative, or you can go to the text itself and read it there:

The Joseph Narrative: Genesis 37-50.

Joseph & His brothers:	*Gen 37:1-14, 23-4, 28-36.*
Joseph & Potiphar's wife:	*Gen 39:2-4, 6b-7, 10-15, 19-23.*
After Joseph interprets dreams:	*Gen 41:38-45, 53-4*
Joseph's brothers come to Egypt:	*Gen 42:6-9, 17-24*
The brothers' dilemma:	*Gen 43:1-5, 15, 29-31*
Joseph forgives his brothers:	*Gen 45:1-15*

Discussion points:

a) 'My brother Esau is a hairy man while I have smooth skin'
   (Genesis 27: 11).

   Esau and his brother Jacob, like Joseph and his brothers,
   seem to represent two different kinds of masculinity – the
   alpha and the beta male. As the narratives unfold this
   construction is shown to be a stereotype as the younger sons
   emerge as the leaders of their nation. Portraying Rebekah
   as guilty of the 'feminine trait' of putting a person before a
   principle (Robertson 1903: 89) by promoting Jacob over Esau
   is a gender stereotype. 'Subversive' would be more accurate.
   Rebekah and Rachel are agents of God's own subversion of
   the status quo.

- Have you been affected by gender stereotyping? If so, how
  did you deal with it?
- Were you able to find biblical paradigms to help you?
- Gender studies tend to speak of masculinities and femininities
  (plural). Have you come across this gender plurality: a) in the
  Bible; b) in your own experience?
- The Church today increasingly insists on 'gender
  complementarity', as if the options were simply male/
  masculine or female/feminine, overlooking even the two
  types of masculinity and the far from straightforward
  construction of femininity in the Joseph narrative. How might
  the Joseph story help to broaden understanding of gender?

b) 'All of you who were baptised into Christ have clothed
   yourselves with Christ' (Galatians 3:27).

   The Joseph story tells of a 'dressy' young man – with his
   gender bending coat; then a garment – not described – that
   Potiphar's wife pulls off him; finally, Pharaoh clothes him in
   fine linen and puts a gold chain around his neck.

- Have clothes ever landed you in trouble – as Joseph's princess
  dress did?
- Being stripped of his garment (as Jesus would be during
  his Passion) 'exposed' Joseph to lies about himself and his
  behaviour. Have you been 'stripped' of your reputation for
  being trans or for another reason?

- Pharaoh's robing of Joseph is reminiscent of the father, in Jesus' parable, clothing his younger son in the best robe, and the baptismal robe in early Christianity. What does it mean to you to be clothed with Christ as a beloved child of God?

c) 'Joseph kissed all his brothers and wept over them' (Genesis 45:15).

- Joseph had to experience rejection by his family and was forced to relocate before his dreams could come true. How might this relate to the experience of some trans people?
- Chris's research shows that forgiveness is often exercised by trans people to those, especially other Christians, who have rejected them: very like Joseph, who forgave his brothers. Has this been your experience too, either as a trans Christian or someone with a pastoral heart for trans people?

d) 'Then a new king, to whom Joseph meant nothing, came to power in Egypt. 'Look,' he said to his people, 'the Israelites have become far too numerous for us' (Exodus 1:8,9).

Joseph's exile, which saves his family from death by famine, and through which his people are blessed, sets the scene for the next generation and the enslavement of the people of Israel in Egypt. Indeed, Joseph is sold into slavery in Egypt early on in his story. The Exodus narrative, in which God sets his people free from oppression, is the biblical basis for many theologies of liberation: Black, African, Asian, Latin American, Feminist, Women of Colour, and Queer.

- What do you see as the specific oppressions trans people experience?
- What sort of liberation might gender variant people be looking for?
- How might belief in Christ as liberator contribute to trans people's quest for self-determination?

3: Formed in our mother's womb: Psalm 139

Psalm 139 does not obviously fit into one of the literary categories that have been applied to the psalms: hymns, thanksgiving psalms, laments, royal psalms, wisdom psalms and liturgies. G.W Anderson (1962: 442) argued that it belongs with the laments because of the reference to 'the wicked', who are at enmity with the author and with

God (verses 19-22). Praying for (verse 23) and being aware of God's scrutiny of one's life (verses 1-12), especially when one is maliciously accused, is typical of the lament. He then continues: 'But its intensely individual and personal character puts this psalm in a class by itself.'

The sense of intimate personal connection with God in this psalm means that it is profoundly meaningful for many people. The thought of God's creativity, present during our time in the womb, and even before our conception, is deeply 'precious' (verse 17). God knows us personally (verse 3), and is 'present', even when our experience is hellish and we anticipate God's absence, or when we prefer the darkness to the light. Indeed, the binaries of light and dark, day and night, apparently so sharp and clear in the Genesis 1 account of creation, begin to dissolve in our prayerful experience of God. The experiential character of this psalm, which is daunting in its extremes, and the sheer immensity of God's creation and plan, is a riposte to those who would deny the author's integrity. In this it resembles the closing chapters of the Book of Job, where Job's encounter with God vindicates him, and communicates mystery and wonder in contrast to the narrow, judgemental vision of his 'comforters'.

The Bible frequently appears masculinist, or has often been interpreted through a male gaze, so this psalm is refreshing in that it references the female body, specifically the womb. Many women love this psalm because of that. Pregnancy can be an intensely spiritual experience for women, and all of us have been shaped by the time we spent in the womb. For some life in the womb was not idyllic, and their birth experience traumatic rather than beautiful. This psalm assures us that, whatever the circumstances of our physical birth, we were birthed in God.

In the initial stage of pregnancy, the human foetus is ungendered with 'indifferent gonads' that have the potential to become either ovaries or testes, and the presence of both Mullerian (female) ducts and Wolffian (male) ducts, one or other of which will be inhibited in due course. Hormonal changes, related to the presence of XY or XX chromosomes, are responsible for male or female development, but there are various chromosomal and hormonal variations which affect intersex people. The evidence for a pre-natal hormonal, or another biological basis for trans people's experience is sometimes fiercely contested, thus rendering their time in the womb problematic. The reassurance of God's love from womb to tomb in this psalm is a healing antidote to that.

Psalm 139

1   You have searched me, Lord, and you know me.

2   You know when I sit and when I rise; you perceive my thoughts from afar.

3   You discern my going out and my lying down; you are familiar with all my ways.

4   Before a word is on my tongue you, Lord, know it completely.

5   You hem me in behind and before, and you lay your hand upon me.

6   Such knowledge is too wonderful for me, too lofty for me to attain.

7   Where can I go from your Spirit? Where can I flee from your presence?

8   If I go up to the heavens, you are there; if I make my bed in the depths you are there.

9   If I rise on the wings of the dawn, if I settle on the far side of the sea,

10 even there your hand will guide me, your right hand will hold me fast.

11 If I say, 'Surely the darkness will hide me and the light become night around me,'

12 even the darkness will not be dark to you; the night will shine like the day, for darkness is as light to you.

13 For you created my inmost being; you knit me together in my mother's womb.

14 I praise you because I am fearfully and wonderfully made; your works are wonderful, I know that full well.

15 My frame was not hidden from you when I was made in the secret place, when I was woven together in the depths of the earth.

16 Your eyes saw my unformed body; all the days ordained for me were written in your book before one of them came to be.

17 How precious to me are your thoughts, God! How vast is the sum of them!

18 Were I to count them, they would outnumber the grains of sand – when I awake, I am still with you.

19 If only you, God, would slay the wicked! Away from me, you who are bloodthirsty!

20 They speak of you with evil intent; your adversaries misuse your name.

21 Do I not abhor those who hate you, Lord, and abhor those who are in rebellion against you?

22   *I have nothing but hatred for them; I count them my enemies.*
23   *Search me, God, and know my heart; test me and know my*
     anxious thoughts.
24   *See if there is any offensive way in me, and lead me in the way*
     everlasting.

Discussion points

- Being trans does not mean being especially broken compared to others (though a few religious people actually do claim that it does), but being gender variant may involve many struggles due to prejudice and lack of understanding. What kinds of things lead you to lament?
- Trans people are often scrutinised by others because they look or sound different compared to current gender norms. What does it feel like to be scrutinised by other people, and how do you deal with that?
- Why might it feel different to be scrutinised by God?
- Heaven/hell; day/night; dark/light. The Bible often presents us with binaries in which one polarity (heaven, day, light) seems superior to the other (hell, night, dark). This psalm subverts that with the paradox that God is to be found in both. How might that message be hopeful for trans people? For everyone?
- The psalm recalls our earliest life in the womb, and even before that, our conception. It is very fleshy and earthy – and God was always there. Some Christians seem keen to question the scientific evidence base for trans people's experience. Aren't Christians better qualified to talk about what this psalm tells us: that God's love surrounds us, even before we are born?
- 'I praise you because I am fearfully and wonderfully made' (verse 14). If this is a psalm of lament, then verse 14 strikes a note of praise. Trans people are often assumed to have a problematic relationship with their body. Even if that were true it's not unique to gender variant people. In any case, many trans people are at ease with themselves, especially when they accept their gender identity. How might this psalm help everyone to be at peace with themselves?
- The psalmist is honest about feeling anger for enemies. It's expressed as prayer. How do you deal with your anger at other people, especially those who question your integrity?

4: Trapped within but then set free – the raising of Lazarus: John 11

St John's gospel opens with a cosmic hymn about the creative Word which becomes flesh in Jesus. Abstract themes of darkness and light, above and below, are rooted in intimate encounters between Jesus and particular people, like Nicodemus, the Samaritan woman, and in this passage, with his friends Martha and Mary, the sisters of Lazarus. Jesus is intimately involved with this family at Bethany. Indeed, John is quite explicit about their intimacy when he says, 'Jesus loved Martha and her sister and Lazarus' (11:5). Moved by Mary's tears at her brother's death, John also records that Jesus 'was deeply moved in spirit and troubled' (11:34) and that 'Jesus wept', which led the Jews to respond, 'See how he loved him!' (11:35,36).

Family dynamics are apparent in Jesus' initial encounter with the forthright Martha, and then with her more reflective sister, Mary. Both are able to express their heartfelt disappointment: that if Jesus had been there, their brother would not have died. Jesus is able to draw from Martha an expression of trust in him and his hold on the future. The raising of Lazarus is an emotional story. It is a family narrative. It is about death and mourning. It speaks of God's love and compassion, and invites faith in Christ's presence in our sorrow and in Christ's power to raise us to new life.

That Jesus stands at the tomb and calls to his dead friend, 'Lazarus, come out' (11:43) has inevitably invited readings of the text that interpret it as a coming-out narrative (Guest et al. 2006: 554). When Lazarus emerges, bound from head to foot 'in strips of linen … in accordance with Jewish burial customs' (John 19:40), Jesus says, 'Take off the grave clothes and let him go' (John 11:44). As Goss notes (Guest et al. 2006: 555), Lazarus needs the assistance of the community to do that, just as 'coming out' involves a renewed relationship with family and friends. The Lent section of the *Weekday Missal* has an image of the risen Christ, standing upright wrapped in linen burial bands, but which is also evocative of Lazarus emerging from the tomb. The tightly wound linen cloths wrapped around Lazarus can symbolise oppression, secrecy, a self that is concealed from others, and being dead on the inside. More hopefully, as they are unwound, they signify bandages which, once removed, reveal a person made whole, healed and restored.

As Goss also observes, just as Jesus' raising of Lazarus was the event that led the religious authorities to plan Jesus' death, coming out as queer can have dire consequences. The death toll among trans women is horrifyingly high and institutional religion can contribute to this 'through narrow definitions, dogmatic regulations and violent exclusions' (Guest et al. 2006: 555).

John 11:32-39a, 41-44

[32] *When Mary reached the place where Jesus was and saw him, she fell at his feet and said, 'Lord, if you had been here, my brother would not have died.'* [33] *When Jesus saw her weeping, he was deeply moved in spirit and troubled.* [34] *'Where have you laid him?' he asked. 'Come and see, Lord,' they replied.* [35] *Jesus wept.* [36] *Then the Jews said, 'see how he loved him!'* [37] *But some of them said, 'Could not he who opened the eyes of the blind man have kept this man from dying?'* [38] *Jesus, once more deeply moved, came to the tomb. It was a cave with a stone laid across the entrance.* [39a] *'Take away the stone,' he said. ...*

[41] *So they took away the stone. Then Jesus looked up and said, 'Father, I thank you that you have heard me.* [42] *I knew that you always hear me, but I said this for the benefit of the people standing here that they may believe that you sent me.'* [43] *When he had said this, Jesus called out in a loud voice, 'Lazarus, come out!'* [44] *The dead man came out, his hands and feet wrapped with strips of linen, and a cloth around his face. Jesus said to them, 'Take off the grave clothes and let him go.'*

Discussion points:

- Emotions can run high when a family member, or a church member, comes out as trans. How might Jesus' interaction with the sisters at Bethany offer a model for honest but hopeful conversations in these or similar circumstances?
- Jesus' love and compassion for the whole family, both the grieving sisters and their dead brother, is strongly emphasised in this passage, but Jesus was also 'troubled'. When someone comes out as trans their families can feel overlooked. The trans person often wants to celebrate their self-acceptance, while family and friends are still grieving the person they feel they have 'lost'. Other people may simply be puzzled. How should churches address these mixed emotions and reactions?
- The raising of Lazarus inspired hatred in some. Coming out as trans, transitioning, acting on one's non binary identity, or being publicly gender nonconforming can all lead to rejection, ridicule, hostility and even violence. What kinds of things might churches do to encourage a safer environment for trans

people to come out to their family and community, and help
them to flourish on the various stages of their journeys?

Radical Christian Equality

This series of Bible studies began with the inclusive humanity of
Christ. Christians are incorporated into the Body of Christ through
sacramental participation in Christ's dying and rising in the rite of
Baptism. Being a member of Christ's mystical body does not erase
one's ethnicity, social status, or gender, but these and other aspects of
our identity are dethroned and transcended by the identity we share
in Christ. This dethroning of human social structures within the life
of the baptised community can involve a tremendous struggle, as
shown by the battles for the abolition of slavery and, more recently,
for the admission of women to all three orders of ordained ministry.
Some Christians argue that our identity is in Christ and 'that's all that
matters', but gender, ethnicity and social status don't just disappear
when we are 'in Christ'. They do, though, lose their potential to distort
our common life, and this made Christianity highly attractive to the
marginalised from the start.

At the Council of Nicaea, held in 325 CE, a decade or so after
Christianity had found favour with the Roman Emperor, the very
first Canon, or church law, enacted ruled that those who had been
involuntarily castrated could be ordained. Those, however, who had
chosen to do this, other than on grounds of health (which would, of
course, apply to modern trans people who have undergone gender
confirmation surgery) could not be ordained, and if they were already
a member of the clergy should cease to minister. Why did the Council
Fathers enact such a decree? Deep down it appears they were ashamed
of the Church's origins, of the Church Jesus called into being, which
Christianity's enemies had mocked as a religion for slaves, women,
children, and for ... eunuchs. Fear of what others might say lies behind
much Christian uncertainty about trans people, but gender variant
people have always existed and evidently found a special welcome
in the early Church, where union with Christ mattered far more than
social differences, and even neutralised social stigma.

Chapter 9

Liturgies

Introduction

At the General Synod of the Church of England in July 2017 a resolution was passed that recognised that 'some nationally commended liturgical materials' might be needed to mark trans people's transitions. Chris and Tina had already identified a need for several rites. These liturgies were written in response to the stories gathered in the Transfaith project.

Please feel free to use them or adapt them for your purposes.

Rite 1: A Liturgy of Communion

Opening Prayer

The earth is God's and all that is in it.
Who shall stand in the high places of God?
Those with clean hands and pure hearts
Those do not lift their soul to what is false
Or speak with deceit.
It is they who will receive blessing and vindication from God,
Come God and be with us today. Our hearts and minds are open.

(based on Psalm 24)

Hymn

Suggestions are :

- In Christ Alone
- Great is thy faithfulness
- Amazing Grace
- Lord for the years

Readings (as many as required)

- Genesis 15:1-8 God's Promise to Abram
- Genesis 32:22-32 Jacob's Name Is changed to Israel
- Acts 9:1-9 Saul Becomes a follower of Christ

Responsorial Prayer

The God we call both Father and Mother can do great miracles.
With wisdom he made the skies.
She spread out the earth on the seas.
He made the sun and the moon.
She made the sun to rule the day.
He made the moon and stars to rule the night.
God remembered us when we were in trouble and freed us from our
enemies of doubt and fear.
*She gives food to every living creature and comes to us in bread and
wine.*

Give thanks to the God of heaven.
The Father/Mother's love continues forever.
Based on Psalm 136

Time of preparation

Now in the stillness and the silence we recall what separates us from God, ourselves and others.

Silence

Therefore, if anyone is in Christ, they are a new creation.

Old things have passed away. All things have become new.

All this is from God, who has reconciled us through Jesus Christ and has given to us the ministry of reconciliation.

Communion

Some parts of creation are born with the intention of sacred transformation. Wheat transforms to sacred bread, Grapes transform to sacred drink. God calls something from its original form to its true purpose and causes it to be named with its true name. If we believe this of bread and wine how can we not also believe this of people?

God called barren Abram and Sari, struggling Jacob, and the murderous Saul and transformed them into Abraham and Sarah whose descendants are more numerous than the stars, the patriarch Israel whose name became a nation, and the Apostle Paul, genius missionary of the Early Church. If we believe this of those whose stories are recorded in the Bible, how can we not believe this of people now?

We are people who understand the infinite transforming power of God. We celebrate God's desire to call all creation to its true nature and purpose. We recognise this can be a difficult, uncomfortable yet sacred process. We recognise it challenges preconceptions and disrupts comfortable assumptions. We recognise that transformation means discarding and laying down what has seemed important and even essential, believing in the goodness of God even when parts of the Church mistakenly pronounce it folly, as did the friends of Job.

Some of us here have experienced this at first hand, others have watched and prayed and loved and sometimes struggled to understand. But we have all been touched by the God breathed imperative to find true name and sacred purpose in transformation.

We recognise that while we gather here there are some still in the wilderness who have yet to experience their Shaveh, Peniel or Damascus Road. There are some who still struggle. We pray for the healing hand of God to rest upon them lightly and bring them peace.

On the night before his passion, Jesus took a piece of bread and called it to its true name and purpose saying 'This is my Body'. He then took a cup of wine and did the same saying 'This is my Blood'. He then asked us to do this and remember him, remembering the transformative love of God.

At this the Last Supper all were invited and here in memory of him all are invited also.

Come take and eat.

Here is Food for your journey and Drink for your celebration.

Communion is shared

Closing Prayer

May the name of God protect you.
May God send you help and support from on high.
May God remember all your prayers and secret struggles.
And fulfil your deepest longings and bring to reality your most hopeful plans.
May God answer your deepest prayers.
For God helps and sustains.
For those who trust in God shall be raised up.

Amen

(Loosely based on Psalm 20)

Rite 2: Preparation for Surgery

Opening Psalm

God is my shepherd, I lack nothing.
He makes me lie down in green pastures,
he leads me beside quiet waters,
he refreshes my soul.
He guides me along the right paths
for his name's sake
Even though I walk
through the darkest valley,
I will fear no evil,
for you are with me;
your rod and your staff,
they comfort me.
You prepare a table before me
in the presence of my enemies.
You anoint my head with oil;
my cup overflows.
Surely your goodness and love will follow me
all the days of my life,
and I will dwell in the house of God
forever.

Friends, we gather here today to mark a stage in the life of N who has decided to undergo surgery to affirm their gender. It is a serious decision based on years of preparation and soul searching. This service seeks to confer a blessing on N as they prepare spiritually for the surgery that they will undergo.

Let us pray

Jesus Christ healer and restorer
Help us and heal us
Jesus who travelled with your band of men and women healing the sick and preaching God's Kingdom

Help us and heal us
Jesus who raised to life Jairus's daughter and the widow's son
Help us and heal us
Jesus who cured the centurion's servant because of his faith
Help us and heal us
Who healed his friend's mother-in-law
Help us and heal us
Jesus who restored the sight of Bartimaeus
Help us and heal us
Jesus who healed the ten lepers and restored them to their society
Help us and heal us
Who healed the lame man brought by his friends
Help us and heal us
Who healed the man thought possessed
Help us and heal us
Who raised his friend Lazarus to life
Help us and heal us
Who healed the man with the withered hand on the Sabbath despite
  the Law
Help us and heal us
Who healed the bleeding woman who people thought unclean
Help us and heal us
Who healed the blind and deaf
Help us and heal us
Jesus who refused to condemn but directed others to look to
  themselves first before throwing stones at others
Help us, heal us and save us.
Amen

Reading

Luke 7:1-17

Song

We cannot measure how you heal or *Amazing Grace*

Anointing

Come and strengthen N through this holy anointing:
Help them and heal them
Free N from all harm:

Help them and heal them

Free N from fear and anxiety

Help them and heal them

Give courage and faith to N as they prepare for surgery

Help them and heal them

Assist all those dedicated to the care of the sick

Help them and heal them

Let us pray: Loving and healing Jesus, the gospels are full of your healing miracles. We ask you to keep safe our beloved N as they prepare for surgery. Be with them and all who are engaged in the care of N in this time. And with oil I now anoint them as a symbol of your healing:

Let us pray

Our **Father Mother** *who art in heaven*
Holy is your name
Your Kingdom Come
Your will be Done
On Earth as it is in Heaven.
Give us what we need today and forgive us
As we forgive those who have wronged us
Save us from the times of trial and deliver us from evil
For yours is the dominion, power and glory for ever and ever
Amen.

Final Prayer

Praise to you Creator God who made everything and called it good.

Blessed be the Creator who heals and saves us

Praise to the Son who preached and healed in the name of the
   Dominion of God

Blessed be the Son who heals and saves us

Praise to the Spirit whose Pentecost gifts were gifts of
   understanding and healing

Blessed be the Spirit who heals and saves us.

Amen.

Rite 3: Acknowledging Loss

Friends, we come here today to mark a change. While this is a positive and healing change, like many important changes in our lives it has come at a cost. While we rejoice, we may also have difficult feelings such as anger, grief and loss.

This is a rite of ending and beginning, in which we acknowledge both sorrow and joy and try to come to a place where we can free ourselves from feelings that are not helpful to carry into the future.

It is also a rite where we come face to face with the fact that none of us are always the people that we have wish to be. Part of the human condition is that sometimes we act in ways we later recognise have been hurtful, angry and unloving in thoughts, words and deeds.

This is a rite to lay all this to rest so that we can walk into a future as freed people. As we come together today to mark endings and beginnings, we acknowledge that both finding and losing has its proper time.

As we hear from ancient wisdom:
There is a season for everything, a time for every occupation under heaven:
A time to give birth and a time to die;
a time to plant and a time to uproot what has been planted;.
a time to kill and a time to heal;
a time to knock down, and a time to build up;
a time to weep and a time to laugh;
a time to mourn and a time to dance;
a time to throw stones away and a time to gather them in;
a time to embrace and a time to refrain from embracing;
a time for to seek and a time to lose;
a time to keep and a time to discard;
a time to tear and a time to sew;
a time to keep silent and a time to speak;
a time to love and a time to hate;
a time for war and a time for peace.

(Ecclesiastes 3:1 - 8)

Let us pray: O God, in this moment where we mark change we realise that there may be many emotions that are swirling around. Feelings of hope, love and joy but also feelings of grief, loss, anger and hurt. The season for these has past but we cannot let them go without acknowledging them. So we call to mind the times that we have felt sad and angry, lost and hopeless, wounded and wounding as we say:

Is it nothing to you, all you who pass by
 Look and see if there is any sorrow like my sorrow,
which was brought upon me,
 For these things I weep;
 my eyes flow with tears;
for the comforter, who should relieve my soul,
is far from me.

-Lamentations

In this quiet time, we call to mind all those times that have been difficult, recognising that we are human and we don't always get it right, no matter how hard we try.

In this quiet time, we recall our dashed hopes and dreams of what we hoped would happen that now in the light of revealed reality cannot happen.

In this quiet time, we recall all those thoughts, words and deeds that have been hurtful, unhelpful, whether known or unknown, and lay them aside.

In recognition that this season has passed we bring tokens of things we wish to put away that we now recognise will be hard to take into the future.

There is a box in which symbols of the past, such as letters, photos and trinkets can be placed. Once everything has been placed in the box it is tied securely with ribbon and covered over. At the end of the liturgy the celebrant should take this box away and ensure it is destroyed without opening it.

Therefore, if anyone is in Christ, they are a new creation.

Old things have passed away. All things have become new.

All this is from God, who has reconciled us through Jesus Christ and has given to us the ministry of reconciliation.

2 Corinthians

As we leave let us hear from scripture:

'I have told you these things so that in Me you may have peace. In the world you will have tribulation. But be of good cheer. I have overcome the world.'
John 16:33

Go in peace into the future, freed and empowered to love, laugh and dance again. **Amen.**

Rite 4: Affirmation of marriage vows

Music

Both partners walk down the aisle.

Reading:

Ecclesiastes 4:9-12

Introduction

In Ecclesiastes, we are reminded that it is better to have a partner than to be alone. While relationships are rewarding, they are never straightforward if they are lived fully.

This service is a rededication of the relationship of N and N who have come to ask for God's blessing as they embark on a new stage of their journey together.

Today they will declare that despite the difficulties and hardships of life, they come today to seek God's help to continue to love and be faithful to one another. They renew their covenant to accept each other and to create a safe and loving home together.

Let us pray:

God of infinite love and life-giving hope,
We bring you thanks for faithful relationships.
Relationships that stand the test of time and
prioritise the importance of love over all else.
Bless N and N today as they promise again to live in faithful relationship with each other, looking forward to what will come.
Amen.

Readings

Song

Renewing the Wedding Pledge:

(to each) Will you, N recommit yourself to this holy relationship and its solemn obligations and responsibilities? Will you continue to be a loving, faithful and helpful life partner, in sickness or in health, in prosperity or in adversity?

Response: I WILL

Vows

Own vows or:

I receive you again as my life partner. I promise to love you, honour you and with God's help, hold you close for the rest of my life.

Blessings of the Wedding Rings

In the Old Testament, God made a rainbow covenant with Noah once storms had finished, water receded and life flourished again.

On (original wedding date), N and N selected rings as a sign of the covenant they made to each other. These rings were fitting symbols of the promises recited on that day because they were made of precious things and were without end. On that first day they were bright and shiny in their newness.

Now they are perhaps a little battered, scratched and scuffed but now also speak of a life lived together. They are more precious than on that first day because they also speak of the endurance and hard work that is needed to continue loving as the years inevitably change us all.

Both join their left hands together and the Minister will bless the rings with these words:

God of Loving Kindness, bless these rings which serve as reminders of lives loved and of vows reaffirmed today. Amen.

Blessing upon the Marriage

Before God and this congregation N and N have renewed their marriage vows. They have re-confirmed their covenant by spoken vows and the holding of hands.

N and N, may you grow from this time on in kindness and love, respecting each other and supporting each other in your life journey together. May God the Creator, Redeemer, Sustainer, bless and keep you as you leave this place to continue your life together.

Amen.

Bible readings suitable for the service

1 Corinthians 13:4-7

Love is patient; love is kind and envies no one. Love is never boastful, nor conceited, nor rude; never selfish, not quick to take offence. Love keeps no score of wrongs; does not gloat over other's sins, but delights in the truth. There is nothing love cannot face; there is no limit to its faith, its hope, and its endurance.

John 15:9-12

As the Father hath loved me, so have I loved you: continue in my love. If you keep my commandments, and abide in his love; even as I have kept my Father's commandments, and abide in his love. These things have I spoken unto you, that my joy might remain in you, and that your joy might be full. This is my commandment: That you love one another as I have loved you.

Additional Readings

'The world, for me, and all the world can hold
Is circled by your arms: for me there lies,
Within the lights and shadows of your eyes,
The only beauty that is never old.'
James Weldon Johnson

What greater thing is there for two human souls than to feel that they are joined for life, to strengthen each other in all labour, to rest on each other in sorrow, to minister to each other in all pain, to be with each other in silent unspeakable memories at the moment of the last parting? *George Eliot*

See Dr Iannis's speech in *Captain Corelli's Mandolin* by Louis de Bernières: 'When you fall in love ... But it is.'

Rite 5: Release from Wedding Vows

On a table there are three candles. One is large and placed at the centre of the table. The other two are smaller and are unlit.

Opening Statements

Sometimes we must acknowledge that promises made cannot always be kept no matter how much we meant them at the time.

As we grow older and life changes us, we recognise that sometimes the gulfs between who we were and who we are now are simply too great to cross.

So it is for N and N today.

After much heartache, they have come to the conclusion that they cannot be their best selves if they remain together.

So they come in a spirit of sadness, forgiveness and resolve to free each other from the promises they made on their wedding day and to depart in peace.

Let us pray:

Loving God, the years are not always kind to us.

No matter how hard we try, sometimes we fail to live up to the dreams we once had.

Sometimes we fail ourselves and others.

Sometimes relationships that cause us pain need to end so we can find peace.

So we come today in sadness and hope;

sadness for the endings and hope for better times.

We pray that you touch both N and N with your healing love and with the spirit of repentance and forgiveness so they forgive each other and leave in peace.

Reading

How long, O God will I be sad?
How long will you hide your face from me?
How long will I harbour pain in my soul?
How long will I have sorrow in my heart?
How long will my troubles loom over me?

Please answer me, O Lord my God!
Show me the way forward!
I have hope my troubles will not overwhelm or defeat me

Because I believe in your compassion;
Because I believe I will dance with joy again.
Because I believe I will sing again,
Because I believe I will laugh again
Because I believe in my heart that you are soothing kindness and healing love.
                                              (loosely based on Psalm 13)

Statements of forgiveness

At this stage both read out a short statement they have written in which they acknowledge the pain and brokenness of the situation and seek forgiveness from the other. A simple statement might be *'I know I have tried but I have failed you and failed myself. Please forgive me.'* It should not be too specific or elaborate. After which the following promises are made:

To each:

N are you freely able to forgive both yourself and N for the hurts and sadness that the end of this relationship has caused?

I am

Are you willing to part in peace and friendship?

I am

(If there are children) Will you commit to be a parent with N, putting the needs of your children (Names) first and foremost?

I will

Do you release N from the promises made on the day of your marriage and bid him / her / them to go freely and in peace?

I do

(*At the end of the promises N and N light a smaller candle from the central candle. Once both have done this the larger candle is extinguished.*)

Reading

From the depths I call on You, O Lord!
O Lord, hear my voice;
let Your ears be attentive
to the sound of my pleas.
If you keep track of iniquities,
Who could stand?
But there is forgiveness with You,
that You may be feared.
So my soul now waits for the dawn,
For mercy is found with the Lord;
God's great redemption.
Redeeming us from all our mistakes.

(loosely based on Psalm 130)

Blessing

Go in peace and friendship to live lives filled with grace, mercy and joy.

Amen

Music

Rite 6: Renaming Ceremony

There are two tables. On one table is a candle and a cloth that will be used to cover the items to be surrendered. On the other table is another candle and items covered by another cloth that signify the gender or non-binary identity that is to be affirmed. Music is playing. The participant is dressed in gender neutral clothing but bearing symbols of their natal gender which can be put on the table.

Opening Scripture

God will wipe away every tear from their eyes, and death shall be no more, neither shall there be mourning, nor crying, nor pain anymore, for the former things have passed away. (Revelation 21)

Opening Statements

Friends, we come here today to mark a change of name. It is a recognition of a pre-existing truth that has been obscured, one in which we have all played our part in uncovering. Today we witness a sacred transformation in which the true purpose of PN's (natal name) life has been revealed.

What we do here has echoes in the Bible. God called barren Abram and Sari, struggling Jacob and the murderous Saul and transformed them into Abraham and Sarah whose descendants are more numerous than the stars, the patriarch Israel whose name became a nation and the Apostle Paul genius missionary of the Early Church. Both true nature and God's purpose was recognised in a change of name and recognition of the calling the new name symbolised. Today PN joins this honoured and holy tradition.

We come to watch God's sacred purpose fulfilled in calling PN to their true identity. From this time on they will be called N (changed name) as a male/female/nonbinary/gender queer (use appropriate term) servant of God.

Let us pray

Loving God, there are times when we need to mark that things have changed significantly in our lives. There are times when old ways of living need to be put to aside so that new and affirming ways of living, loving and being can be taken up.

Be with us as we celebrate the journey that PN has made and bless this faithful step they are making this day.

Bless each one of us that are here to witness this miracle of faith and transformation and keep us in love with each other now and in the future. Amen

Reading

There is a season for everything, a time for every occupation under heaven:
A time to give birth and a time to die;
a time to plant and a time to uproot what has been planted;.
a time to kill and a time to heal;
a time to knock down, and a time to build up;
a time to weep and a time to laugh;
a time to mourn and a time to dance;
a time to throw stones away and a time to gather them in;
a time to embrace and a time to refrain from embracing;
a time for to seek and a time to lose;
a time to keep and a time to discard;
a time to tear and a time to sew;
a time to keep silent and a time to speak;
a time to love and a time to hate;
a time for war and a time for peace.

(Ecclesiastes 3:1 - 8)

We hear in our reading that there is a God-appointed time for everything under heaven. We recognise that this is the time for you to put away the identity that feels like an ill-fitting garment and no longer serves God's purpose for you. We recognise that it is the time to cast the identity known as PN identity away. I will now ask you to affirm your intention to lay down this identity so that your calling to live as N can be realised.

PN do you wish to be known by another name?

I do

Have you prayed and heard the whisper of the Spirit calling you to this transformation?

I have

Have you prayed, struggled and discerned that this is the will of God?

I have

Do you freely lay down the name PN but embrace all that has happened up until this moment in your life?

I do .

(to those assembled) And do you, family and friends recognise that it is time to lay this identity aside so that God's sacred purpose for this Child of God can be achieved?

We do.

At this stage PN places the symbols of gender on a table and a cloth is drawn over them. At this stage PN takes a light from the candle and extinguishes the flame. They then move to the other table and light the candle. The items are uncovered. The following questions are asked.

So what is the name that God has gifted you with in this new stage of your journey.

N

And is it your calling to live as a woman/man/non-binary/gender-queer person? (use which is applicable)

It is

Are you willing to accept yourself as a child of God in this stage of your life, seeking God's will for your life and acting with faith, love, mercy and kindness to all those you meet?

I am

Then, we welcome you N among us. As tokens of this welcome, we gift you with symbols of your new calling (at this stage family friends come and present symbols of the new identity and gift them to N)

Song

('One more step along the world I go' or 'Morning has broken' are suggestions)

Blessing

N, go with the blessing of God the Creator
who dreamed of this day at the beginning of time
Of God, the Child who lived and laughed amongst us
And of God the Spirit who dances ahead of you lighting the way into new life.
Amen.

Rite 7: Trans Day of Remembrance

Introduction to Vigil

Transgender Day of Remembrance began in 1999 as a result of the increasing anti-transgender violence and discrimination. The first memorial event was held in November 1999 to remember and honour Rita Hester, who was murdered on November 28th, 1998 in Boston, USA. Rita Hester's murder — like most anti-transgender murder cases — is still unsolved.

Reading

My eyes fail from weeping,
  I am in torment within;
my heart is poured out on the ground
  because my people are destroyed.

(Lamentations 2)

Act of Remembrance

This, is our time to remember. We remember:

Some parts of creation are born with the intention of sacred transformation. Wheat transforms to sacred bread, Grapes transform to sacred drink. God calls something from its original form to its true purpose and causes it to be named with its true name. If we believe this of bread and wine how can we not also believe this of people?

God called barren Abram and Sari, struggling Jacob and the murderous Saul and transformed them into Abraham and Sarah whose descendants are more numerous than the stars, the patriarch Israel whose name became a nation and the Apostle Paul genius missionary of the Early Church. If we believe this of those whose stories are recorded in the Bible how can we not believe this of people?

We are people who understand the infinite transforming power of God. Of God's desire to call all creation to its true nature and purpose. We recognise this can be a difficult, uncomfortable yet sacred process.

We recognise it challenges preconceptions and disrupts comfortable assumptions. We recognise that transformation means discarding and laying down what has seemed important and even essential, believing in the goodness of God even when parts of the Church mistakenly pronounce it folly as did the friends of Job.

Some of us here have experienced this at first hand, others have watched and prayed and loved and sometimes struggled to understand. But we have all been touched by the God breathed imperative to find true name and sacred purpose in transformation. We recognise that while we gather here there are some still in the wilderness who have yet to experience their Shaveh, Peniel or Damascus Road. There are some who still struggle. We pray for the healing hand of God to rest upon them lightly and bring them peace. We remember them by lighting a candle.

We lift up all those who have gone before us to bring about the full human rights of transgender people and all other oppressed groups. We remember those who have worked to bring about the passage of the Gender Recognition Act and other important legal victories. We remember those who do not get access to the health care they need. We remember all those who are rejected by their families, friends and communities. We remember those who died not knowing truly that they were loved and affirmed as gender variant people. We remember all those lovers, friends, families and communities that support gender journeys. We remember that the journey is not over and that we will continue to work towards full human rights and equal services for all transgender people. We celebrate together for our human spirit and our ability to change the world we live in.

Pause for people to name names and light candles

Our stories

Invite people to share their stories

Closing Prayer

We will not forget them, those who hate has killed.

We will not forget them, those who lived in silence

We will not forget them, those who have not told their stories

We will carry them in our hearts

We will sing with them and for them

Songs of liberation and joy.

Amen.

Bibliography

Akena, F.A. 2012. Critical analysis of the production of western knowledge and its implications for indigenous knowledge and decolonization. *Journal of Black Studies*, 43:6: 599–619.

Alexander, A. & P. Alexander. 1999. *The New Lion Handbook to the Bible*. Oxford: Lion.

Alsop R., Fitzsimons A. & K. Lennon. 2002. *theorizing gender*. Cambridge: Polity Press.

Althaus-Reid, M. 2003. *The Queer God*. New York & London: Routledge.

Anderson, G.W. 1962. The Psalms. In *Peake's Commentary on the Bible*. Black, M. & H.H. Rowley eds. London & Edinburgh: Thomas Nelson & Sons.

Anderson, H. & E. Foley. 2001. *Mighty stories, dangerous Rituals: Weaving Together the human and the divine*. San Francisco: Jossey-Bass.

Althaus-Reid, M. 2000. *Indecent theology*. London: Routledge.

Barlow, D. H., Abel, G. G., & E. B. Blanchard. 1977. Gender identity change in a transsexual: an exorcism. *Archives of Sexual Behavior*, 6:5: 387-395.

Beardsley, C. 2007. *The transsexual person is my neighbour*. Brighton: The Gender Trust.

Beardsley, C. 2005. Taking issue: The Transsexual Hiatus in Some Issues in Human Sexuality. *Theology*, 108: 845: 338–346.

Beardsley, C., O'Brien M. & J. Woolley. 2012. Exploring the interplay: the Sibyls' 'gender, sexuality and spirituality' workshop. *Theology & Sexuality*, 16:3: 259–283.

Bennett, J. 2000. Love me gender: normative homosexuality and 'Ex-gay' performativity in reparative therapy narratives, *Text and Performance Quarterly*, 23:4: 331-352

Bettcher, T.M. 2007. Evil deceivers and make-believers: on transphobic violence and the politics of illusion. *Hypatia*, 22:3: 43–65.

Billings, D.B. & T. Urban. 1996. The Socio-Medical Construction of Transsexualism: An Appreciation and Critique. In Ekins R. & D. King, Eds. *Blending Genders: Social Aspects of Cross-Dressing and Sex-Changing*. New York & London: Routledge, pp. 99-117.

Bischoff, G., Warnaar B., Barajas M. & D. Harkiran. 2011. Thematic analysis of the experiences of wives who stay with husbands who transition male-to-female. *Michigan Family Review*, 15:1: 16–34.

Bockting, W.O. & C. Cesaretti. 2001. Spirituality, transgender identity, and coming out. *Journal of Sex Therapy and Education*, 26:4: 291–300.

Bockting, W.O., Knudson G. & J. Goldberg. 2006. Counselling and mental health care for transgender adults and loved ones. *International Journal of Transgenderism*, 9:3-4: 35–82.

Bosch, D. 1995. *Believing in the future: towards a missiology of western culture.* Leominster: Gracewing.

Bornstein, K. 1994. *Gender Outlaw: On men, women and the rest of us.* New York & London: Routledge.

Bornstein, K. 1998. *My Gender Workbook: how to become a real man, a real woman, the real you, or something else.* New York & London: Routledge.

Bosinski, H.A., Schröder, I., Peter, M., Arndt, R., Wille, R., & W.G. Sippell. 1997. Anthropometrical measurements and androgen levels in males, females, and hormonally untreated female-to-male transsexuals. *Archives of sexual behavior*, 26:2: 143-157.

Bowker, J. 1969. *The Targums and Rabbinic Literature: An Introduction to Jewish Interpretations of Scripture.* Cambridge University Press.

Brooker, W. 2017. *Forever Stardust: David Bowie Across the Universe.* London & New York: I.B. Tauris.

Brown, G. 1966. *I Want What I Want.* London: Weidenfeld & Nicolson.

Brown G. 2006. Transsexuals in the military: flight into hyper masculinity. In S. Stryker & S. Whittle, Eds. *The transgender studies reader.* New York: Routledge, pp. 537–544.

Browne, A. 2007. The Call of Christ. Reading the New Testament. In Dormor, D. & J.N. Morris (Eds.) *An Acceptable Sacrifice? Homosexuality & the Church.* London: SPCK.

Browne, A. 2010. Welcome one another: The Scriptures and Sexual Diversity. In Proceedings of a Conference on Sexuality and Human Flourishing. Saturday February 6th 2010, Church of the Ascension, Stirchley, Birmingham: 6-13.

http://www.lgbtac.org.uk/events/Conference6feb10/SuA0421bper cent20Proceedings2SexualityAndHumanFlourishing.pdf (21 September 2017)

Brownson, J.V. 2013. *Bible, Gender, Sexuality: Reframing the Church's Debate on Same-Sex Relationships.* Grand Rapids, Michigan & Cambridge: Eerdmans.

Brush S. 1993. Indigenous knowledge of biological resources and intellectual property rights: The role of anthropology. *American Anthropologist*, 95:3: 653–671.

Buchanan H. 2009. Christian experience as a transsexual. In L. Isherwood & M. Althaus-Reid, Eds. *Trans/Formations.* London: SCM Press, pp. 41–45.

Bullough, B. & V. Bullough. 1998 Transsexualism: Historical Perspectives, 1952 to the Present. In D. Denny, Ed. *Current Concepts in Transgender Identity*. New York & London: Garland Publishing, pp. 15-34.

Butler, J. 2006 [1990]. *Gender Trouble: Feminism and the Subversion of Identity*. New York & London: Routledge Classics.

Califia, P. 1997. *Sex Changes: The Politics of Transgenderism*. San Francisco: Cleis Press Inc.

Carmichael, C. 2010. *Sex and Religion in the Bible*. Yale University Press.

Carpenter, E. 1948 [1896] *Love's Coming of Age: A Series of Papers on the Relation of the Sexes*. London: George Allen & Unwin.

Cass, V.C. 1979. Homosexuality identity formation: a theoretical model. *Journal of homosexuality*, 4.3: 219-235.

Chase, L. 2011. Wives' tales: the experience of Trans partners. *Journal of Gay & Lesbian Social Services*, 23:4: 429–451.

Clifford, J. 2009. God's new frock. In L. Isherwood & M. Althaus-Reid, Eds. *Trans/Formations*. London: SCM Press, pp. 168–201.

Cohen-Kettenis, P. T. & W.A. Arrindell. 1990. Perceived parental rearing style, parental divorce and transsexualism: a controlled study. *Psychological Medicine*, 20:03: 613-620.

Conroy M. 2010. Treating transgendered children: clinical methods and religious mythology. *Zygon*, 45:2: 301–316.

Cornwall S. 2009. Aphophasis and Ambiguity: the 'unknowingness' of transgender. In L. Isherwood & M. Althaus-Reid, Eds. *Trans/Formations*. London: SCM Press, pp. 13–40.

Cornwall S. 2010. *Sex and uncertainty in the Body of Christ: Intersex Conditions and Christian theology*. London: Equinox.

Crites S. 1971. The narrative quality of experience. *Journal of the American Academy of Religion*, XXXIX:3: 291–311.

Cupitt, D. 1999. *The New Religion of Life in Everyday Speech*. London: SCM.

Daly, M. 1985. *Beyond God the Father: Toward a Philosophy of Women's Liberation* (Vol. 350). Beacon Press.

Daniels, B. 2013. A poststructuralist liberation theology?: queer theory & apophaticism. *Union Seminary Quarterly Review* 64: 2-3: 108-117.

Devor, A. 2004. Witnessing and mirroring: a fourteen stage model of transsexual identity formation. *Journal of Gay & Lesbian Psychotherapy*, 8:1-2: 41–67.

de la Huerta, C. 1999. *Coming out Spiritually. The Next Step*. New York: Tarcher/Putnam.

Dietert, M. & D. Dentice. 2013. Growing up Trans: socialization and the gender binary. *Journal of GLBT Family Studies*, 9:1: 24–42.

Dillon, M./Jivaka, L. 1962. *Imji Getsul: An English Buddhist in a Tibetan Monastery.* London: Routledge & Kegan Paul.

Dillon, M./Jivaka, L. 2017. *Out of the Ordinary: A Life of Gender and Spiritual Transitions.* J. Lau & C. Partridge, Eds. New York: Fordham University Press.

Dörner, G., Poppe, I., Stahl, F., Kölzsch, J. & R. Uebelhack. (1991). Gene-and environment-dependent neuroendocrine etiogenesis of homosexuality and transsexualism. *Experimental and Clinical Endocrinology & Diabetes*, 98:05: 141-150.

Doxtater, M. 2004. Indigenous knowledge in the decolonial era. *American Indian Quarterly*, 28:3/4: 618–633.

Doyal L., Anderson J. & S. Paparini. 2008. 'Elvis died and I was born': black African men negotiating same-sex desire in London. *Sexualities*, February (11): 171-192.

DSM: 1994. *Diagnostic and Statistical Manual of Mental Disorders.* Fourth Edition (DSM IV) American Psychiatric Association: Washington DC.

Ekins, R. & D. King. 1996. *Blending Genders: Social Aspects of Cross-Dressing and Sex-Changing.* New York & London: Routledge.

Ekins, R. & D. King. 2006. *Virginia Prince: Pioneer of Transgendering.* Binghamton New York: The Haworth Medical Press.

Ettner, R. 1999. *Gender Loving Care: A Guide to Counselling Gender-Variant Clients.* New York & London: W. W. Norton.

Evangelical Alliance Policy Commission. 2000. *Transsexuality.* Carlisle: Authentic Media.

Faith, R. 2001. Religion, family and ritual: the production of gay, lesbian, bisexual and transgender outsiders-within. *Review of Religious Research*, 43:1: 39–50.

Feinberg, L. 1998. *Trans Liberation: beyond pink and blue.* Boston: Beacon Press.

Fisk, N. 1973. Gender dysphoria syndrome (the how, what and why of a disease. In D. Laub & P. Gandy, Eds. *Proceedings of the second interdisciplinary symposium on gender dysphoria syndrome.* Palo Alto, CA: Stanford University Press, pp. 7-14.

Flores, A.R., Brown, T.N.T. & J.L. Herman. 2016a. *Race and Ethnicity of Adults who Identify as Transgender in the United States.* Los Angeles, CA: The Williams Institute.

Flores, A. R., Brown, T.N.T. & A. S. Park. 2016b. *Public Support for Transgender Rights: A Twenty-Three Country Survey.* The Williams Institute.

Forcier, M. & Johnson M. 2013. Screening, identification, and support of gender non-conforming children and families. *Journal of paediatric nursing*, 28:1: 100–2.

Ford, A. 2013. *Transitional belief*. Amazon UK: Marston Gate:

Foucault, M. 1998. *The Will to Knowledge: The History of Sexuality, Vol: 1*, trans. R. Hurley. London: Penguin Books.

Foucault, M. 2003. *The Birth of the Clinic: An archaeology of medical perception*, trans. A.M. Sheridan. London: Routledge.

Francis, L. 1992. Male and female clergy in England. Their personality differences: gender reversal? *Journal of Empirical Theology*, 5:2: 31–38.

Francis, L. & M. Robbins. 1995. Survey response rate as a function of age: are female clergy different? *Psychological Reports*, 77: 499–506.

Frazer, M. 2005. Some queers are safer than others: correlates of hate crime victimization of lesbian, gay, bisexual and transgender people in Britain. *Conference Paper from the proceedings of the American Sociological Association Meeting in Philadelphia.*

Futty, J. 2010. Challenges posed by transgender-passing within ambiguities and interrelations. *Graduate Journal of Social Science*, 7:2: 57–75.

Gagnon, R.A.J., 2007. 'Transsexuality and Ordination'. http://www.robgagnon. net/articles/TranssexualityOrdination.pdf (22 August 2017).

Gallarda, T., Amado, I., Coussinoux, S., Poirier, M. F., Cordier, B., & J.P. Olie, 1996. The transsexualism syndrome: clinical aspects and therapeutic prospects. *L'Encephale*, 23:5: 321-326.

Gendered Intelligence. Issues of bullying around Trans and gender variant students in schools, colleges and universities. Available from http://cdn0. genderedintelligence.co.uk/2012/11/17/17-43-56-trans_youth_bullying_ report1108.pdf (10 October 2013)

Gilbert, O.P. 1926. *Men in Feminine Guise: Some historical instances of female impersonation*, trans. R. B. Douglas. London: John Lane.

GIRES 2015. Terminology. https://www.gires.org.uk/assets/Research-Assets/ TERMINOLOGYper cent202015per cent20April.pdf (22 August 2017)

Glasser G. & A. and Strauss. 1967. *The discovery of grounded theory: Strategies for qualitative research*. New York: Aldine de Gruyter.

Goss RE. 1993. *Jesus acted up. A gay and lesbian manifesto*. New York: Harper Collins.

Graham E, Walton H & F. Ward. 2005. *Theological Reflection: Methods*. London: SCM Press.

Green, R. 1998. Mythological, Historical, and Cross-Cultural Aspects of Transsexualism. In: Denny D., Ed. *Current Concepts in Transgender Identity*. New York & London: Garland Publishing Inc, pp. 3-14.

Greene, D. & P. Britton. 2013. The influence of forgiveness on lesbian, gay, bisexual, transgender, and questioning individuals' shame and self-esteem. *Journal of Counselling & Development*, 91:2: 195–205.

Grossman, A. & A. D'Augelli. 2006. Transgender youth: invisible and vulnerable. *Journal of Homosexuality*, 51:1: 111-128.

Guest, D., Goss, R.E, West, M. & T. Bohache (eds). 2006. *The Queer Bible commentary*. London: SCM.

Guest, D. 2006. Deuteronomy. In D Guest et al, Eds. *Queer Bible commentary*. London: SCM Press, pp. 122–143.

Hattie, B. & B. Beagan. 2013. Reconfiguring spirituality and sexual/gender identity: 'It's a feeling of connection to something bigger, it's part of a wholeness'. *Journal of Religion & Spirituality in Social Work: Social Thought*, 32:3: 244–268.

Hay, D. & R. Nye. 2006. *The spirit of the child*. London: Jessica Kingsley.

Himschoot, M. 2009. Action and reflection: one pastor's method of creating Trans Day of Remembrance liturgy. In L. Isherwood & M. Althaus-Reid, Eds. *Trans/Formations*. London: SCM Press, pp. 139-147.

Hipsher, B.K. 2009. God is a many gendered thing: an apophatic journey to pastoral diversity. In L. Isherwood & M. Althaus-Reid, Eds. *Trans/Formations*. London: SCM Press, pp.92–104.

Hirschfeld, M. 1991 [1910] *Transvestites: The Erotic Drive to Cross-Dress*, trans M.A. Lombardi-Nash. Amherst, New York: Prometheus Books.

Holder, R. 1998a. The ethics of transsexualism. Part 1. *Crucible*. London Board of Social Responsibility, pp. 89-99.

Holder, R. 1998b, The ethics of transsexualism. Part 2. *Crucible*. London Board for Social Responsibility, pp. 125-135.

Home Office. 2000. Report of the Interdepartmental Working Group on Transsexual People 2000. The Home Office Communications Directorate. London.

Horton, D. 1994. *Changing Channels? A Christian response to the Transvestite and Transsexual*. Nottingham: Grove Books.

House of Bishops. 1991. *Issues in human sexuality: a statement by the House of Bishops*. 5th Impression. London: Church House Publishing.

House of Bishops. 2003. *Some issues in human sexuality: A guide to the debate*. London: Church House Publishing.

House of Bishops. 2013. *Report of the House of Bishops Working Group on human sexuality* [The Pilling Report]. London: Church House Publishing.

Hubbard, R. 1998. Gender and Genitals. In D. Denny, Ed. *Current Concepts in Transgender Identity*. New York & London: Garland Publishing Inc., pp. 45-61.

Hutchins, C.K. 2001. Holy ferment: queer philosophical destabilizations and the discourse on lesbian, gay, bisexual and transgender lives in Christian institutions. *Theology & Sexuality*, 8:15: 9–22.

Hutchison, A.J, Johnston L.H. & J.D. Breckon. 2010. Using QSR-Nvivo to facilitate the development of a grounded theory project: an account of a worked example. *International Journal of Social Research Methodology*, 13:4: 283–302.

Iacovino, L. 2010. Rethinking archival, ethical and legal frameworks for records of indigenous Australian communities: a participant relationship model of rights and responsibilities. *Archival Science*, 10:4: 353–372.

Iantaffi, A. & W.O. Bockting. 2011. Views from both sides of the bridge? Gender, sexual legitimacy and transgender people's experiences of relationships. *Culture, health & sexuality*, 13:3: 355–370.

Israel, G.E. & D.E. Tarver. 1997. *Transgender Care: Recommended Guidelines, Practical Information and Personal Accounts*. Philadelphia: Temple University Press.

James, S. E., Herman, J. L., Rankin, S., Keisling, M., Mottet, L., & M. Anafi. 2016. *The Report of the 2015 U.S. Transgender Survey*. Washington, DC: National Center for Transgender Equality.

Jasper A. 2005. Theology at the freak show: St Uncumber and the discourse of liberation. *Theology & Sexuality*, 11:2: 43–53.

Jennings, T.W. 2005. *Jacob's Wound: Homoerotic Narrative in the Literature of Ancient Israel*. London & New York: T&T Clark International.

Jesurathnam, K. 2011. A Dalit interpretation of Wisdom Literature with special reference to the underprivileged groups in the Hebrew society: A mission perspective. *Asia Journal of Theology*, 25(2): 334–358.

Joranson, K. 2008. Indigenous knowledge and the knowledge commons. *The International Information & Library Review*, 40:1: 64–72.

Kandel, E. & R. Hawkins. 1992. The Biological Basis of Learning and Individuality. In *Scientific American*. 267:3: 53-60.

Kennedy, N. & M. Hellen. 2010. Transgender children: more than a theoretical challenge. *Graduate Journal of Social Science*, 7:2: 25–43.

Kessler, G. 2005. Let's Cross that Body When We Get to It: Gender and Ethnicity in Rabbinic Literature. *Journal of the American Academy of Religion*, 73:2: 329-359.

Kidd, J.D. & T.M. Witten. 2008. Understanding spirituality and religiosity in the transgender community: implications for aging. *Journal of Religion, Spirituality & Aging*, 20:1-2: 29–62.

King, D. 1996. Gender Blending: Medical Perspectives and Technology. In R. Ekins R & D. King, Eds. *Blending Genders: Social Aspects of Cross-Dressing and Sex-Changing.* New York & London: Routledge, pp.79-98.

Kolakowski, V.S. 1997a. The concubine and the eunuch. Queering up the breeder's Bible. In R. Goss & A.A.S. Strongheart, Eds. *Our Family, Our Values.* New York: Haworth Press, pp. 35–49.

Kolakowski, V.S. 1997b. Towards a Christian ethical response to transsexual persons. *Theology & Sexuality,* 3:6: 10–31.

Kolakowski, V.S. 2000. Throwing a party. Patriarchy, gender and the death of Jezebel. In Goss, R & West M, Eds. *Take back the word: A queer reading of the Bible.* Cleveland: Pilgrim Press, pp.103-114.

Komesaroff, P., Kath, E. & P. James. 2011. Reconciliation and the technics of healing. *Journal of Bioethical Inquiry,* 8:3: 235–237.

Kranemann, B. & S. Moore. 2013. Liturgy in a pluralistic society. *Worship* 87: 5: 414-428.

Kundtz, D. & B. Schlager. 2007. *Ministry among God's Queer Folk. LGBT Pastoral Care.* Cleveland: Pilgrim Press.

Lawrence, A.A. 2003. Factors associated with satisfaction or regret following male-to-female sex reassignment surgery. *Archives of Sexual Behavior,* 32:4: 299-315.

Levy, D.L. & J.R. Lo. 2013. Transgender, transsexual, and gender queer individuals with a Christian upbringing: the process of resolving conflict between gender identity and faith. *Journal of Religion & Spirituality in Social Work: Social Thought,* 32:1: 60–83.

Lings, K.R. 2013. *Love Lost in Translation: Homosexuality and the Bible.* Bloomington, IN: Trafford Publishing.

Lothstein, L.M. & S.B. Levine. 1981. Expressive psychotherapy with gender dysphoric patients. *Archives of General Psychiatry,* 38:8: 924-929.

Magdalene, F.R. 2006. Job's wife as hero: a feminist-forensic reading of the Book of Job. *Biblical Interpretation: A Journal of Contemporary Approaches,* 14(3): 209-258.

Mann, M.J. 2013. The nexus of stigma and social policy: implications for pastoral care and psychotherapy with gay, lesbian, bisexual and transgender persons and their families. *Pastoral Psychology,* 62: 2: 199-210.

Mann, R. 2012. *Dazzling darkness: Gender, sexuality, illness and God.* Glasgow: Wild Goose Publications.

Martin, J. & S. Ehrenkranz. 2003. Applying ethical standards to research and evaluations involving lesbian, gay, bisexual and transgender populations. *Journal of Gay & Lesbian Social Services,* 15:1-2: 181–201.

Mason, N. 1980. The transsexual dilemma: being a transsexual. *Journal of Medical Ethics*, 6: 85-89.

McCall Tigert, L. & M. Tirabassi. Eds. 2004. *Transgendering Faith: Identity, Sexuality & Spirituality*. Cleveland: Pilgrim Press.

Methodist Church UK. 1990. The Report of the Conference Commission on Human Sexuality.

Metzger, B.M. & M.D. Coogan (eds) *Oxford Companion to the Bible*. Oxford University Press.

Meyerowitz, J. 2002. *How Sex Changed: A History of Transsexuality in the United States*. Cambridge MA & London: Harvard University Press.

Millspaugh, S. 2009. Pastoral care with Transgender People. In Kujawa-Holbrook, S. & K. Brown Montagno. Eds. *INJUSTICE AND THE CARE OF SOULS. Taking Oppression Seriously in Pastoral Care*. Minneapolis: Augsburg Fortress.

Mollenkott, V. 2001. *Omnigender: a trans-religious approach*. Cleveland: Pilgrim Press.

Mollenkott, V.R. & V. Sheridan. 2003. Transgender journeys. Eugene, Oregon: Resource Publications.

Morrison, E.G. 2010. Transgender as ingroup or outgroup? Lesbian, gay, and bisexual viewers respond to a transgender character in daytime television. *Journal of homosexuality*, 57:5: 650–665.

Namaste, V. 1993. Undoing theory: the 'transgender question' and the epistemic violence of Anglo-American feminist theory. *Hypatia*, 24:3: 11–31.

Nataf, Z.I. 2006. Selections from Lesbians Talk Transgender. In S. Stryker & S. Whittle, Eds. *The transgender studies reader*. New York: Routledge, pp. 439-448.

Norris, R.A. 2008. Some notes on the current debate regarding homosexuality and the place of homosexuals in the Church. *Anglican Theological Review*, 90:3: 437–512.

Norwood, K. 2012. Transitioning meanings? Family members' communicative struggles surrounding transgender identity. *Journal of Family Communication*, 12:1: 75–92.

O'Donovan, O. 1982. *Transsexualism and Christian Marriage*, Bramcote Nottinghamshire: Grove Books. Reissued in 2007 as *Transsexualism: Issues and Argument*.

O'Keefe, T. & K. Fox. 1996. *Trans-x-u-all: The Naked Difference*. London: Extraordinary People Press.

Paglia, C. 1991. *Sexual Personae: Art and Decadence from Nefertiti to Emily Dickinson*. London: Penguin Books.

Perry, G. 2016. *The Descent of Man*. UK: Allen Lane. Penguin.

Pfäfflin, F. 2015. Transgenderism and Transsexuality: Medical and Psychological Viewpoints. In J.M. Scherpe, Ed. *The Legal Status of Transsexual and Transgender Persons*. Cambridge: Intersentia: pp. 11-23.

Pfeffer, C. 2008. Bodies in relation--bodies in transition: lesbian partners of transmen and body image. *Journal of lesbian studies*, 12:4: 325–45.

Pfeffer, C. 2010. 'Women's work'? Women partners of transgender men doing housework and emotion work. *Journal of Marriage and Family*, 72:1: 165–183.

Piacenza, J. and R.P. Jones. 2017. Americans on Discrimination Against and Social Construct with Transgender People. PRRI, July 26, 2017, https://www.prri.org/spotlight/transgender-military-ban-discrimination-social-contact/, (11 September 2017).

Raymond, J. 1979. *The transsexual empire*. Boston: Beacon Press.

Reay, L. 2009. Towards a transgender theology: que(e)rying the eunuchs. In L. Isherwood & M. Althaus-Reid, Eds. *Trans/Formations*. London: SCM Press, pp. 148–167.

Reed, T. 2016. Gender Incongruence in the changing social and medical environment. In: C. Beardsley & M. O'Brien. *This is My Body: hearing the theology of transgender Christians*. London: Darton, Longman & Todd, pp. 95-100.

Reid, R., di Ceglie, D., Dalrymple, J., Gooren, L., Green, R. and J. Money. 1996. *Transsexualism: The Current Medical Viewpoint*. London: Press for Change.

Reinsmith-Jones, K. 2013. Transsexualism as a model of spiritual transformation: implications. *Journal of GLBT Family Studies*, 9:1: 65–99.

Rekers, G. A., Mead, S. L., Rosen, A.C., & S.L. Brigham. 1983. Family correlates of male childhood gender disturbance. *The Journal of genetic psychology*, 142:1: 31-42.

Riley, E.A., Clemson, L., Sitharthan, G., & M. Diamond. 2013. Surviving a gender-variant childhood: the views of transgender adults on the needs of gender-variant children and their parents. *Journal of sex & marital therapy*, 39:3: 241-263.

Rosser B.R.S., Oakes, J.M., Bockting, W.O. & M. Miner. 2007. Capturing the social demographics of hidden sexual minorities: An Internet study of the transgender population in the United States. *Sexuality Research & Social Policy*, 4:2: 50-64.

Roberts, V. 2016. *Transgender*. The Good Book Company.

Robertson, F.W. 1903. *Notes on Genesis*. New Edition. London: Kegan Paul, Trench, Trübner.

Roscoe, W. 1998. *Changing Ones: Third and Fourth Genders in Native North America*. New York: St Martin's Griffin.

Roth, J.D. 2007. Forgiveness and the healing of memories: an Anabaptist-Mennonite perspective. *Journal of Ecumenical Studies*, 42:4: 338–339.

Ryan C. & I. Rivers. 2003. Lesbian, gay, bisexual and transgender youth: victimization and its correlates in the USA and UK. Culture. *Health & Sexuality*, 5:2: 103–119.

Schweitzer, C.L. 2010. 'For-giving' and forgiving: process and practice in pastoral care. *Pastoral Psychology*, 59:6: 829–842.

Schuck, K. & B.J. Liddle. 2001. Conflicts experienced by lesbian, gay, and bisexual individuals. *Journal of Gay and Lesbian Psychotherapy*, 5:2: 37–41.

Sen, B. 2005. Indigenous knowledge for development: bringing research and practice together. *The International Information & Library Review*, 37:4: 375–382.

Sheehan, N.W. 2011. Indigenous knowledge and respectful design: an evidence-based approach. *Design Issues*, 27:4: 68–80.

Sheridan V. 2001. *Crossing over: liberating the transgendered Christian*. Cleveland: Pilgrim Press.

Shotwell, A. & T. Sangrey. 2009. Resisting definition: gendering through interaction and relational selfhood. *Hypatia*, 24:3: 56-76.

Simpson, L.R. 2004. Anticolonial strategies for the recovery and maintenance of indigenous knowledge. *American Indian Quarterly*, 28:3/4: 373–384.

Simpson, R.H. 2005. How to be fashionably queer: Reminding the Church of the importance of sexual stories. *Theology & Sexuality*, 11:2: 97-108.

Singh, A., Richmond K. & T.R. Burnes. 2013. Feminist participatory action research with transgender communities: fostering the practice of ethical and empowering research designs. *International Journal of Transgenderism*, 14:3: 93–104.

Smith, B. & S. Horne. 2007. Gay, lesbian, bisexual and transgendered (GLBT) experiences with earth-spirited faith. *Journal of Homosexuality*, 52:3-4:.235–248.

Steinmetz, K. Why LGBT Advocates Say Bathroom 'Predators' Argument is a Red Herring, *Time*, May 2, 2016, http://time.com/4314896/transgender-bathroom-bill-male-predators-argument/

Stevens, A. 2008. A different way of knowing: tools and strategies for managing indigenous knowledge. *Libri*, 58:1: 25–33.

Stone, S. 2006. The empire strikes back: a post transsexual manifesto. In S. Stryker & S. Whittle, Eds. *The transgender studies reader*. New York: Routledge, pp. 221–235.

Stonewall. 2017. A Vision for Change: Acceptance without exception for trans people 2017-2022. http://www.stonewall.org.uk/sites/default/files/stw-vision-for-change-2017.pdf (22 August 2017)

Stotzer, R.L. 2009. Violence against transgender people: A review of United States data. *Aggression and Violent Behavior* 14: 170–179.

Stryker, S. 2008. *Transgender history*. Berkeley: Seal Press.

Sullivan-Blum, C.R. 2008. Balancing acts: drag queens, gender and faith. *Journal of Homosexuality*, 46:3-4: 195–209.

Super J.T. & L. Jacobson. 2011. Religious abuse: implications for counselling lesbian, gay, bisexual and transgender individuals. *Journal of LGBT Issues in Counselling*, 5:3-4: 180–196.

Symonds, J.A., 1896. *A Problem in Modern Ethics: Being an enquiry into the phenomenon of sexual inversion, Addressed especially to Medical Psychologists and Jurists*. London: privately published.
https://ia801408.us.archive.org/9/items/aprobleminmoder00symogoog/aprobleminmoder00symogoog.pdf (22 August 2017).

Tanis, J. 2003. *Trans-Gendered: Theology, ministry and communities of faith.* Cleveland: Pilgrim Press.

Tanner, K. 1997. The religious significance of Christian engagement in the culture wars. *Theology Today*, 58:1: 28–43.

Taylder, S. 2009. Shot from both sides: theology and the woman who isn't quite what she seems. In L. Isherwood & M. Althaus-Reid, Eds. *Trans/Formations*. London: SCM Press, pp. 70–91.

Tiller, K. 2010. Towards an understanding of transsexual behaviours. Available from http://ia600504.us.archive.org/32/items/KT-IA-Wordpress/Towards-an-understanding-of-transsexual-behaviours.pdf (October 2013).

Toscano, Peterson, Transfigurations – DVD. https://petersontoscano.com/portfolio/transfigurations/

Truluck, R. 2000. *Steps to Recovery from Bible Abuse.* Gaithersburg: Chi Rho Press.

Vidler, A.R. 1966. *F.D. Maurice and Company: Nineteenth Century Studies*. London: SCM.

Watts, F. 2002. Transsexualism and the church. *Theology & Sexuality*, 9:1: 63–85.

Weiss, J.T. 2014. The Transgender Tipping Point: An Overview for the Advocate. Issue Brief for the American Constitution Society for Law & Policy.
https://www.acslaw.org/sites/default/files/Weiss_-_The_Transgender_Tipping_Point.pdf   (26 August 2017)

West, G.O. & B. Zengele. 2004. Reading Job 'positively' in the context of HIV/AIDS in South Africa. *Concilium*, 4: 112-124.

West, P. 2004. Report into the Medical and Related Needs of Transgender people in Brighton and Hove: The Case for a Local Integrated Service. Spectrum-LGBT Forum & Brighton and Hove City NHS Teaching Primary Care Trust.

West, P. 2015. The Spirit and the Flesh.
https://persiawestwords.net/2015/06/03/the-spirit-and-the-flesh/
(18/09/17)

Whitehead, N. & B. Whitehead. 1999. *My Genes Made Me Do IT!* Lafayette: Huntington Press.

Whittle, S. 1996. Gender Fucking or Fucking Gender: Current Cultural Contributions to Theories of Gender Blending. In Ekins R. & D. King, Eds. *Blending Genders: Social Aspects of Cross-Dressing and Sex-Changing*. New York & London: Routledge, pp. 196-214.

Whittle, S. 2002. *Respect and Equality: transsexual people and transgender rights*. London: Cavendish Publishing.

Whittle, S. & L. Turner. 2007. 'Sex Changes': Paradigm Shifts in 'Sex' and 'Gender' Following the Gender Recognition Act. Sociological Research online, 12:1. http://www.socresonline.org.uk/12/1/whittle.html (26 August 2017)

Wilcox, M.M. 2002. When Sheila's a lesbian: religious individualism among lesbian, gay, bisexual and transgender Christians. *Sociology of Religion*, 63:4: 497–513.

Wilson, W.A. 2004. Indigenous knowledge recovery is indigenous empowerment. *American Indian Quarterly*, 28:3/4: 359–372.

Wojciechowska, K. 2016. 'The first human and the perfect human as an androgynous character', In *Queer Ways of Theology*. Warsaw: Wydawnictwo Newsroom.

World Professional Association for Transgender Health, Standards of Care, Version 7:
https://s3.amazonaws.com/amo_hub_content/Association140/files/Standardsper cent20ofper cent20Careper cent20V7per cent20-per cent202011per cent20WPATHper cent20(2)(1).pdf (26 August 2017)

Yarhouse, M.A. 2015. *Understanding Gender Dysphoria: Navigating Transgender Issues in a Changing Culture*. Downers Grove, Illinois: InterVarsity Press Academic.

Zauzmer, J. 2016. The rabbis of Conservative Judaism pass a resolution supporting transgender rights. *The Washington Post*, June 1, 2016, https://www.washingtonpost.com/news/acts-of-faith/wp/2016/06/01/the-rabbis-of-conservative-judaism-pass-a-resolution-supporting-transgender-rights/?utm_term=.f3fd3e0b3e2b.

Zhou, J., Hofman M., Gooren, L., & D. Swaab. 1995. A sex difference in the human brain and its relation to transsexuality. *Nature*, 378: 68-70.

The Holy Bible: New International Version (NIV).

The Qu'ran: A New Translation. 2004. Trans T. Cleary. USA: Starlatch Press.